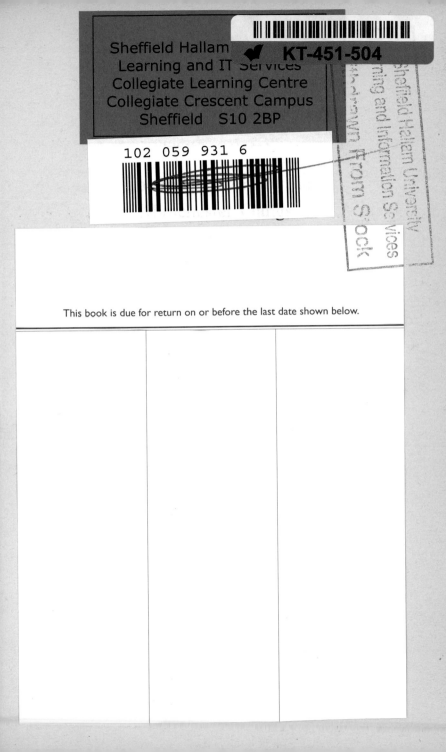

First published in June 2003 by Milo Books

This paperback edition published February 2005

ISBN 978-1-9038-5429-7

Typeset in Plantin Light by Avon DataSet Ltd,
Bidford on Avon, Warwickshire, B50 4JH

Printed and bound in Great Britain by
CPI Group (UK) Ltd, Croydon, CR0 4YY

MILO BOOKS LTD
info@milobooks.com

GANG WAR

The Inside Story of the Manchester Gangs

Peter Walsh

MILO BOOKS LTD

'We go around at night, and are consumed by fire.'
Karline Smith, *Moss Side Massive*.

Contents

Prologue

ONE NIGHT IN the early eighties, a young man burst through the doors of a police station in Moss Side, Manchester. He was frantic with fear. *Some men are coming with machetes*, he shouted. *They're going to chop me up.* The desk officer flattened a buzzer, and within seconds bobbies were pulling on their jackets and running outside. They peered into the damp night. There was no-one around. Whoever was doing the chasing had vanished.

Back in the security of the station, the agitated young man – brown-skinned, of mixed race – slowly calmed down. The bobbies joked that he must have been seeing things, but they could tell he was scared. In the climate of the times, such incidents were not unknown. Recent weeks had seen a rising number of street woundings on 'the Moss', many with the machete, the favoured weapon of the area's West Indian immigrants. Local bobbies put it down to individual disputes that had just become a bit more intense than usual. The young man wasn't the first to dash into the nick for protection late at night, and he wouldn't be the last.

Though it was now one o'clock in the morning, two senior detectives were called in to interview him. They sat him down, gave him a cup of tea, asked the usual questions, and got the usual answers – nothing. Yet there was something about the demeanour of the young man that hinted he had something to say. The two officers – a detective chief inspector and a sergeant – made sure he got home safely and, a couple of weeks later, paid him a follow-up visit. Then something unusual happened, something that would write the first page in the story of the Manchester gang wars. The young man began to talk.

The story he told astounded the hard-bitten detectives. The

city, he said, was being 'carved up' by two black gangs. One was from Moss Side itself, an area a mile south of the city centre, and could call on up to eighty young men, though most of these were bit-players. The hard-core were involved in armed robbery, drug dealing, pimping and thieving. The other gang was based in Cheetham Hill, a couple of miles north of the city centre, and in particular on a couple of modern but already rundown council estates. The core members of the Cheetham Hill mob had graduated from street crime and petty theft to high-level robberies, favouring raids on security vans making payroll deliveries. They were well organised, with strong leaders and, the young man claimed, could put up to 130 'soldiers' onto the streets.

Many gang members on both sides knew each other well, and some were friends; much of the black population of Cheetham had been moved from Moss Side during slum clearances in the sixties, and maintained family ties in the area. Others knew each other from their early teenage years hanging around the indoor Arndale shopping centre, a popular meeting place for some of the more unruly black teenagers. It had seemed sensible for the leading figures on both sides to form a loose alliance, agreeing not to carry out robberies on each other's turf, and this was what they had done.

The more senior of the two detectives, the DCI, listened with scepticism. Though he had transferred only recently to the Moss from nearby Longsight, his father had been a Moss Side cop twenty-five years earlier, and he knew the area and its people. This tale didn't tally with any of his assumptions. 'The informant said the robbers got together and said, town isn't big enough for this, so they co-ordinated their activities,' recalled the DCI. 'There was an alliance and a division of territory. They controlled the prostitution, the robberies, the drugs and the "tax" activities. They were well structured.'

Something, however, then caused the two sides to fall out. 'It started with a robbery close to the BBC building on Oxford Road, on a cash-in-transit van,' said the DCI. 'One side was hitting on the ground of the other and refused to pay tax. This was followed by a series of woundings on the street, and that was when this fellow ran into the police station seeking sanctuary.'

Though the officers hid their disbelief, it sounded like he was spinning them a yarn. *How could this have been happening without their knowledge?* The numbers involved, for a start, seemed implausible. It was also unlikely that any young group could control the crime in an area as unruly as Moss Side; the older guys would not have stood for it. 'It came right out of the blue – there was no perception of organisation until then – and at first it was assumed the informant was gilding the lily. Before, we just thought it was disorganised.'

Yet the young man was adamant – and there had been all those machete attacks. Manchester had also been plagued by a spate of violent armed robberies, many of them in Cheetham Hill. A Cheetham sub-post office was relieved of £10,000 in January 1983 when men with shotguns forced staff and customers to lie facedown and rifled the safe. A month later, a balaclava-clad gang struck two guards with pickaxe handles and took £20,000 outside a Cheetham cash-and-carry. Then a security guard was shot in the shoulder outside Barclays Bank in Cheetham Hill Road; the gang escaped in style in a stolen Porsche. These were heavy-duty jobs, and as the informant continued, the detectives' ingrained cynicism gave way to growing excitement. Perhaps they were onto something big.

Their next problem was to convince their boss. The DCI reported to his chief superintendent, Frank Halligan, a vastly experienced officer who also knew Moss Side inside out: as a detective, he had led the investigations into the riots there in 1981. Halligan was even more sceptical; he was most familiar with the Moss Side underworld of the sixties and seventies, with its shebeens and illicit blues clubs, its gambling dens and raucous card schools, its genial Jamaican dope dealers and exotic madams. The idea that young gangs were vying for control of the rackets was a new one on him and, frankly, sounded ludicrous. 'When I put the report in, Halligan simply didn't believe it,' said the DCI.

★   ★   ★

Moss Side is a flat expanse of housing a mile south of Manchester city centre, split into two parts by Princess Road, now Princess Parkway. 'Old' Moss Side, largely constructed before the First World War in a grid pattern of back-to-back houses, is in the eastern part. On the western side – 'new' Moss Side – is the Alexandra Park estate of mainly terraced housing, built in the 1970s to a peculiar layout that restricts traffic flows into many of the streets by means of cul-de-sacs and walkways.

As a whole, Moss Side is home to around 14,500 people, an unusually high proportion of them young: almost forty-five per cent are under twenty-five and there are four times more single-parent families than the national average. While many are Irish, Asians, students or born-and-bred Mancunians, it is the forty per cent of Afro-Caribbean descent that most influence the district's character. For all the stereotypes of indolent, come-day go-day Caribbeans that many white cops believed, most of the original black immigrants worked hard, some holding down several jobs, and the ghetto, though a little wild, was not unwelcoming to the police. Even those who broke the law often did so for cultural, rather than criminal, reasons.

'When the immigrants came over, a lot came off sugar plantations and had certain skills to manufacture liquor,' said Frank Halligan, who would eventually command the CID central division, covering Manchester and Salford. 'They knew all about running stills and shebeens. They had a culture where they didn't get married. They had very loose relationships. They were all big strong lads. And they smoked cannabis – they even used to give it to their kids for coughs. It is part of their culture. In those days, prostitution was the big money maker. You would get people running a number of prostitutes and someone would try to muscle in and you would get the odd shooting, with shotguns. But mostly it was the machete: it comes from the plantations. And they all carried knives.

'Then the drug scene started to develop. Manchester University is right next door and middle-class kids were going in buying cannabis. You didn't really see heroin. The whole of that part of Manchester ran on vice, shebeens and brothels. You didn't get that in Hulme next door, which was mainly white and terraced houses, where there were a few very hard men like Scotch Dave and a few car dealers. They would have links into the city and they would defend their territory with guns.'

Poverty was unconcealed. 'There were children without shoes in the middle of winter, in just a vest and trousers. The police would collect money and distribute it to the poor. It was a mature population of immigrants who had come here as adults and there wasn't a great racist problem. The police by and large got on with them very well. The problems occurred with the offspring of that generation; not just the police but the parents had problems with them.'

Illegal drinking dens known as shebeens were the arteries of Moss Side social life, where man gathered in bare-roomed walls to play cards, smoke and listen to music, drink Red Stripe and eat goat curry. 'Certain major players ran Moss Side, and they definitely weren't "community leaders",' said Halligan. 'Running clubs were men like Scarface Shine, Pereira and Tunde. Salow Sabe ran the Nile, he was very influential. There was a coloured lady called Mary Robinson who was very well known, ran shebeens, a great person. People could go to her with all kinds of problems.' Robinson had a wooden chute out of the back window down which booze and customers would slide if police raided through the front. 'The shebeens were very useful for the police. The people who ran them didn't want trouble inside because then they would get shut down, and they were very good sources of information. The criminals and prostitutes would go in there. If we got a bad spate of robberies that we couldn't connect up, you would go in there and they would be openly boasting.'

In the late sixties, the city embarked on a massive programme of slum clearance, flattening many of the old back-to-backs in Moss Side and Hulme to build grey, featureless, high- and mid-rise flats. Residents were moved out to Cheetham Hill and to overspill estates in Hyde and Hattersley while the work was carried out. 'They made the classic mistake of building high-rise flats,' said Halligan. 'What they did with Hulme was devastating. There were certain structures holding it together; families that knew each other, but they moved a lot out. They used to come back for years to the pubs in Hulme, even when they lived miles away.'

The notorious Hulme Crescents, huge semi-circular blocks of mid-rise flats with thin walls, urine-soaked stairwells and rubbish-strewn balconies, became the most notorious symbol of the re-build. 'The Crescents were built on the architecture of Bath [but] they had small ginnels and were havens for crime. Decent people would feel very isolated. There were open grass areas in the middle with dogs running around and prostitutes streetwalking. The whole place started to go down.' This was not Bath. The drab uniformity of the brutalist architecture sapped the soul from the area, and rising unemployment deepened the malaise: in parts of Moss Side, four out of every five young black people had no job by the early eighties. Employers were routinely accused of 'post code prejudice' against the district. Add to that racial tensions, the rise of the National Front in the late seventies and a growing black consciousness inspired by the Rastafarianism of reggae idols such as Bob Marley, and a chill wind was rising.

Many shebeens survived the clearances, while others appeared in the new flats at Hulme. They remained an important source of intelligence, and detectives could still move freely in them, but the owners sometimes put minders on their shoulders, and occasionally the young bucks would smash their car windows while they were inside. Many of the children of the hard-working first-generation immigrants were in no mood to accept the cultural norms of white society that seemed to offer them little. The open smoking of ganja was no longer just a tradition but two fingers to authority: Stop us if you dare. Afros were pulled into dreadlocks.

The Moss Side Frank Halligan knew was passing. The riots sounded its death knell. For several nights Toxteth in Liverpool had been consumed by an orgy of violence, so it was not entirely a surprise when, in the early hours of 8 July 1981, a group of youths left the Nile Club and attacked shops along Princess Road. Daylight saw crowds gather on the stretch of grass separating the Alexandra Park estate from Princess Road. Police in riot gear were greeted by missiles. That night the police station in Greenheys Lane was besieged by up to 1,000 black and white youths. Shops were looted and vandalised as far away as Rusholme. The police disappeared.

The next day they returned hard and heavy, determined not to abdicate control of the streets. More than 200 people were arrested. It was later held that the speed and aggression of the police response – after the first night – was instrumental in avoiding another Toxteth and in quelling the disturbances. 'The CID follow-up was first-rate,' said Halligan. 'There were hundreds of people put before the courts.' Some cops felt that their response to the riots enhanced their 'power' in the area, but it also destroyed their community links. 'After the riots, there was a distancing,' said the DCI. 'There was patrolling by the police but they weren't as intrusive and didn't get to know about as much, and I wonder if that allowed the gangs to flourish. There was also a lot about corruption then and people began to assume you were bent if you went in shebeens.' One high-profile corruption case involved nearby Platt Lane police station. James Anderton, a puritanical, no-nonsense chief constable, also disbanded his vice squad after reports of some senior officers drinking after time in city pubs. The effect was that, for two or three years after the riots, the CID lost touch with the streets.

That was why Frank Halligan found the informant's story so hard to swallow: these young gangs were a mystery to him. But when the young man was able to put officers at the scene before several pre-arranged fights, Halligan came on board. It soon became clear that a major public order problem was brewing and that something had to be done. 'These gangs were the top for street disorder at the time,' said the DCI. 'They were affecting the city.' The two detectives and their boss had discovered that Manchester was in the opening stages of gang warfare unlike anything it had known before: a conflict that would last for more than twenty years, cost dozens of lives and leave hundreds injured. It would make headlines around the world, blight the reputation of one of Europe's most famous cities and see the coining of the sinister and unwanted epithet 'Gunchester'.

Yet the officers and their colleagues knew nothing about it. It seemed to have come from nowhere.

CHAPTER ONE

Hell Is A City

THE GANGS OF Manchester were born, like the city, in the Industrial Revolution, that huge, unnatural upheaval in the way people lived and worked. Manchester was a mildly prosperous cotton and market town until the excavation of the Bridgewater Canal and the invention of contraptions for spinning and weaving textiles. The canal, which saw the world's first steamboat in 1780, allowed coal to be brought to the town from pits at nearby Worsley, providing fuel for the recently designed, steam-powered spinning mule and the power loom. The cotton trade, the traditional employer of the townspeople, was lifted to an industrial footing, and the factory rather than the home or workshop became the place of labour. Soon Manchester was 'Cottonopolis', the most important textile trading centre in the world.

There had never been such a city before. People had never worked in such immense, roaring mills, nor lived beside them in such numbers or such squalor. The population of Manchester and neighbouring Salford rose from 18,000 in 1752 to 400,000 a century later, as farm labourers, impoverished immigrants and previously home-based textile artisans were drawn like ants to syrup. The cotton trade generated immense wealth, but life for many of the newcomers was unspeakable, denied even the necessities of clear light and clean air. 'A great proportion of the poor lodge in cellars damp and dark, where every kind of filth is suffered to accumulate, because no exertions of domestic care can ever make such homes decent,' wrote the poet Robert Southey in 1802. 'Imagine this multitude crowded together in narrow streets, the houses all built of brick and blackened with smoke; frequent large buildings among them where you hear from within the everlasting din of machinery and where when the bell rings it is to call wretches to their work instead of to their prayers.'

By the middle of the nineteenth century, Friedrich Engels, author with Karl Marx of *The Communist Manifesto*, had identified a 'girdle of squalor' surrounding the central commercial district, with the 'most horrible spot' being an area called Little Ireland, south-west of Oxford Road near the River Medlock. Others contended that the nadir was Angel Meadow, a depraved area of less than a square mile around the Victoria Station end of Deansgate that housed scores of thousands of people and armies of rats and was labelled 'the Place of Terror' by the yellow Press. Beyond this girdle lived the upper and middle classes, in a band of towns and villages. As the town centre overflowed, so the inner suburbs – Chorlton-on-Medlock, Ardwick Green, Hulme – were gradually swallowed up, and the wealthier moved yet further away to escape the sun-blotting smoke of the chimneys and the dead-animal stench of the tanneries. Manchester became two cities, rich and poor.

Bound to the mills for their wages and hence their survival, the workers sought escape in their free hours. The biggest growth industries after cotton were brothels and beerhouses: there were hundreds of prostitutes, or 'factory girls', and according to an 1843 police report, 330 whorehouses. In the same year, Manchester had 920 retailers of beer, 624 public houses and thirty-one inns and hotels. Coupled with drinking and debauchery was a reputation for rebelliousness dating from the Civil War. There were food riots, wage strikes, the Plug Riots, the Peterloo Massacre and the radical reform movement known as Chartism. Soldiers struggled to keep order from barracks around the town amid an atmosphere of political discontent, wild nightlife and an existence of 'raw poverty, rough conditions and seething violence'.[1]

Into this unstable mix came the scuttlers, strangely dressed youth gangs that appeared suddenly and aggressively around 1870 in the poverty-stricken Rochdale Road area. Their name may have referred to the sound they made when they ran in their clogs, like scuttling insects. The scuttlers had their own look and style; indeed they may have been the first urban youth cult, their clothes an outlandish affront to older generations. Boys and girls wore bell-bottomed trousers, pointed-toed clogs, silk neckties and long fringes plastered over one eye, topped with pointed caps pulled down at a jaunty angle. The fashion and the gangs spread across the Manchester-Salford conurbation and were unique to the region, with its huge demand for juvenile labour. Most of the gang members were aged between fourteen and nineteen; anyone over twenty was a veteran. At any one time there were twenty or thirty gangs, with names like the Bengal Tigers, the She Battery mob and Buffalo Bill's Gang.

It was an era of widespread casual brutality, fuelled by heavy male drinking. Wives and children in working-class families were routinely beaten, while fistfights were an accepted means of settling arguments and mass street brawls were not uncommon. The youth gangs aped this behaviour, marking out their territory by pubs and street corners. Entering enemy turf was a sure way of provoking a fight. 'Suppose you want someone to fly at you,' a youth told the *Manchester Guardian* in 1898, 'you just soap your hair down over your left eye and put on a pigeon-board cap. Then you go into Salford.' Other battling arenas were the city centre dancehalls, where scuttlers from all over the city would gather. They tended to settle rows in three ways: a stand-up between a selected fighter from each side, a full 'scuttle' involving up to 500 youths, in which weapons would be used, or an attack by a gang of scuttlers on a lone rival. The gangs were led into battle by 'captains' and used a range of weapons, especially knives and leather belts with heavy brass buckles. Another feature of the gangs was the intimidation of witnesses giving evidence against them in court and they had a strong code of not 'grassing'. However, they were not overtly criminal; the modern parallel would be the football casual firms, with their emphasis on male bonds, mass fighting and fashion.[2]

Scuttling had faded by 1900 and it would be eighty years before a gang phenomenon as persistent reappeared, though Manchester and Salford always had territorial street crews, with names like the Ikey Boys and the largely Italian Napoo Gang. Ray Rochford grew up in Salford in the 1930s and was involved in street gang fights from the age of eight. 'You had to fight or there would be open season on you. There was half a dozen gangs round the area where I was born. There was Dalfy Street gang, Chapel Street gang, Cross Lane gang. And every few weeks there'd be chalked up on the wall "gang fight". I was absolutely terrified, but you daren't show it. I remember one fight, I got hit in the eye with a bolt, I was only about ten. I was taken to Salford Royal Hospital; I had eight stitches.'[3]

By the 1950s, the Teddy Boys were the new demons of the media. 'The first time I noticed major gang conflict in Manchester was with the Teddy Boys,' said former police chief Frank Halligan. 'They used to have massive fights. You would get a mob from Wythenshawe coming up to a dance in Northenden and there would be a hundred-a-side fighting. They hid bike chains in their drape collars and used cut-throat razors.' Rambunctious though they were, however, the Teds were another youth cult, into music and clothes, not a criminal conspiracy. Most were mere 'kids' compared to the hard men who began to make their names in the post-War rackets of the 1950s. The Second World War and rationing had brought huge opportunities for black market dealing, and crime records show that theft soared as the police clear-up rate collapsed. Even as the British Empire crumbled and Manchester's industrial and commercial importance declined, the city's spirit of *laissez faire* liberalism survived, though often subverted to illegal ends. Organised crime was beginning to emerge.

The best-remembered 'face' of the post-War years was Bobby McDermott, self-styled King of the Barrow Boys. 'Mac' was the archetypal Manchester character: generous, gregarious, a man with a swagger. He started in business at the age of twelve, selling fruit from his father's stall, and eventually acquired sites all over the city. By the mid-fifties, he was said to own three-quarters of all the fruit and veg barrows in Manchester. He became a father figure to the city's many market traders, and a spokesman for their rights. The market porters were notoriously handy with their fists but Mac himself was not known as a hardman. Instead he was reputed to be the city's biggest fence, a clever wheeler-dealer who was too canny to be caught. When nabbed with a cellar full of stolen apples, he paid someone else to take the fall for him. His appetite for business increased rather than diminished as he got older, and he became Manchester's leading ticket tout at a time when the city's two football clubs were becoming powers in the land. 'The 1947 United team was on its way to a Cup semi-final in Sheffield and the coach was travelling along Cannon Street,' recalled his son Terry. 'He wished them luck and handed out two boxes of black cherries which were hard to come by at the time. Two of the players gave him a bunch of tickets and he suddenly realised he was onto a winner.'[4]

McDermott mixed freely with people from all walks of life in the villagey atmosphere of central Manchester, and was a regular at big sporting events, with his entourage in tow. He acquired a club, the Cellar, which became a popular gambling haunt, and one local newspaper described him as 'on first-name terms with everyone from judges to hardened criminals and from mayors to football players.' When he died, at the age of seventy-seven, in July 1980, former boxers, ticket spivs and men from racing circles all over the country joined dozens of street traders to pay their respects. Scores of floral tributes and more than 200 mourners arrived, some flying in from London and at least one arriving in a Rolls-Royce. 'He was a monument of Manchester,' said his son Terry. 'He knew and was respected by everyone. He had an incredible appetite for work, for people and for the city.'

McDermott and one or two others such as Bobby Critchley, who made his money in used cars and allegedly drove a bullet-proof version himself, were the closest the city had to 'godfathers', but this was still mild roguery compared to what would follow. One of Mac's many acquaintances was the actor Stanley Baker, and the pair spent time together when Baker came to Manchester in 1960 to play a detective in the atmospheric film noir *Hell Is A City*. The sepia-tinged world it captured was already dated: smoky snugs in bare corner pubs, uniformed bobbies raiding organised pitch-and-toss games on strips of wasteland, Black Marias, and honest cops who went home to their wives at lunchtime for a cooked meal. In truth, Manchester's nocturnal world was fast-changing. The impetus for this came first from the cabaret and gaming clubs. They transformed the city centre economy, bringing in gamblers, prostitutes, bouncers and all that went with them. Hard on their heels came the juke-box coffee shops of the rock 'n' roll era, aimed at a younger market.

In London, modern organised crime was taking hold for the first time under gangland bosses Billy Hill and Jack Spot. Manchester had no-one similar, and its booming clubland offered possibilities for the London men. On at least three separate occasions in the fifties and sixties, London hoodlums came to Manchester in force looking for a toehold in the city's expanding club scene. Three times they left empty-handed, and each time Owen Ratcliffe was in the thick of it.

★ ★ ★

'Don't make me out to be some kind of nutter,' said Owen Ratcliffe sternly from an armchair at his cosy bungalow near Blackpool. Still dapper and articulate in his eighties, with swept-back grey hair, zip-up cardigan and brown slippers, Ratcliffe was a big man, and occasionally his eyes showed the glint of latent steel. A nocturnal life had taught him the value of a close mouth and a flinty stare. 'He feared no-one,' said his former partner Paddy McGrath.

Born in Blackpool, Ratcliffe seized opportunities in the seaside resort after World War Two, catering for servicemen still barracked at nearby training camps. He opened a restaurant selling fish and chip dinners for half a crown: 'Blackpool was very busy then and we took a fortune.' Ratcliffe hooked up with Paddy McGrath, a heavyweight boxer from the rough Collyhurst district of Manchester, to open a gaming club in Blackpool. It attracted gamblers from all over the region and some asked why they didn't open something similar in Manchester, so in 1952, McGrath and Ratcliffe bought and converted a vacant restaurant in Cromford Court, in the heart of the city, and named it the Cromford Club. 'I took a hell of a gamble,' said Ratcliffe. 'I had a good business in Blackpool but was putting all the takings from it into the

Cromford. It was the first of its type. It had a restaurant, a stage, a dance floor, a bar and a gambling room with roulette. We used to have acts from the Salford Hippodrome and put on good-class cabaret. It was an exciting place.'

The Cromford opened each evening at eight but wouldn't liven up until late, when crowds arrived after watching the shows around town. It caught a mood of release after the privations of war. Head waiter Arthur Conway buzzed between gents in lounge suits quaffing Double Diamond and Younger's Pale Ale and women in their best gowns sipping gin and tonics. Regulars soon included football manager Matt Busby – 'a real gentleman' – and his Manchester United stars, actors, industrialists, tycoons, singers and showgirls. The city had seen nothing like it. The performers were top-notch for the time – Joseph Locke, Terry Thomas, Charlie Chester – while others would often turn up after their shows elsewhere and put on impromptu late-night performances. The Cromford became a magnet for gossip columnists. 'I remember having breakfast with the editor of the *Manchester Evening News* at six o'clock in the morning,' said Ratcliffe. 'I knew people like Marjorie Proops, columnists read by millions.' The police held parties there too, despite its somewhat dubious status as a gambling house: the Betting and Gaming Act would not provide a legal basis for casinos and off-course betting until 1961. 'The law was all upside down until then. After the Gaming Act, you had to have a licence. Before that, they didn't know where the law stood; gambling was all right in one town but not another. We also had the call-over there. In the Victoria Club in London, all the bookmakers would get together, swap information and set the odds, and it was known as the call-over. It was quite an honour to have it.'

As other clubs appeared – the Continental, the Cabaret, the Stage and Radio, Chez Joey and many more – it was only a matter of time before the gangland leaders of the day came to take a look. Top of the heap was Billy Hill, born one of twenty-one children in utter poverty in the Seven Dials district of London. Hill built a formidable army of thieves and tearaways and would, with some justification, call his autobiography *Boss of*

Britain's Underworld. He had friends in Manchester's criminal community and some of them invited him up. 'He came and stayed about three days,' said Ratcliffe. 'They wanted to move in, it was unknown territory to them. They don't say what they want, they feel people out and see how they react.' One of Hill's Manchester contacts was a nark who would spot wealthy patrons out in the clubs and then tip off burglars to screw their houses. Ratcliffe banned the man from the Cromford Club. Hill was not happy, and had one of his middlemen phone Ratcliffe.

'Billy Hill is very annoyed with you,' warned the man.

'I'm very annoyed with him,' said Ratcliffe.

A meeting was held at which it was indicated to Hill that his head might be removed with a meat cleaver if he did not stick to his own patch. According to Paddy McGrath, Ratclifffe even went down to the Astor Club in London and threatened Hill in front of 'Italian Albert' Dimes, another underworld don, saying that if they wanted to take him on, they'd have to kill him. 'I wasn't scared of anyone in those days,' said Ratcliffe. 'I had a rule: I wouldn't stand for certain things, at any cost, and I kept getting away with it. I was surprised, because Billy Hill was in some ways the most powerful man in England. They had done people for a lot less.'

Next came the Kray brothers and their East End firm. They were backing a UK tour by retired boxing legend Joe Louis, which they took as an opportunity to make a few contacts and exert some muscle in the provinces. Both the club bosses and the police in Manchester saw this as a threat. 'We wouldn't let them move in,' said Ratcliffe. 'There were a few club owners by then and they got together and said they wouldn't stand for any nonsense.' After a night on the town during which one club bouncer was punched down a flight of stairs, the Krays were escorted out of the Midland Hotel by police and sent back to London.

The third incursion was by the Nash brothers, a club-owning Islington clan once labelled 'the wickedest brothers in Britain' by a national newspaper. 'The Nash boys only stayed about a week and went. They underestimated the city and thought it would be an easy touch but there was a solid front. The police have a lot to thank us for.' Would the other club owners have backed Ratcliffe up if it came to a fight? 'They said they would but if it had come to the crunch, I don't know. There were no gangs in Manchester then, though there were one or two tearaways.'

Success brought the Ratcliffes a nice home in a posh suburb and a holiday place at the Welsh resort of Abersoch. Owen was so reckless – 'either an idiot or very, very brave,' according to his wife, Judy – that he even expanded into south London, acquiring a night club in Catford called Mr Smith and the Witchdoctor. The club came with problems in the shape of some tough brothers called the Hawards and their friends, who treated it as their own. At the same time 'Mad' Frankie Fraser, chief enforcer for the Richardson mob, wanted to install his fruit machines there. Fraser promised to 'sort out' the bother with the Hawards. In March 1966, one man died and five were badly wounded in a brutal gang battle at Mr Smith's, and several members of the Richardson gang, including Mad Frank, were later jailed for their part in the carnage. 'I was there that night but left about half an hour before anything happened,' claimed Ratcliffe. 'I was staying at the Grosvenor Hotel, and when I got up the next day, I bought a paper and there was the story. I had no idea anything was going on, but then London was all protection rackets.'

Eventually the Cromford ran into debt and was sold to the Playboy group, before being demolished to make way for the Arndale Centre. It marked the end of a way of life. Ratcliffe retired to the Lancashire coast, where he ran a kennels and a cattery. At seventy-five, he was still re-roofing the cats' pens, a hard man with many memories. 'He has the same birthday as the Scottish poet Robert Burns,' said Judy, 'and he always reminds me of the line, "A man's a man for a' that." '

★ ★ ★

A good nickname sticks and is one reason why the Quality Street Gang became and remains so notorious. Some characterise it as a malevolent octopus that manipulated the rackets in Manchester for thirty years. One report compiled by a high-ranking police officer contends, 'The Quality Street Gang is the name given to a group of Manchester criminals who are regarded by a number of senior police officers as being the organisers of incidents of major crime in the city. The membership of the gang appears to be ever changing and many criminals claim membership or association because it enhances their reputation amongst their fellows.'[5] Many crimes have been laid at its door, from well-executed burglaries, hi-jackings and robberies to long-firm frauds, arms running and international drug smuggling. Yet other informed sources, including experienced detectives, contend that the QSG never existed, at least not as an organised entity. They believe that social friendship between a group of men, most with criminal records, was exaggerated into an on-going conspiracy and that 'QSG' was a catch-all term bandied about so loosely that it became meaningless. Separating fact from myth is all but impossible.

The core of the group came to attention in the early sixties, a hard-living bunch of men from poor backgrounds in inner-city districts such as Ancoats and Collyhurst who were involved in market trading, used car sales, boxing, scrap metal and, later on, construction and property. London villain Eric Mason, a Kray associate who spent a lot of time in the north of England, first heard of them at Bobby McDermott's Cellar. 'The impression given was far from sinister – they were spoken of as tough, fun-loving guys who all seemed quite wealthy,' he said. 'One got the feeling that they were respected because although they were tough they never threw their weight about. After an incident at the Wilton Club in 1962, when a noted underworld figure of the day was put in hospital, the QSG were seen as pretty fearless fighting men.'[6]

According to the award-wining television journalist Peter Taylor, who examined the QSG in his book *Stalker: The Search for the Truth*, their label was a typical piece of Manchester humour:

> The QSG – most of them Damon Runyonesque figures with smart suits and shades, gold bracelets and chains – took their name from a television commercial for chocolates which ran

many years ago. A limousine rolls up to a bank; men with long coats, fedoras and dark glasses march in and the frightened cashier holds up his hands; a man with a fat cigar slips his hand inside his overcoat and pulls out . . . a box of Quality Street chocolates. The name originated when several members of the 'gang' walked into a pub one evening, looking incredibly dapper and smart, and someone shouted out, 'Here's the Quality Street gang.' The name stuck.

In the boom years of the sixties, as wallets grew fatter and skirts shorter, the QSG became fixtures at clubs such as Deno's, and some eventually owned pubs and clubs themselves. Twenty years before 'Madchester', the city had become an entertainment capital, with soul venues like the Twisted Wheel pulling in customers from all over the region. 'I was a detective sergeant in the city centre in the mid-sixties and there were ninety-four clubs,' said John Stalker, a Manchester police officer whose name would become inextricably linked with the QSG. 'That is an awful lot. They attracted people from all over the north-west. It kept us very busy, yet in the four years I was a detective sergeant in the city centre I only recall one armed incident at a club, where the doorman was shot.'

From the late sixties to the mid-eighties, the QSG and their crowd were 'faces' in the city, men you didn't mess with. Notoriety gave them glamour – heads turned when they walked into a club – and they rubbed shoulders with entertainers and the more flamboyant footballers of the day. The gang was even immortalised on vinyl: they frequented a Whalley Range hotel run by the mother of Thin Lizzy singer Phil Lynott, and Lizzy's track 'Johnny The Fox Meets Jimmy The Weed' was a reference to Jimmy 'the Weed' Donnelly, one of the better-known faces. They may also have inspired the band's hit 'The Boys Are Back In Town'.

The QSG came under police surveillance in the early seventies, particularly at their car pitch 'headquarters', and this would continue intermittently but with little success for the next ten years. Often the subjects of surveillance seemed to know they were being watched or their phones tapped and there were strong suspicions that bent officers were tipping them off. 'If we were watching them from a room across the road, they wouldn't make themselves scarce; they'd walk right across and put a brick through the window,' a senior detective told Peter Taylor. 'They'd let us know they knew. There were lots of stories about how they got the information out but nobody could put their finger on it.'[7]

Over the next ten years, the Quality Street myth became impenetrable. Some police officers have claimed that this period saw them become the most powerful criminal group in the city's history, moving into both armed robbery and drug importation, the latter partly through contacts with people from the Middle East. Robberies and drugs were the two boom areas of top-end crime, with easier foreign travel and the construction of the domestic motorway network making it easier for criminals to get around. The QSG – or so some officers would claim – often acted as financiers, putting up money for major jobs and taking a hefty cut in return. Yet it was never clear whether the QSG was responsible for all, or indeed any, of the crimes attributed to it. None if its alleged core members were convicted of serious crimes.

* * *

Nineteen eighty-four was the year Lenny Pilot and Fred Scott went supergrass and turned the Manchester underworld on its ear. Scott, a porn dealer in his mid-fifties, and Pilot, twenty years his junior, were part of the white criminal elite, the premier league of 'blaggers' behind an eruption of armed robberies in the north-west. With their sawn-offs, stocking masks and getaway cars, they had brought a higher level of planning and precision, and were instrumental in a jump in robberies of over one-third in the county of Greater Manchester in 1982. The use of guns in such crimes almost quadrupled, to six a week, between 1979–82. One of their rules was that no raid should last longer than ninety seconds, in case they had tripped a security alarm. They often planted one of their gang in a car boot wearing an 'old man' joke mask; at the right moment, the bizarrely dressed accomplice would leap from the boot, terrifying anyone there.

James Anderton, the Manchester chief constable with the biblical beard and fire-and-brimstone rhetoric, was vexed. He told a session of the county police committee that 'ruthless and vicious men' were 'not only prepared to set out on their violent expeditions carrying deadly weapons but are quite ready to use them to maim or murder to achieve their needs or to evade arrest.' He was determined to do something about it. Anderton was Britain's most colourful cop, an outspoken moralist as recognisable during the contentious Thatcher years as left-wing firebrands Arthur Scargill or Derek Hatton. Relishing controversy, he secretly put armed units on patrol to catch the robbery gangs. It was unheard of at the time, and caused a political storm when the news leaked.

A separate armed robbery investigation led to over 160 arrests and six major trials, but it was the capture of Pilot and Scott after a post office raid that had the biggest impact. When they were jailed for ten years each in June 1983, Pilot indicated he was prepared to 'cough' and made a series of statements to Detective Sergeant Harry Exton, an ambitious and determined investigator from the regional crime squad. Exton then turned his attention to Scott, who had never before admitted anything, either to police or to juries. Scott too, despite the danger of reprisals, agreed to tell what he knew, probably in the hope of early parole to see his two young children. He implicated gang members in wage van raids that had netted a total of £130,000. Shots had been fired six times on these raids, though no one had been hit. Armed with the statements from Pilot and Scott, the police launched Operation Belgium – Harry Exton was of Belgian descent – to gather intelligence and evidence against the gang. They planned to arrest them just after New Year, when it was reckoned they would be relaxed and off-guard. One hundred and fifty detectives raided ten homes early in January 1984. As they handcuffed and escorted twenty-five suspects into waiting vans, jubilant officers described it as the one of the most successful operations ever carried out in the region.

The defendants faced a mass trial at Lancaster Crown Court, to avoid the danger of jury nobbling in Manchester. Even so, a senior QSG figure was rumoured to have put a £50,000 'contract' on the lives of Pilot and another supergrass called Cook, and to have then extended it to include the detective Exton. Scott's information led to proceedings against twenty-five people, with Scott giving evidence for the prosecution. The longest sentence, of fourteen years, went to a scrap dealer from New Moston. An indication of how prolific the gang had been was provided by Pilot, who himself admitted twenty-three counts of conspiracy to rob, attempted robbery, robbery, arson by setting fire to a van to assist escape, theft, attempted theft, conspiracy to pervert the course of justice and perjury over alibi evidence, and asked for another thirty cases to be taken into consideration. He was given six and a half years to serve concurrently with the ten he was already doing. The judge said threats on his life meant he would have to serve his time in isolation.

Most of the Operation Belgium defendants were in their thirties or forties, their criminal prime; Anderton and his men had wiped almost the entire top tier of Manchester armed robbers. At the same time, they began a painstaking investigation aimed even higher up the criminal ladder, at the Quality Street Gang, in what became known as the Stalker Affair, one of the most extraordinary police and governmental scandals of modern times. These two events – Operation Belgium and the QSG investigation – would have profound implications for the future direction of gang-related crime in the city.

John Stalker was the newly appointed deputy chief constable of Greater Manchester, number two to Anderton. Pragmatic and capable, he rose swiftly through the ranks and his skills as a detective were so highly regarded that in 1984 he was chosen for a most difficult and politically sensitive assignment: he was to investigate allegations that members of the Royal Ulster Constabulary had assassinated unarmed republicans in Northern Ireland in a so-called shoot-to-kill policy. Stalker pursued his task with vigour. He was determined to do his duty and uncover the truth, even if it meant embarrassing the RUC, British Intelligence and the Conservative government of the day.

Yet by apparent coincidence, two chance conversations were about to spark a separate investigation that would encompass Stalker himself, and would undermine him at a crucial stage in his inquiries. In the first, a conman and police informant called David Burton told Manchester detectives that a prominent businessman and former chairman of the Manchester Conservative Association, Kevin Taylor, was close to the QSG, indeed was instrumental in some of its activities. Taylor was also known to be friendly with John Stalker and his wife; a couple of years before, the Stalkers had attended Taylor's fiftieth birthday party at his home, a converted mill in Summerseat, a village near Bury. At around the same time, in June 1984, a detective superintendent in the regional crime squad called Bernard McGourlay played golf with a businessman he had never met before. Over a pint afterwards, the businessman said that he supposed McGourlay knew all of Manchester's criminals, and mentioned the names of suspected members of the QSG. 'He went on in quite a joking manner about Mr Taylor and parties at his home in Summerseat,' McGourlay would later testify. 'He said one of my bosses went to those parties.' McGourlay asked him who. 'He said it was Stalker. I was very concerned.'

McGourlay wanted to warn Stalker of the gossip but instead went to Detective Chief Superintendent Peter Topping, the head of Y department, which investigated complaints against officers. At the time, alleged QSG members were in the news: one had recently skipped bail and fled to Spain. Police behaviour was also a topical issue and Topping had had to investigate some messy corruption cases. Though the claims of the unreliable Burton and the golf course tittle-tattle amounted to little, Topping wrote a confidential four-page report that was passed to James Anderton. Its contents would be kept secret for over a decade. It referred to the allegations about Kevin Taylor and said, among other things, 'What is particularly disturbing about the activities of the Quality Street Gang is their ever-increasing involvement in drugs and there is now a strong indication the IRA is associating with them in this most lucrative criminal area.' Another extract asserted, 'The involvement of this group in the drugs scene cannot be over-estimated. They have contacts in Africa and have access to their own shipping facilities.' The report also said an informant (Burton) had revealed an association between the gang and a senior police officer named as 'Mr Z'. Mr Z was John Stalker.

Anderton was gravely concerned, yet said nothing to his deputy. In February 1985, he announced the setting up of a drugs intelligence unit, ostensibly to work alongside the existing narcotics squad. Topping, promoted to detective chief super-intendent in charge of CID operations, was put in control of it. It has never been publicly resolved whether this unit was set up to tackle organised crime, or whether its purpose was to investigate the QSG and any possible links with Taylor and Stalker. Certainly it was set up without Stalker's involvement, and all information bypassed him, even though he was the second most senior officer in the county.

Detectives from the unit visited Burton before his death in jail in March 1985 and heard further, utterly unsubstantiated allega-tions of Stalker being 'on a pension' from the QSG. Anderton passed on his concerns to Sir Philip Myers, HM Inspector of Constabulary. Eventually the drugs intelligence unit built up an index of 5,000 names and 7,500 cards and information sheets. Kevin Taylor was put under constant surveillance and the files portrayed him as a Jekyll and Hyde character who would associate with target criminals and entertain Cabinet ministers at his home in the same day. It alleged that he part-financed some QSG operations and laundered money, said his yacht *Diogenes* was used for drug-running, and claimed that gang leaders financed one of Taylor's property developments in Salford, later sold for £2.5 million. One dossier named thirteen members of the QSG syndicate, with numbers one to eight described as the 'inner sanctum', and said they were 'allowed to flourish' because of connections within GMP.

If true, this was a criminal conspiracy at the highest level, involving not just serious offences including drug importation but top-level police corruption and threats to national security.

The problem was the provenance of the information. Much of the material in the intelligence files was based on the highly dubious word of David Burton, now dead. It was worthless without corroboration, which was proving hard to come by. Did it merit further investigation? DCS Topping clearly thought so. Meanwhile Stalker, buried in his RUC inquiry and unaware of his own force's investigation, was oblivious to the storm rising around him. In September 1985, he handed a highly critical interim report to RUC head Sir John Hermon for his comments. The report recommended the prosecution of eleven officers. Hermon was furious.

In May 1986, police raided Taylor's village home and found a leather-bound album of photographs from his fiftieth birthday party. The 150 guests present had included John Stalker – and some convicted criminals. Stalker's wife was on one of the photos with Jimmy the Weed and Steve Hayes, an ex-policeman convicted of corruption, though the Stalkers did not know either man personally. For all that they proved nothing, these photos became something of a 'smoking gun' in the inquiry. A few days later, the axe fell in a startling direction. Stalker, whose RUC probe had reached a critical stage, was working in his garden on a day off when the phone rang. It was the clerk to the police authority. He said curtly that allegations had been made against Stalker that might indicate a disciplinary offence; that Colin Sampson, Chief Constable of West Yorkshire Police, was investigating; and that Stalker was to take an extended 'leave of absence'. Sampson was also taking over Stalker's shoot-to-kill inquiry.

The stunned Stalker was interviewed by Sampson the next day. Stalker later testified that Sampson told him he was merely looking into rumour, innuendo and gossip about his association with Kevin Taylor. 'There was no allegation, no report and no complaint put to me, which tells me that Mr Sampson didn't quite know what his role was,' said Stalker.[8] The suspended officer sank into a Kafkaesque world of sitting and waiting, unable to respond to mounting innuendo because no-one would tell him what he had done wrong. Newspapers and TV programmes were briefed and leaked to. Snippets about Taylor's photo album and the parties at his home appeared in some newspapers. Others speculated that Stalker had been stitched up to discredit his RUC investigation. There were dark hints of Masonic conspiracies.

Sampson's final report exonerated Stalker. He was reinstated in August 1986 but the damage had been done. Unable or unwilling to work any longer with James Anderton, he took early retirement a few months later to pursue other interests and write his autobiography, which was scathing of the entire inquiry. The unfortunate Kevin Taylor, however, would eventually be charged with attempting to defraud the Co-op Bank of £240,000 – even though the bank had made no complaint. He was acquitted with three others in 1990. Taylor, who had been ruined, launched a High Court action against the police for malicious prosecution. In 1995, he received more than £2.3 million in damages and costs when GMP agreed to settle seven weeks into the hearing.[9]

Mob or myth? There is no final word on the QSG. The names of some its alleged members continued to crop up in the newspapers from time to time, and criminals of that generation still carry the label whether they deserve it or not, including a group who hung out at a club in Chinatown in the early nineties. 'All the old QSG boys used to come in there, people with money,' said a former doorman. 'There'd be two limousines, Rollses, Porsches. The QS influenced everything, they were well-respected throughout town, no matter who you spoke to. Even some of the head boys from the Gooch [a much younger black gang] gave them total respect. These blokes were wearing £500 suits, in their early fifties, they'd been around Manchester a long time. The QSG is not a myth. I got to know quite a lot of them personally. They were well-off people, flash cars, big houses.'

Superintendent Bill Kerr, who headed Manchester's drugs squad when the DIU was set up, begged to differ. He was aware of the QSG and who they were supposed to be, but was unimpressed: 'I don't like the title. It is misleading. It gives the impression of an organised gang, which from my information didn't exist on the same scale as other gangs. There was no hierarchical structure. I have no direct information of a gang of that type, comparable with other street gangs and gangs within the Manchester area that presently exist and have existed for the last ten years.'[10]

What is certain is that two events – the success of the armed robbery clampdown and the obsession with the QSG – not only hobbled the old order but also made room for the new. Police resources are finite, and if concentrated in one particular group they cannot be targeted on another. At the same time, a profound change was taking place in British society. The onset of mass unemployment was creating a pool of young men without hope. Violence was rising. Inter-district gang fights were becoming common again. Football hooliganism was a national concern. Guns were being used almost every day to commit crimes in Greater Manchester: in 1984 there had been eighty-nine armed robberies in the county; in 1985, despite the success of Operation Belgium, that figure was 139, and the GMP firearms squad went on twenty-four-hour alert. Someone had taken over.

Removing the city's predominant robbery gangs inadvertently opened the door for younger hoods emerging from the economic wastelands of Thatcherite Britain. 'The big difference between Liverpool and Manchester was that when James Anderton moved in during the eighties, he took out the middle tier,' said a Liverpool solicitor who has represented many major criminals. 'As a result, those below them had no influence or experience to look up to. They just ran wild.'

It was these wild gangs that faced the two Moss Side detectives when that frightened young man ran into their police station seeking sanctuary.

CHAPTER TWO

New Order

HAVING CONVINCED THEIR chief superintendent of the worth of their new informant, the two Moss Side detectives faced an even harder task: to persuade the X department. They would need manpower to stop any further clashes between Cheetham Hill and Moss Side, and X department was responsible for public order, providing the officers to handle protest marches, football matches and large-scale disturbances. The revelation that two large gangs were about to go to war should have tripped an immediate response. Instead, the detectives hit a wall of disbelief.

'A lot of information was in report form and at first no-one believed it,' said the DCI. 'Our boss, Frank Halligan, was beside himself because we were refused X department help. We were telling them about pre-arranged fights between eighty to a hundred a side, and they were saying, "This is bollocks, it can't be right." Halligan did a lot of work to get them to believe it. Then trouble kicked off at a christening in Moss Side and it followed from there.'

An unsanctioned robbery by one gang on the other's turf had caused the initial tension between the two sides. It was now exacerbated by trouble over a woman. A driving force in the Cheetham Hill mob was a prolific robber of mixed race, then aged in his mid-twenties. Tall, fearless and forceful, he became known to police as 'the Gladiator', for obvious reasons. 'He was very sharp, quick and strong,' said the DCI. 'He was doing a lot of very good, muscular armed robberies,' admitted Frank Halligan. 'He was responsible for a lot of good jobs, used a lot of force and caused a lot of problems.' The Gladiator had a long criminal record, beginning in his youth. He served a jail term in the early eighties and while he was inside, his girlfriend went out with one of the top Moss Side men. The Gladiator was furious. 'He felt this was an affront to his manhood, but at the same time it was seen to be uncool to fight over a woman,' said a gang member, on condition of anonymity. 'So he did not immediately do anything about it when he came out of jail, but there was this simmering tension.'

When a family with friends in both communities held a christening party at a house on the Alexandra Park estate in Moss Side, the Gladiator saw his chance. According to one version of events, he was standing in a doorway when a Moss Side man bumped into him and spilt a drink.

'Look at the mess you made,' said the Gladiator.

'Sorry, it was an accident.'

'That ain't good enough.'

Seizing his opportunity to make a statement to Moss Side, the Gladiator dragged the unfortunate man outside and beat him badly. 'Everyone comes out of the party and the two sides are drawn,' said the gang member. 'The Moss Side man who had been seeing his girlfriend comes out also, they have words and another fight kicks off. Then they fuck off back to Cheetham Hill and come back with guns.'

There was no shooting that day but the battle lines had been drawn.

* * *

On Thursday, 19 September 1985, the Cheetham Hill gang gathered in the car park of a pub in Rusholme, the largely Asian area of curry houses, takeaways and shops that borders Moss Side. Most of the group were teenagers, armed with baseball bats and sticks, nervous but charged with adrenalin. Their leaders barked a few instructions and they headed purposefully for Barnhill Street, an old Moss Side terraced street where Don's was located, one of the best-known shebeens. There they found their Moss Side enemies. A running fight broke out but police arrived before anyone was badly hurt.

The X department was suddenly convinced. Several days later, officers arrived in force to disperse a sixty-strong mob gathered at the south end of Alexandra Park, an area of grass, trees and a small lake that divides Moss Side from Whalley Range. 'They were all walking towards Alexandra Park and when the bobbies turned up they threw all their stuff away,' said the DCI. Several parked vehicles were searched and found to contain baseball bats, bricks and knives. Four youths were questioned afterwards. 'They were cruising around the streets in vans with mobs in the back, pulling up and having a battle, then driving off again,' said the DCI. 'We were worried about what could happen if a bobby stopped one of these vans and got done, but the battle was between themselves, not with the law. A characteristic then was that they wouldn't tackle the police. If just one bobby turned up, they would throw all their weapons away.'

Undeterred, the two sides faced off again the next day on a strip of spare land near the Whalley Hotel in Whalley Range, this time on the western rim of the Alexandra Park estate. As insults were exchanged, a Cheetham Hill soldier opened his coat, pulled out a sawn-off shotgun, and fired. The crowd scattered. Nineteen-year-old Roger Jordan, from Whalley Range, was found slumped on the ground by a passing motorist and was taken to hospital, where doctors removed pellets from his leg. There was no more scepticism. Gunshots were still rare in Manchester, and the police response moved up another gear.

Most of the gang members were known not by their real names but by nicknames, so the Moss Side detectives started a card index to keep track of who was who. 'They were all known by streetnames and this was the first time we had indexed them that way,' said the DCI. 'The local lads developed a really good intelligence system, jacked up from nothing. We ran our own intelligence files, keeping it tight because it was coming off informants. We wouldn't have put it in centrally. The lads in the Moss became quite an important little team and earned a fortune in overtime.' Their informant was still crucial. 'He was constantly able to put us on the scene when things were going to happen. Whenever there was an attack, we would know about it.'

They soon learned that, contrary to expectations, Cheetham Hill were the dominant force. 'They were armed robbers and were more organised and businesslike,' said a gang member. 'They had a different mentality. Moss Side were a bit thick business-wise.' In fact the Cheetham Hill mob was, at that time, the most dangerous and well-organised black gang in British history.

* * *

Cheetham Hill lies, like Moss Side, within walking distance of Manchester city centre. It was once a Jewish area, a pleasant suburb between the two main roads heading to the satellite mill towns of Bury and Rochdale. As they became more affluent, its Jewish inhabitants followed the established pattern and moved further out. The large houses they had owned were split into flats and poorer people moved in. Modern estates were also built – cheaply – around Fairy Lane, Hacking Street and Waterloo Road. They housed many black and Irish families who had moved out of Moss Side and Hulme during the clearances and, like Alexandra Park, quickly became havens for criminals.

The Cheetham Hill Gang began to coalesce on these estates in the late seventies and early eighties. It had five or six dominant characters who commanded respect by physical prowess, daring, ambition and, above all, force of personality. Many of its core members had African, rather than Caribbean, roots and their surnames were recognisably African. The same was true to a lesser extent of their Moss Side enemies; indeed many West Indian youths on the Moss did not see it as 'their' conflict and did not take part. This explained why numbers seemed to favour 'the Hill', whose leaders could call out large numbers of followers from housing projects like the Waterloo estate. They were powerful enough to issue an ultimatum to almost all of the young men of the estate: *you are with us or against us, and if you don't join us in the war you will be shot or will have to leave.* It worked.

The Hillbillies, as they became known, started small: muggings at knifepoint, snatches, theft, burglary. Shopkeepers in the early eighties often took their takings in small leather pouches to be

banked and were a prime target. The pickings were not big –
usually a few hundred pounds – but soon they were being turned
over at a rapid rate. The turning point, the step up, came when
the Hillbillies used guns in a raid on an Asda supermarket; they
escaped with £75,000. This showed them where the big money
was: armed robbery. They moved up a gear, became secretive
and dangerous, no longer scallies who dabbled in crime but
proper villains who did it right: balaclavas and boiler suits,
observation of targets, route-planning and fast getaways. There
was no mercy on raids; they were in and out in a ferocious wave
of energy, flashing machetes, ramming shotguns in faces, telling
staff they'd blow their *fucking* brains out if they didn't co-operate
– and looking and sounding like they meant it.

Most jobs involved no more than four people, often including
a white driver, a quirk copied to some extent by Moss Side. White
lads were perceived to be better wheelmen and were also less
likely to be pulled up by traffic police. The police called these
small squads 'domino teams' because of their mixed racial make-
up. A white driver and two black accomplices battered a Security
Express guard with a pickaxe handle and escaped in a Porsche
with £23,000 from a bank in Ancoats. Another domino team had
held school staff captive while waiting to rob a security van in the
south of the city, and a third, clad in boiler suits and ski masks,
attacked the owner of a clothing firm in Cheetham with baseball
bats and a hammer, fracturing his skull.

'It had been assumed that Moss Side was pre-eminent but the
lads from Cheetham Hill were actually a lot more violent,' said
the DCI. 'One guy lived near the Whalley pub [in Whalley Range]
and two of the Cheetham Hill leaders broke in through his patio
doors. He locked himself in an armoured loo but they broke in
and macheted him. He had over a hundred wounds. They also
didn't abuse drugs, didn't drink, and when we raided their houses,
a typical trick was to leave the phone off the cradle so they could
hear our conversations. They were good. They had communica-
tions interception before we did. They were always on the move,
and used an overspill estate at Handforth in Cheshire for safe
houses.'

Some did not live in Cheetham Hill, which complicated police attempts to understand who was allied to whom. They had ties in Moss Side and friendships criss-crossing the city. 'There were a series of woundings in Wythenshawe [in south Manchester] where people had gone to live with relatives. There had been an unwritten rule that they wouldn't break into each other's houses. One side broke it and after that all hell let loose.'

They also had no fear of the police. Members of the serious crime squad staked out a rent office after a tip-off that it was going to be hit by a Cheetham Hill team. Sure enough, they arrived, only to be pursued by the police. Officers cornered them at a parade of shops, and hand-to-hand fighting ensued. 'They threw some of the serious crime squad men over a balcony and they ended up in hospital,' said the DCI. The Hillbillies were fit, athletic lads and they could fight. 'There was another fight at the leisure centre at Stretford Baths, where the serious crime squad went to get one of the Cheetham Hill leaders and a couple of others,' said the DCI. 'They were wrestling with these guys who were stripped to their shorts and soaking wet. It was almost comical.' The Moss Side men, too, were openly hostile to the uniform, though generally detectives were out of bounds. One night on the Alexandra Park estate, a police sergeant and a constable were leaving a pub where they had been making enquiries when they saw a drugs deal taking place. They went to question two men and were attacked by a crowd. One suffered a broken nose, the other a bruised face. All of their attackers escaped.

'As the streets were kicking off, they were withdrawing uniformed officers from the streets and only the CID could patrol,' said the DCI. 'There were threats to gang-rape policewomen. Yet CID could go in at will, there was never a problem. We had an armed response team stationed with us to do the inquiries but there was never any aggravation. People would take refuge in a shebeen and if a strange cop walked in they would get robbed in the toilets, but the local detectives could move at will. Our informant was constantly able to put us on the scene when things were going to happen. Whenever there was an attack we would know about it. It went on for years. We took him out for a few good meals but he was paid nothing. Without him we would have had nothing.'

In January 1986, four months after the shooting of Roger Jordan, armed police battered down the door of a house in Wythenshawe, a vast south Manchester housing estate, where they believed the gunman was hiding out. He wasn't there, but two men were taken away for questioning. In all, the police raided more than a dozen homes in search of the man over several months. Two months later, police in Leeds chased a high-powered stolen car. The driver, the man they wanted for the Jordan shooting, escaped and the car was found abandoned. Armed officers staked it out, and early the next morning saw a man approach the vehicle. He then went to a nearby flat but fled through a first-floor window. A week later, the police spotted him again, this time driving through the Fitton Hill district of Oldham. Officers from the Tactical Aid Group were called out and the quarry was cornered in a street, but suddenly rammed an unmarked CID car and tried to speed off. His vehicle overturned but he crawled out and ran until he was brought down by a bevy of officers. He was held in custody and questioned about a number of serious offences.

His arrest was one of a number of factors that calmed the gang war for about twelve months. Others factors included continued police interventions based on intelligence from their informant, and some successes against some of the more prolific Moss Side armed robbers. The calm allowed other businesses to flourish. In May 1986, three-quarters of a kilo of brown heroin, worth around £100,000 when cut and sold, was seized in a car that had arrived on the Alexandra Park estate from Toxteth in Liverpool. It was the largest amount of heroin seized on a Manchester street up to that time. Smack had hit Moss Side.

★ ★ ★

Heroin and crime are today synonymous, yet for much of the Twentieth Century the United Kingdom took a medical, rather than legal, approach to opiate addiction. While in the United States it was a criminal offence for a doctor to prescribe narcotics for a patient, in Britain addicts were deemed to be sick, not feckless or immoral. Their care was left to the professional judgement of doctors, who decided on appropriate treatment and were allowed to maintain the habits of the relatively small number of addicts. Usage of 'soft' drugs, particularly cannabis, did slowly increase but heroin and cocaine were rare. 'The drug scene in the fifties was virtually non-existent,' said John Stalker. 'It involved a few seamen and a bit of hash and a few Jamaican elders who smoked it all their lives. You could count the number of drug arrests on two hands in the City of Manchester in the fifties.

'Life changed in the sixties with the big clubs. The Twisted Wheel was a good example, that size of club that attracted anything up to two thousand people from all the north of England. That was when the chemical drugs became more prevalent, amphetamines and so on, and became part of the club scene. That really was the beginning of the heavier drug scene, when it became more of a need and less of a social event. The Chief Constable at the time formed a full-time drug squad and, like all drug squads, they found there was a bigger problem than they had known about: if you don't look for it, you don't find it. Because these clubs in Manchester were national institutions, we got national salesmen as it were, drug operators, coming from all over the north and the Midlands to sell drugs in Manchester and it brought problems which have never gone away.'

The Twisted Wheel opened in Brazennose Street in 1963 before relocating to Whitworth Street, where it remained until its closure in 1971. It was a beatnik venue before becoming a mod club and later the birthplace of Northern Soul. It pioneered all-nighters and with that came drugs, especially amphetamines pills. Harder drugs remained rare. As late as the mid-sixties, there was virtually no smuggled heroin in the UK because the legal provision of low-cost drugs had largely eliminated the profit incentives supporting such traffic. Crime by addicts was also almost non-existent; they did not need to become thieves or prostitutes to fund their habits.

Everything changed when the Brain Committee, convened under neurologist Lord Brain, recommended in 1964 that the right to prescribe opiates be denied to GPs, and instead restricted to psychiatric specialists operating in an environment in which the addict was subjected to regimes of discipline and surveillance. A policy of notification was instituted similar to that for infectious diseases. The Dangerous Drugs Act of 1967 and its successor, the Misuse of Drugs Act 1971, followed. They were Britain's equivalents of the Volstead Act, which outlawed the sale of alcohol in the USA after the First World War. Doctors were banned from prescribing heroin and cocaine and had to notify the Home Office of anyone known or suspected of being addicted. It drove access to hard drugs completely underground and created an entire world, an underworld, underpinned by the drug economy. Illegal drugs would become Britain's Prohibition, making millions for criminals and creating a climate where gangsterism could flourish.

'We thought we could police the drugs problem off the streets,' said a former detective chief inspector, Ron Clarke, who would write a drugs strategy for Greater Manchester Police in the 1990s. 'Overnight, treatment for people with drug problems was removed. We started to get an increase in burglaries at chemists and drug stores. That led to a hue and cry by the police and drug enforcement agencies. We weren't skilled to deal with drug addicts. That led to the Misuse of Drugs Act. That was when we really started policing drugs in this country.' The seventies saw the gradual ending of prescribed opiates; users could instead be given the synthetic heroin substitute methadone. Yet if the changes were intended to reduce the number of addicts, they failed – spectacularly. The first major seizures of smuggled heroin came in 1971 and soon criminal gangs saw the profits that could be made – including, allegedly, the Quality Street Gang. The mass media announced the onset of a drugs epidemic.

Smack became a big problem in Manchester around 1979, at the time of the revolution in Iran, when thousands fled the Ayatollah's men and opium poured out of the country. It was easier to conceal from Customs checks than the far bulkier cannabis. 'About eighty-nine per cent of all drugs targeted at this country get through,' said Ron Clarke. 'We estimate Customs get ten per cent and the police get one per cent. We catch very, very few of the Mister Bigs of this world. What we are very good at is catching the street dealers [but] the majority we deal with are addicts themselves.' Hard drug prosecutions nationwide rose ninefold between 1981 and 1983. Amounts seized were consistently higher and of better quality than in previous years. Labour MP Alf Morris, whose constituency covered Wythenshawe, said to be the largest housing estate in Europe, claimed a 'tidal wave' of cheap heroin was being sold in pubs and colleges in South Manchester. The main players were now conscious of police activity, using safehouses for their stashes and 'clean faces' unknown to the police to sell their stuff.

In April 1984, the Home Office posted a senior police officer to The Hague in Holland 'to improve operational intelligence about drug smuggling operations targeted on the UK' and a senior Customs officer was sent to Karachi in Pakistan. Both postings were overdue. Early 1985 saw the first major seizures of cocaine at Manchester Airport, and Amsterdam was considered the main source of entry. Nationally, cocaine seizures rose fivefold between 1982–3. At the same time, Asia had become a prime source of heroin for the Manchester market. In one early case, two white brothers teamed up with three Pakistanis living in Longsight to arrange the importation of £2.25 million of heroin, a huge amount for the time. It was driven from Pakistan to Calais in France by a private in the Ulster Defence Regiment but was seized at Dover. All of the conspirators received long jail terms: the judge told them that every packet of drugs they sold 'sowed the seeds of death'. The south Manchester connection was significant. 'A lot of problems with the Moss Side riots were against Asian property,' said Frank Halligan. 'Really it is the Asians that probably started the heroin trade. A lot of the real big fellers were Asians. I don't know how they then made selling links with the blacks but Rusholme was just a derelict road with a few shops and it absolutely mushroomed with a huge amount of money from nowhere.'

Manchester's distribution of drugs once they had arrived from abroad was controlled largely by white criminals, men like Robert 'Rab' Carruthers, a thirty-seven-year-old Scot whose criminal record began at the age of ten. He joined the violent Cadder Young Team, a Glasgow gang, before fleeing the city after being implicated in a murder and settling in Eccles, Salford. His partner Terry Jeffries was an ageing Manchester villain who had also been in trouble since childhood yet who could afford to spend £12,000 on private cardiac surgery. Just a week after having three new valves put into his heart, he was flying to Paris to tie up an international deal bringing in heroin from Pakistan. Carruthers, who sold on to a network of suppliers in the north of England and Scotland, was his partner, while finance was put up by an eight-man syndicate. They were caught when a consignment of drugs was found hidden in a suitcase at Heathrow and both received nine years. Carruthers, who at one time was tipped as the prospective Mr Big of the Glasgow underworld, would reappear ten years later in another big heroin case and would eventually die from his own addiction to the drug in 2004.

By the mid-eighties, Britain was in the grip of a drugs epidemic and nowhere was hit harder than Manchester. James Anderton warned in his 1984 annual report of 'a horrifying explosion' of trafficking and predicted that many more crimes were going to be attributable to drugs. Arrests for heroin possession were doubling every year, partly because of an increase in smoking rather than injecting. By the summer of 1985, the Department of Health was saying that the north-west had the worst record in the country for drug-related admissions to treatment units and mental hospitals. The Home Office described Manchester as an 'area of prime concern' and the city council called a summit of police, customs officials, probation officers, education experts, welfare workers and social services heads to discuss the drug problem. 'We have an international airport which is now extending its flight network to areas where drugs emanate, so it is imperative we recognise the dangers now and discover the scale of the problem we already have,' said GMC deputy leader Peter Kelly. Customs officers claimed more than £100 million of heroin and cocaine was passing through the city and its airport every year.

Anderton and his force were struggling to hold back a rising tide of lawlessness, fuelled by social inequality and rising unemployment: in Greater Manchester, sixteen per cent of the workforce was without a job. As crime in England and Wales soared to record levels, the north-west had the highest rate of any region: overall crime rose by thirty-nine per cent between 1981 and 1986, while robberies almost doubled. The region had the most burglaries and criminal damage and the second highest rates of theft, fraud and forgery. Serious woundings rose equally rapidly and the number of villains carrying firearms had reached 'frightening proportions,' according to Anderton. When the Chief Constable announced the setting up of his shadowy drugs intelligence unit, coincident with a Government advertising campaign against heroin, it was already too late for some Manchester officers. 'The horse has already bolted,' one detective commented. 'Firm action was needed at least four years ago.' Britain had created its Prohibition, and now had its Chicago. Manchester had become Britain's crime capital.

Primed to exploit this were the new gangs. As the *Manchester Evening News* put it, 'The old white underworld, dominated in Manchester by a federation with its roots in 50s Ancoats, still runs most of the money but has competition at street level from the black-dominated gangs formed in the city's new smelting grounds of desperation, greed and anarchy.' The judiciary was in little doubt where the chief smelting ground was. 'If the police force were to man a vigilant watch on the area circumscribed by Wilmslow Road, Princess Parkway, Wilbraham Road and Moss Lane East, they would kill the drugs problem in Manchester overnight,' remarked senior judge Ivan Taylor QC while jailing a cannabis dealer at Manchester Crown Court. The area he described was Moss Side.

* * *

The Cheetham Hill-Moss Side war re-ignited one night in a row over a girl at a 'blues' – an illicit club. 'She was dancing with a Moss Side lad and some of the Cheetham Hill weren't happy about it,' said a source. 'The lad was white, which also offended some of Cheetham men. It turned nasty but some of the Moss Side spoke up for the white lad and stood their ground. From that incident, it escalated.' Women would be a recurring source of friction between the two sides.

After a year-long lull, the clash at the blues sparked fresh fighting. Many of the incidents during this phase of the conflict are hazy, as attacks were often not reported to the police, but one of the worst was an attack by Cheetham Hill on the Reno, a colourful late-night joint on Princess Road. One of the main Hillbillies had driven his car into a mob of Moss Side and been macheted in the head, and the Reno attack was apparently revenge for that. The Hillbillies gathered at a house where they put on their boiler suits and laid out an array of bats, machetes, knives and meat cleavers. Then they put on a violent video and watched it together to pump themselves up. Some began to shout out what they were going to do to their enemies. Then they set off for the Reno. It was carnage. 'They steamed in and started indis-criminately beating people,' said an ex-gang member. 'People were getting chopped and beaten over the head with bats.' At least fifteen were injured.

Still top of the Hillbillies' hit list was the Moss Side man who had dated the Gladiator's girl. On a Sunday evening three weeks before Christmas 1986, twenty-seven-year-old Melvyn Adai left his terraced house in Rusholme and slid into a waiting Ford Escort XR3 driven by a friend. They were about to pull away when a figure padded up behind the car on soft-soled shoes. He was wearing a full-faced balaclava, what appeared to be dread-locks, and a quilted jacket. He levelled a shotgun at the window. The driver saw him, threw open his door, and ran. 'He was supposed to get the car in gear but instead he got himself in gear,' commented one gang member. The gunman fired twice in an explosion of lead shot and glass. One blast almost severed one of Adai's legs; the other tore up his arm. The gunman then ran, startling a nosey neighbour so much that the terrified man jumped back through his own glass door, and was picked up by a waiting car. More residents alerted by the shots ran out to find Adai a bloody mess. 'He was in a terrible state,' neighbour John Heinz told the *Manchester Evening News*. 'A hole had been blown clean through his leg.'

The shooting of Melvyn Adai seemed to herald another quietus. Precipitate police action again deterred the few who were bent on conflict and so prevented others from being dragged into it. In 1987, the Gladiator was jailed for robbery, a Cheetham Hill domino team was caught robbing a supermarket in Nottingham, and the most dangerous Moss Side leader also went down for robbery: 'He was the one they really feared because he was a proper calculating geezer who could do some serious damage,' said a gangland source. 'That knocked the stuffing out of the older lot in Moss Side.' It seemed that the war was over. At least no-one had been killed.

★ ★ ★

Ivanhoe Preston worked as a bouncer at a shebeen in Broadfield Road, in the heart of Moss Side. Though he lived in Cheetham Hill, Preston knew many people on the Moss and in some ways represented the old order that was rapidly fading: he was forty-nine years old and, at six foot four, kept order by his size and bearing rather than how many weapons or 'soldiers' he could call on. That was no longer enough. Late one night in March 1987, he turned away a man whose attitude he didn't like. At 4.30am, the man returned, carrying a shotgun. Ivan Preston saw him and quickly shut the door, but the man fired through the flimsy wood, blowing away part of Preston's thigh and severing a main artery. The mortally wounded doorman lay in agony for fifteen minutes before anyone called the police, and no-one dared venture from the club in case the gunman was still outside, even though several others had been injured by pellets. Preston, a father of three, eventually received thirty pints of blood in hospital, but it was too late. He died soon afterwards.

Ivan Preston's death marked a break with the past. The shebeens had always been moody places, where slashings and cuttings were common enough to be unremarkable. Now, however, the new gangs were bringing their beefs into the drinking dens, and could no longer be intimidated into behaving by the older heavies. 'The old shebeen bosses who ran the places in Moss Side, and the one in Cheetham Hill run by a Nigerian called Banjo, they had no time for this,' said the DCI. 'They thought the gangs had no respect and didn't like them in the premises. There was a bit of hash in those places but they were stable and it wasn't in their interests to have disorder, but the young bucks would walk in and machete everyone and it was bad for business. They had a big cult following. You would get fifteen woundings in a night. They would stretch people across a car and cut their tendons.' Worse than that, they were now prepared to use 'shooters' almost indiscriminately.

The deadly triangle of drugs, guns and gangs had formed.

CHAPTER THREE

The Pepperhill Mob

'A MATE OF mine's sister used to live in Alexandra Park estate, on the east side of it, and that is where we used to hang out. We used to stash guns and drugs at her house. There was a pub across the road called the Pepperhill. That's where we used to drink, so people trying to describe that group of lads, instead of going through their names, they would just go, "the Pepperhill lot'. That is how that came about. It wasn't like we would sit there and say, "We need a name, what do we call our gang?" '

Anthony Stevens, a stocky, bullet-headed black man, was born and raised in Whalley Range, in a close and disciplined family environment. 'We weren't angels but we knew what it was like to have to grow up with manners and respecting people around you.' He had to attend church every week, address adults respectfully, be polite and well-mannered in public. The rod was rarely spared and backchat earned a backhander. 'A friend of mine did some graffiti all over the park wall and I remember seeing his mother stood there beating him whilst he was trying to scrub it all back off again.'

Stevens and his close friends formed a tight-knit group of eight or nine, many from Whalley Range, who came to adulthood at a time of the highest unemployment since the 1930s. Jobs for black youths with a Moss Side postcode were almost non-existent, despite the efforts of bodies such as the Moss Side and Hulme Task Force, which spent large sums on employment schemes. The area had a high percentage of single-parent families and more than a quarter of its population was aged between fifteen and twenty-five. If any zone was ripe for an American-style gang culture, it was this. Its bored, disenchanted young men turned to whatever means they could to make money: opportunist crime, drug dealing, whatever. The fortnightly £32.50 Giro cheque was never going to be enough.

'When it came to the Thatcher years, young black males were at the bottom of the pile,' said Stevens. 'There was no hope. I was in the top class all the way at school but I couldn't get a job. I can honestly say that when we all left school and college, we were actively trying to find employment, and because we couldn't, we saw other ways to fund our lives. We wanted flash cars. What am I supposed to do with thirty-two pounds fifty a fortnight?

'A lot of us tried – I'm talking about some very notorious gangsters, some of them now dead, some in jail and some still on the street. One tried to start a garage business, fixing cars. I tried to start a PA business because I was always interested in music.' Nothing worked; it was a bad time to start a business as well as to look for a job. 'The ones who had the balls turned to armed robberies and God knows what, and those who had the brains thought, there is the drugs market. Up to that point, hardly any of us knew what heroin or cocaine was. There was no sort of gang culture. People just did what they did to make money.'

Their base became the Pepperhill, a squat, brick-built public house with living accommodation above that was part-owned by Great Britain rugby league star Des Drummond. It sat in a secluded position in a tiny road on the Alexandra Park housing estate, which lies beside the main Princess Road thoroughfare and just north of the parkland from which it takes its name. Alex Park had been built in the seventies to a Radburn layout, a style pioneered in the United States to separate pedestrians and cars and emphasise secluded areas, cul-de-sacs and patches of green. It was meant to provide an attractive, calming, natural environment. Instead the estate had poor lighting, dangerous walkways and a lack of clear definition between public and private space.

The Pepperhill lads were of West Indian descent, younger and distinct from the local 'Africans' who warred with Cheetham Hill. 'They were the big, old-style gangsters and they didn't mix with us,' said Stevens. 'They were a bit classier than our lot, in flash BMWs. Their women were always beautiful. Our lot came raw off the streets, every low-down critter you can imagine, though I don't know why. We were all raised well.' The older Africans were more anglicised: they listened to rhythm and blues and soul, went to the Reno and drank Guinness stout. 'They were very English and didn't seem to have much of a connection with us on a cultural level. I was unaware at the time that quite a few of them did have connections with their homelands, with Gambia and Nigeria. They were heavy characters, guys we had heard of on the street, but their world was different from ours.' The younger West Indians were into reggae, spliffs and Red Stripe lager, frequented nightclubs in the city and riffed in patois, which the Africans couldn't understand. When the first war kicked off with Cheetham Hill, the Pepperhill lads stayed out of it. 'We were smoking ganja and weed and arguing over sound systems,' said Stevens. 'What did this fighting have to do with us? There was a big African influence among Cheetham Hill as well and many of their leaders had African surnames. It didn't involve us.'

A trait the Pepperhill boys shared with the older crowd was the urge to look good. Moss Side lads generally regarded Cheetham Hill as scruffy – loud gold necklaces and bracelets that had gone out of fashion on the Moss were referred to disparagingly as 'Cheetham Hill chains'. The more businesslike Hillbillies might have earned the money but they didn't have the style, or so the Moss lads believed. They cultivated a 'rude boy' demeanour: good clothes worn well, a devil-may-care attitude, and take no man's disrespect. 'Cheetham Hill, with all their money from crime, couldn't understand why the women still looked over their shoulder at us,' said another Moss Side gangster. 'That caused a lot of conflict.'

On a typical day, Stevens and his mates would rise late, make a few phone calls to see who was around, perhaps run a couple of family errands, then amble over to the Pepperhill in the early afternoon. There they would smoke weed, drink, play pool, sell drugs, perhaps duck out for a pattie or fish and chips, while the resident sound system churned out leaden-bass roots reggae.

'Every day was like a holiday. You don't realise it at the time but you are in a permanent state of being stoned. We sold anything. We didn't give a shit. The cops didn't raid us; they didn't care. They would rather know where we were and not have us troubling other people. This was when they had what I call Operation Container, which was to keep the drugs problem on the estate and not let it spread, though they deny it.' It would become Moss Side folklore that the police allowed the drug trade to flourish there in the mid to late eighties and so kept it away from more affluent, white areas.

At weekends, the Pepperhill lads would head for the Gallery, the most popular black club, on the corner of Peter Street and Deansgate. 'The Gallery was maybe intimidating if you weren't used to it, and jeeps parked up outside the club on a Saturday night blocked the highway, but the music was pure gold and the club rocked,' according to DJ and author Dave Haslam.[11] The crew would spend the night dancing in a fug of marijuana smoke before ending the night at one of the many shebeens, often until sunrise. 'On Friday and Saturday nights, people just cruised around listening for the bass. That told you where the party was,' said Stevens.

The Pepperhill crew may have had respectable family back-grounds but they hung out in one of the toughest inner-city areas in Britain, and they were ruthless when crossed. 'Anyone who fucked with us got severely, severely dealt with,' said Stevens. 'When people troubled us, we annihilated them. We were tight and we were insular. No-one knew that much about any of us.'

* * *

Their first sign of serious trouble came when a fresh teenager called Julian Bradshaw took to hanging out with some older Pepperhill lads. They found him funny. Bradshaw liked to wind up the 'yardies', native-born Jamaicans who drank in the Big Western pub on the estate, and would skit their accents and mannerisms. Had he been older, he would have known it was a mistake. The Jamaicans were not to be messed with: while their homeland is a tropical paradise for tourists, its ghettoes or 'yards' are among the most violent places on earth. One day one of the yardies slapped Bradshaw and threw him out of the pub. The next day, the teenager walked into the bookmakers in the shopping precinct and, in retaliation, hit Anthony 'Soldier' Baker over the head with a baseball bat.

Soldier was over six feet tall, a former British infantryman who took no shit. So when Bradshaw also took two of the Pepperhill to assault his girlfriend, he snapped. Two of the men were arrested, and Baker and his girlfriend called at Moss Side police station, where they were being held. She told officers she did not want to pursue the complaint, but Baker shouted across the cell area to the two men to go to his home 'to sort something out'.

The two men were released and two hours later drove with Bradshaw and a fourth man to the Alex Park estate. Bradshaw was belligerent, bragging he was going to give Baker 'some Englishman's licks'. No doubt they felt there was strength in numbers, but when Baker arrived he was in no mood for talking. He pulled up a hood to cover his face, produced a shotgun and fired. Bradshaw and one of his companions, a Pepperhill stalwart called Ian McLeod, jumped into their car while the others fled. McLeod knew Baker and tried to reason with him but Baker fired again through a window and hit McLeod in the stomach. Bradshaw, who was wounded in the arm, drove off but crashed. He abandoned the car and ran into a small close but Baker tracked him down and found him leaning against a wall. He fired again. Bradshaw fell and lay on the pavement, bleeding, as Baker approached.

'Please, please don't,' begged Bradshaw. 'No more.'

'You were warned,' muttered Baker. Then he shot the teenager dead.

Baker would strongly deny involvement, claiming he was at a friend's house at the time of the shootings, but was later jailed for life for murdering Bradshaw and wounding McLeod. 'You were persistent and merciless,' said the judge.

The Pepperhill had let someone into their tight crew and it had cost them. It was a lesson they failed to learn. Anthony Stevens later saw it as the beginning of the end for him. 'My influence with my lads was diminishing. I was always the more business-minded. I wanted us to have money. The less I was about, the more trouble crept in. The first skirmish they had was when we opened our borders to outsiders. The very thing that brought us together was being eroded.'

That July saw a Manchester record: four armed robberies in one day. Guns were becoming ubiquitous and the average robber was no longer the experienced villain in his thirties but a young man or even a teenager. Some were just fifteen. 'We are now in the shotgun era and the pickaxe handle is almost a thing of the past,' commented Assistant Chief Constable Ralph Lees. There seemed to be robberies almost every day: kidnappings, jewellery snatches, payroll heists, post office stick-ups, and they were more and more violent, with shots often fired. Both Cheetham Hill and Moss Side had teams out regularly, scouring for targets. The gun was also replacing the knife and the machete in inter-gang disputes. Summertime was always especially edgy.

* * *

One Cheetham Hill stronghold was the Apollo public house on the Waterloo estate, a base for drug dealing, fencing stolen goods and planning robberies. On a Thursday night in July 1987, two traffic cops stopped an eighteen-year-old outside on suspicion of a motoring offence. He was one of the Cheetham crew and a hostile crowd emerged from the pub. Local beat bobby John Piekos went to assist his two colleagues. A punch broke his nose. Back-up was quickly on the scene and the cops arrested three men and bundled them into a van. The Hillbilly mob of thirty split up and the police pulled out.

Shortly afterwards, another constable was driving through the area in a panda car when a brick came through one of his windows, breaking his arm. A police dog handler on stand-by was attacked in his van and hit on the head with another brick, and a traffic patrol car was dented by another missile. Two parked cars, one a police vehicle, were turned on their sides and another was stolen and set alight. The local inspector activated contingency plans put in place after the Moss Side riots and police from other divisions were drafted in. They had the desired effect; as night set, in the incident fizzled out and the crowds drifted off.

The next day, Collyhurst Division commander Walter Elder played it down as a 'routine incident', but a city council report asserted that 'police harassment and misconduct' had worsened problems in the area. Only one in 100 GMP officers was non-white and accusations of racism were routine. Jim Anderton had a terrible relationship with the left-wing city council, and the chairman of the police committee and certain councillors delighted in undermining him, or holding him to account, depending on which side of the fence you sat. Privately, officers were furious about the report, blaming a hard core of between eighteen and thirty local men who persistently broke the law. 'We police the Cheetham area as sensitively as we can,' said a superintendent. 'We don't harass or wish to offend but we have a duty to protect all people and if people break the law, whatever their colour, we have to act accordingly.'[12]

* * *

A growing contempt for the police spread to the Moss. On a Sunday night that September, a patrol car spotted four men in a Ford Escort reportedly stolen from Cheetham. They gave chase and tailed the vehicle to the car park of the 8411 Centre, a community building near Moss Side's so-called Frontline, where the men in the car knew they would get help. As they piled out of their vehicle, the officers managed to grab two of them; one butted a policeman in the face.

The other two got away and shouted to groups nearby. Some piled out from a party at the 8411. The outnumbered officers came under a hail of bottles, bricks and clubs and were forced to release the arrested men. Three hundred rioters gathered in the street and in the ensuing battle eleven police officers were injured. Reinforcements were called in but eventually made what was described as a 'tactical withdrawal' to let the rioters disperse. Nine police vehicles were damaged, including one that was burned out.

It was open war between the cops and the gangs.

★ ★ ★

'It happened so quickly. It was very violent. I thought I'd been punched. It was a knife in the chest.' Three weeks after the battle at the 8411, twenty-six-year-old PC Allan Donohue was in the car park of the Great Western Hotel on the Alex estate, trying to make an arrest. The Moss Side lads had other ideas. Forty of them closed in and one plunged a knife into the officer. The radio in his breast pocket deflected the blade into a rib and probably saved his life. Another thrust severed an artery and soaked him with blood. Someone hit him over the head with a bottle. 'I was very dazed. My colleagues dragged me away. If they hadn't helped, I'd have been dead.'[13] As his constable lay strapped up and recovering in Manchester Royal Infirmary, James Anderton declared, 'It is impossible to provide routine policing of the character we are so often told is desirable if our officers, often working alone and always unarmed, stand to be attacked whenever they seek to arrest someone in the street.' Once again, not one witness came forward.

The reason for this overt hostility towards the uniform was that Moss Side had become Manchester's centre for dealing hard drugs, which carried potentially bigger jail sentences than cannabis and pills, and so dealers would go to greater lengths to escape arrest. One of those who noticed the change was a young detective called Tony Brett. Tall, slim and articulate in a mildly-spoken way, he was a keen observer of the streets. 'I went on the drugs squad around 1984. There didn't appear to be any drug gangs then. There was small-scale drug dealing going on all over the place on a self-financing basis; it tended to be addicts who sold themselves. What changed it was the entry of people who came in purely for profit. And the first time I really noticed that was in and around the Moss Side shopping precinct in 1988. There had always been cannabis dealers in Moss Side but now we were seeing people selling heroin in the street.'

The Moss Side Leisure and Shopping Centre, an unprepossessing, indoor block of shops and a small covered market, provided an important service for the community in an area ignored by supermarket chains. It had also been yardie territory for weed-dealing purposes, as the Jamaicans liked a bet and hung out at the bookies there. When Class A powders began to arrive in significant quantities, a younger element began dealing by the Hotpot pub at the back of the precinct. Another main dealing area, in front of a row of shops on Moss Lane, became known as the Frontline.

Heroin, which had fallen in price, was the drug of a disenchanted generation. The young men who started selling it did not really know what they had but soon a ghostly army of addicts was patrolling the city, 'grafting' and stealing to feed their insatiable habits. Addicts or users in outlying districts and towns might once have bought locally from other users but now a market was consolidated in a single location, with a regular supply guaranteed. 'In amongst the weed-sellers of Moss Side, there began to appear a new type of dealer who was using the market place to hawk heroin and who was a businessman, not a user,' wrote BBC journalist Jon Silverman. 'As word spread, the Moss Side shopping precinct became a magnet for heroin addicts firstly from all over the city, then Greater Manchester, then eventually the entire region, stretching from the Midlands up to Cumbria. By the time the police mounted a major undercover operation, codenamed Corkscrew, in 1989, Moss Side had become a heroin bazaar where the traders were raking in a fortune.'[14]

A number of impromptu businesses sprang up to serve the dealers, their hangers-on and their customers, including the Chicken Run, a makeshift fast food outlet. 'At any one time there was fifty people dealing around the bookies, along Southcombe Walk and around the Hotpot,' said Anthony Stevens. 'Then there was the other lot around Medlock Court, which was attached to the precinct and was where the Chicken Run was. There were that many dealers out that one of the women who lived round there, they smelt her cooking and said it smelt good, so she started selling her cooking out of her house. The next thing, she had tables up and it was a proper business. Then an ice cream guy started coming there, and he would sell Rizlas and foil as well as his ice cream.'

Detective Tony Brett saw it all escalate. 'I was probably the officer who pressed the button. You stood and watched and thought to yourself, *There are people selling heroin here in a shopping parade. How can this be?* Then you got people with established streetnames. That is everything in that area; it is like Marks and Spencer. To have a good name, you have got to sell good quality gear, give no hassle to your customers and be available virtually twenty-four hours a day. And the only way you get to that stage is if you market it. The precinct was the embryo of it. People realised that if they had twenty bags of heroin on a corner, someone would approach them. To this day, I don't know how Moss Side became the centre for it, but the market established itself.'

The Hillbillies and the Pepperhill lads had no personal beef with each other yet but it was kindling: the drugs, and the money and power they bought, were too attractive for the Cheetham crew to ignore. They began to 'tax' the occasional dealer on the Frontline. 'People will watch to see what amounts you're getting through, and try to find out who you're buying from to see how big you buy,' one Moss Side dealer told the *Independent*. 'Then they put two and two together and set you up. They'll wait till you come home, burst into your house all masked-up, tooled-up, and basically put a piece to your head and say, "Where's your money," and you've to give it 'em. It's quick money to be made and there's no risk unless the guy fights back. There's no risk of the law being involved. I've heard up to sixty grand's been taxed.'[15] The dealers soon stopped flaunting their gold jewellery, realising it could make them a target. Others tooled-up themselves, ready for war. The streets were waiting for the conflagration. It needed only a spark.

* * *

Delroy Brown arrived in Manchester 'dripping in gold and driving a BMW,' in the memorable phrase of one police officer.[16] A young black man from Birmingham, he'd endured an unsettled childhood and had lived in children's homes in North Wales and, latterly, Manchester, where he fell in with some of the Moss Side boys. Good-looking and self-assured, Brown was soon hanging out on the Frontline, where he hooked up with a couple of the Pepperhill crowd. Not all of them were impressed. 'He came to Manchester because apparently he was in a load of trouble in Birmingham and had to leave for his own safety,' said Anthony Stevens. 'He was an absolute nothing in my eyes. What saw him rise to prominence was that he was attacked for no other reason than an argument over a woman.'

Brown, known as 'D', began dating a beautiful ex-girlfriend of the Cheetham Hill leader. This alone was viewed as an affront, but when he was also seen with the girl of another Cheetham Hill man serving time for robbery, there was outrage. The jailbird sent word that, though he couldn't do anything about it, he expected his boys to. A pack of Hillbillies caught up with Brown in the street five days before Christmas, 1987. They beat him to the ground, stomped him, chopped his face and arm, took his money and jewellery worth £1,000, and left him with wounds needing twenty stitches. His BMW was driven away, trashed and abandoned.

It was the kind of reprisal the Hillbillies had carried out many times before. Usually the victim kept his mouth shut, licked his wounds and tried to forget about it. Had the Hillbillies left it there, what followed might never have happened, but they next sent word to Brown that he was to pay them £1,000 a week, or he was dead. He missed his first payment, so they fired a shot through his front window, then informed him that the amount had gone up to £2,000 a week and would keep rising if he didn't pay.

* * *

Another night, another blues. A few weeks after Delroy Brown's beating, a car pulled up outside a noisy shebeen popular with a younger crowd in Gretney Walk, Moss Side. Anthony 'Scratch' Gardener was in the passenger seat. Gardener lived a double life. He had been raised in a law-abiding, God-fearing family and earlier that evening had been to a church service. Scratch was a good-looking, well-dressed young man, popular with women, and had two young children. He hid from his parents his convictions for assault, theft and burglary. He had also apparently fallen out with the Cheetham Hill leader over money and had made the mistake of telling him where to get off.

Unseen in the shadows, a dark-browed, white-skinned young gunman stood waiting. He had been there for half an hour, silent and still, watching as people arrived. When he saw Gardener's car pulling in, he stiffened, reached inside his coat and stepped from the gloom. He walked past the car once to eyeball his target, then turned. His gun cracked. Scratch Gardener was shot dead.

More than fifty people were in the blues, but in the early days of their investigation, the police could trace only six. They even put out appeals on Moss Side's illegal pirate radio station, ICR, which broadcast from addresses in Moss Side and Hulme and reached a big Afro-Caribbean audience. 'They have taken a great part of us away,' said Gardener's mother, Floris. 'Sometimes we sit down and we cry and we groan.'[17] Police kept hearing one name: that of a virtual unknown on the gang scene, a teenager called Tony Johnson, who was from the south side of the city but seemed to have teamed up with the Hillbilly boys.

Gardener's death was still news when the Hillbillies called again at Delroy Brown's home for payment. They were greeted by a man with a pump-action shotgun, who chased them into the residential street, firing from the hip. The Cheetham Hill leader was hit in the head; while he did not report the attack to police, they later discovered he had sought medical treatment to remove pellets from his scalp. Detective Chief Superintendent Grange Catlow, who led a team investigating what the Press were calling 'Mafia-style shootings', encountered the usual wall of silence. 'We knew who had done it and why,' he said. 'When we interviewed the victim, he denied he had been shot and he certainly wouldn't make a complaint.'[18]

It was the crucial moment. The counter-attack showed that the Hillbillies could be hit and hurt by someone with the nerve to take them on – and Brown certainly had the nerve. He also won the backing of the Pepperhill boys, some of whom decided to take his corner. Anthony Stevens, a powerful figure within the group, was moving away from his friends, while Brown became more influential. The attacks on Brown 'sort of created a monster, which is how it all came about, unfortunately,' said Stevens. 'I never saw the sense in going to war with someone over something as silly as a woman and, even more to the point, going to war with a gang of people who, half of them have nothing to do with the actual argument.' But friends were drawn in through misplaced loyalties and through the heavy-handedness of the Cheetham crew. 'There was a load of threats, and gunplay started between all our boys and Cheetham Hill, but I can honestly say that all our lot were just defending themselves at the time. They were not the aggressors.' The Pepperhill Mob became the defenders of the Frontline. So began the second Moss Side-Cheetham Hill war.

* * *

On Friday, March 18, a dozen Hillbillies arrived at the PSV Club in Hulme, a reggae and soul venue popular with young black people and students. They were on a mission. Six of them entered the club while the rest waited outside. Inside were Delroy Brown and his cohorts. Menacing stares soon escalated to threats. According to media reports gleaned from the police, a Moss Side man produced a shotgun, one of the Cheetham contingent whipped out a handgun, and both opened fire. According to people who were there, Cheetham Hill pulled out their weapons first and disarmed the Moss Side lads at gunpoint, before seizing Delroy Brown. In the melee, Stephen Jackson, twenty-six, from Hulme, took a shotgun blast in his lower abdomen and fell groaning to the floor. Fighting spread as the Hillbillies dragged Brown outside, where they tried to cut off his head with a machete. He escaped, once more badly injured. The man with the shotgun left in a Ford Sierra, while club customers spilled out and ran for their lives through the Crescents.

A short time afterwards, an identical Sierra containing three black men pulled up outside a house in Fallowfield. They kicked through a panel in the wooden front door and fired into the hallway, peppering the stairs with shot. Thirty minutes later, someone shot out a window of Brown's council house in Roker

Avenue, Longsight. Brown wasn't there; he had apparently fled to hide out with friends in another city, where he treated his machete wounds with Dettol.

An unnecessary conflict had become uncontrollable. Anthony Stevens spoke to his crew the next day but sensed a growing rift. He could see where the madness was heading but they were bent on payback. 'In the first war, it was mainly one-way traffic, Cheetham Hill attacking Moss Side. Moss Side defended themselves but didn't really hit out. This time, they properly took the fight to Cheetham Hill.'

Police believed that while the war may have started over a woman, at its heart was drugs. 'Hard and soft drugs costing tens of thousands of pounds are involved,' said Detective Superintendent Arnold Beales, announcing Operation Sheriff, a gung-ho name for the police response. 'The argument is over drug-dealing territories or rivals ripping each other off.' The situation was now deemed so serious that drugs squad detectives were given armed escorts on raids. They seized five firearms, ranging from rifles to sawn-off shotguns. At the end of March they had another stroke of luck when two shotguns were found, one behind a shop, the other hidden on an allotment. Still the shootings continued.

* * *

'There will be a bloodbath if you don't check a Vauxhall Commander car being driven by four black men who are driving between Moss Side and Cheetham Hill. They have guns.' Minutes after that short, anonymous 999 call was made to a police switchboard operator, a car pulled up outside the house of Stephen Jackson, who had been badly injured at the PSV. Four men armed with a shotgun blasted through a window as his girlfriend and her four young children cowered inside. Jackson was not at home.

The next day, Claudius Shajobi was shot in the foot with a .38 revolver outside a taxi rank in Hulme. Shajobi was a friend of Jackson. He kept his mouth shut. 'We are dealing with a black mafia which is a threat to the whole community,' said Clive Atkinson, deputy head of the city's CID, announcing a reward of £1,000 to help catch the shooters. It was not the first time that emotive phrase 'black mafia' had been used, but it over-stated the case. Neither side was anywhere near the level of the US or Italian Mafia. The numbers involved most intensely were small – perhaps half a dozen on each side – while others were dragged in only through friendship or loyalty.

A week after the Shajobi shooting, Delroy Brown parked his BMW outside his house in a small cul-de-sac in Longsight. It was shortly after eleven o'clock at night and Brown was wary. His wounds had only just healed, and he didn't want any more. He scanned the area as he got out of the car – and spotted three figures in nearby bushes. Two of them had shotguns. 'As soon as I saw the guns I ran for my life,' Brown later told the *Manchester Evening News*. 'They were out to kill me. I jumped across the nearest fence as the first shot was fired. I hit my leg on the fence and rolled over.' He leapt back to his feet and ran for his life. 'The men were chasing me and I was running as hard as I could. Three more shots were fired. When the shooting stopped I stayed put for about five minutes until I heard the sound of cars screeching into the road and I saw it was the police. I'm paranoid at the moment and that was why I was on my toes so quickly. I'm not involved in drugs in any way and I haven't done anything wrong.' A report of the shooting made the front page of the *Manchester Evening News*, which called it part of a 'mafia feud' in Moss Side and Hulme.

That June, *Manchester Evening News* crime reporter Paul Horrocks, later the paper's editor, wrote a full-page feature under the headline, '£1m drugs racket in gang's "mini Chicago"'. It described a shooting war between gangs from Cheetham Hill and Moss Side that had left one man dead and four shot. 'We know the people responsible for these attacks but we need people to come forward as witnesses with proof,' Detective Superintendent Arnold Beales told the newspaper. 'It's got to the stage where people are being shot in the street and yet, incredibly, they don't want to make a complaint. In some cases we have only found out about shootings while making inquiries into other incidents. We believe that most of the gun attacks are intended as frighteners but it is only a matter of time before an innocent bystander is murdered.' The *Evening News* was then the biggest-selling evening paper outside London and the national Press often followed up its stories. The word 'Gunchester' had not yet been coined but the image was being formed.

That summer a man was stabbed in Moss Side in a gang fight and there was a shooting in the car park of the Great Western Hotel. An invisible line was drawn across the city centre: Cheetham Hill men could not safely venture south without weapons and back-up, and Moss Side men could not go north. The pressure was turned up when some of the Pepperhill warmongers decreed that no-one from their side of the city – even those not involved in the war – could do business with Cheetham Hill. 'Certain members of my group decided that if we catch anybody from south of the border doing business with Cheetham Hill, we are going to do them in as well,' said Anthony Stevens. 'The whole thing started to get ridiculous.'

This heavy-handed approach caused a split on Alexandra Park, as some young dealers from the west side of the estate continued to trade with Cheetham Hill. They resented being told what to do. For Anthony Stevens, it was the final straw. 'I began looking for a way out. I remember being with my boys one day, I was looking at how they were talking, where they were going, what they were doing, how they were dressed, how they were conducting themselves. I thought, there is a massive gulf now between me and my boys, and the time has come that I've got to pull away. Because I was not prepared to go around having people trying to kill me, and me trying to kill people, over some guy's argument over an ex-girlfriend. No way.'

★   ★   ★

With Moss Side increasingly hostile and clubs such as the Nile and the Reno virtually out of bounds, the Hillbillies began to socialise more in the city centre at weekends. One notorious 'black' club was Parliament, a disused cinema in Ardwick, another of the inner-city's decayed wards. 'Parliament was rough as anything,' said a doorman who worked there. 'There was a lot of heavy music, and they'd be smoking the weed. Most of the doormen were black and there was a black girl bouncer as well, Janice, from Moss Side. She was hard as nails, had no front teeth and could knock men out for fun. She was there for searching girls coming in. People were bringing more and more weapons into the club, also pills, cannabis. They can always sneak things in. We confiscated all sorts, not guns but machetes, knives. They used to sharpen up steel combs for jibbing people. And one of the most lethal weapons was a woman's stiletto heel; I've seen blokes with holes in their heads from them. But you had to be careful what you said if you found a machete on someone, because a lot of gangs came in. I got to know certain heads of gangs and if they give you respect, they get it back.'

The main black club remained the Gallery, which, despite the odd incident, had somehow avoided becoming a battleground for the two factions. 'All the grief that had been going on on the streets now developed into trouble in night clubs as well,' said Anthony Stevens. 'It wasn't that a guy would have a load of grief during the daytime and then put on his gladrags and go out at night and have a good time. He'd take the same grief with him into the nightclubs.'

The badmen of Cheetham Hill and Moss Side had operated in their own hermetic world, baffling to the police, their elders and the white criminal elite. In 'town', however, they were not the only gangs around. They came across heavy doormen, often years older than them, with their own networks of muscle and steel, and encountered volatile white tribes from the city's terminal zones of industrial decline and housing overspill: Ancoats, Benchill, Blackley, Gorton, Langley, Newton Heath. The two underworlds, black and white, had thus far existed separately, with no interface; black lads had stuck to their own clubs and anyway were often turned away by the bouncers at mainstream venues. Now, as the club scene opened up and dress (and race) restrictions disappeared, they began to converge.

The black gangs soon discovered that one white tribe stood out from the others: bigger, rougher, harder. A city barman recalled the moment he became aware of them.

'I was at a club and someone kicked the door off and seventeen or eighteen people just walked in, in front of all the bouncers. I turned to a guy and said, "What the hell's going on?"'

'Well, he just turned to me and he said, "Salford." '

CHAPTER FOUR

A Proper Rum Outfit

PAUL MASSEY WAS once publicly labelled the 'Mister Big' of Salford gangland. For twenty years, Salford Police tried to lay many crimes at his door: riots, attacks on pubs and nightclubs, prison breakouts, intimidation, mass brawls. Most of the allegations failed to stick. Massey does not fit the stereotype of a 'godfather': he is not big, does not look especially intimidating or sinister. Of medium build, he has short hair, watchful eyes and a face marked by the occasional small scar. He dresses like a Salford lad: sweatshirt, jeans, trainers. Only the expensive cars he favours and the obvious respect, even deference, he commands reflect some kind of status.

Massey was born at home on 7 January 1960 in inner-city Salford, near the old docks and quays at the end of the Manchester Ship Canal. It is a tough area, as all docklands are. Massey's family was large and close-knit. 'My mam's family, they're all close, and we was brought up respectable, we was brought up with discipline, we was brought up to show respect by my father,' he said. 'We was brought up with, you know, morals.'[19] Despite this, he found it easy to fall into crime on the streets of an inner-city district in one of Britain's hardest cities. When he was eight, he committed a burglary with his older brother Steven.

> That was the first time I got caught. My mam was actually watching across the road and we're getting carried by the cop. She didn't know it was me until the neighbour said, 'I'm sure that's your Paul.' I'm trying to keep my head down because the copper had me over his shoulder. Oh, she whacked me. My friend, his mam was in the back of the van

whacking him. It used to be the old Black Marias then. And I thought, *Wow, first time I've been caught, this.* It just went from there. I ended up going out with the young kids and the older kids, you get a bit of boredom and you go and wander.

Parts of Salford were being cleared for wider roads and new houses and there were derelict buildings to explore. When he was ten, Massey was badly injured when he smashed down some walls in a house and it collapsed on him. He recovered, but didn't change his ways.

> That was our hobby, knocking houses down. I was walking down Chapel Street in Salford, I think I was about twelve years old, and I seen this building, loads of kids in it. Kids were jumping off the roof into these polystyrene things, getting paint, writing their names. Anyway, the doors come off. We got done for criminal damage. It was a building what the kids had broken into and smashed up but we didn't know, we thought it was an old building. We got charged and I went to the approved school.

Massey's anger at authority stemmed from that moment.

> The thing that hurt me more than anything was . . . my mam and dad and my family being there and [me] being dragged off by the police, took out of the family to be took away. That made me bitter against the system. I know I'd got a bit of a record by then but I didn't open them doors, I didn't let everybody into that building. Them doors was wide open. We told the police that when we got arrested. How would you like your son dragged out of your house and your mam and dad stood there, not knowing where he's going to go? You know, it was hard.

Massey's father had kept him in some kind of check by beating him brutally, but as he grew older even that sanction no longer held any fears for the young street hoodlum.

When I was about ten years onwards, my dad used to kill me. He used to beat me up. There was no messing about, I was black and blue. And as soon as he beat me up, put me in that bedroom, I was out that window and gone . . . [then] I'd just got out of approved school, I was fourteen and my dad took me to the school. I was only in there an hour and some fucking bully was throwing something at my head. So I turned around, bang, done him in. And I just got off from the school because I thought, *I'm not sitting around with all that shit, I've better things to do.* And I remember seeing my dad coming down the road and I jumped under a car. He come up and grabbed me from under the car and I was waiting for him to do me in. He just put me in the car and drove me home and said, 'I'm not going to hurt my hands on him any more.' My dad just give up.

An old head on young shoulders, Massey hung out with a crowd of like-minded lads who were a law unto themselves. They were contemptuous of authority, disdained physical injury and ostracised 'grasses' and snitches. Another of the group was Paul Doyle, a stocky, heavy-boned man with an aura of latent strength. He was the same age as Massey and had a similar childhood as one of seven brothers from Lower Broughton, an uncompromising district that sits on the northern bank of the Irwell, the polluted river that divides Salford from Manchester. He was a handful from the time he could walk. 'Me and my brothers robbed our first shop, I was about six, they were seven and eight. It was a cake shop. I was that young I didn't even understand what money was and went straight for the cakes.'

Doyle also ended up in approved school. 'You cope with it. Believe it or not, when I left I was a bit lonely. I missed the place. I was institutionalised by the time I got out. So becoming a thief never bothered me, going back to prison never bothered me, because I'd just meet my same old friends I was brought up with.' He would get home leave from the approved school, then steal from houses or shops on his way back. 'Just before I left for the last time, one of the bosses – you have to call them boss – said to me, "With your upbringing, you've got a one in a thousand chance of not being in prison all your life."

'I've left approved school and I've gone out there wanting to earn money. Going back to borstal or prison never scared me. What I had to do was graft and earn money. You come across friends who are the same as you, and that's what we like to call ourselves: not the old-fashioned word gangsters, but grafters. Being from Salford, everybody I drank with was more or less grafters. There was a group of about twenty that went out grafting every day. When it comes to the weekend, they'd tell you what they had planned for the week coming and ask if you wanted to have any involvement in it. So sometimes if you fancied it, you'd do it with them. It was between a group of twenty but the number that would go out on a particular job was probably three.'

This group and their associates were behind a disproportionate amount of crime in the area. They included Doyle and his brothers, Massey and his close friends, the young but wild Paul Corkovic, the McDonalds and others – 'a proper rum outfit,' as Doyle describes them. They saw crime as inevitable, even natural: a fact of life. 'No straight job would have me,' said Doyle. 'I've been thieving from a very early age and I don't want to stack shelves. I won't work in an office, I'm not capable of that, I don't want to work on a building site. I want much more than that. There's no shame in being a thief from Salford.

'Burglaries were easy, I don't mean on houses but on warehouses. The other thing was snatches: in them days the shopkeepers used to have to take the takings to the bank and they was all in leather pouches, so they was easy to suss out. We used to snatch the bags and off you go with the leather pouches. The security was pathetic. It was robbery without weapons.' Arrest was an occupational hazard. At one stage some of them were in a detention centre at the same time as some Hillbillies, who were up for armed robberies. 'Cheetham Hill were very clever, they were into money whereas the Salford firm was into violence. We were just a load of hyenas, fighting for fun. There were no guns about then so no-one could compete with Salford. There were no drugs.' Even though many from the two gangs lived less than half a mile apart, they were oil and water: Salford was a largely white area and there was some racial tension between the two groups, though this would decline in later years.

The Salford lads frequented pubs and clubs in Manchester and became notorious fighters. Paul Massey wasn't big but was dead game and did not seem to care about pain. Once the skin was torn completely off one side of his face, leaving a huge scab.

I've had some beltings off older guys when I was younger. I've had some kickings off fucking ten guys . . . when I was street fighting. That's where I got my scars from. But I didn't lie down; I got back up. A lot of people haven't had that experience. You get a lot of people in town who walk around and once they get a good kicking, I'll tell you now, nine out of ten of them don't come back. When I have a fight, pain doesn't come into it. It's like it doesn't affect me. I've got tired and emotional pain, like anybody else, but I'm talking fighting pain. I've been hit with bottles on many occasions over the head, I've been hit in the face with glasses, I've had knives pulled, I've been slashed around the arse, slashed round the back with knives. But what always used to surprise me, especially when I was younger, like sixteen . . . I was fighting fellers and I was beating them. I used to go home scratching my head, *how did I beat that big bastard?*

Doyle was even an more formidable brawler, a stocky young man with tattooed arms, a concrete jaw and a pile-driver right hand; he flattened so many men that Massey nicknamed him 'One-Punch'. One of their haunts was a club called Pips in Fennel Street, a warren of rooms where they were regularly in brawls. 'Fighting was a pleasure,' said Doyle. 'We was young, wild, been brought up in approved schools, all you've learned is to stick up for yourself. And you come out, all you know is violence, and you go out on the nightlife in Manchester, you come across idiots, the straight members, and . . . they got beat up.' The lads saw themselves as different from the 'straight members', the law-abiding majority. They acknowledged no authority but their own, no code but the unforgiving law of Salford's white ghettos.

'We used to hang out at a pie van in town after the clubs shut,' said Doyle. 'I saw more violence there than anywhere else. On one occasion a load of huge black geezers came towards us. We were only young and thought we were going to get it but we stood there and faced them and they just walked through and did nothing. We weren't scared of anyone. Salford people have already got a reputation. It's through our fathers, our grandfathers, they've all been brought up as fighters. You could be somebody from the other side of Manchester, so big deal, you're a hard kid from Altrincham. Being a hard kid from Salford means you're capable of putting a gang together in no time.'

★   ★   ★

The River Irwell roughly separates Salford from Manchester, yet the two cities are bound like Siamese twins, with Salford cast as the poorer relation. The opening of the ship canal in 1894 to bypass Liverpool turned Salford into a vital port – and ports are unruly places. Some of the worst scuttler mobs came from Salford and the gang culture never died out there. The police had their own way of dealing with it. 'Salford was a law unto itself,' said John Stalker. 'It introduced zero tolerance before anybody ever invented the phrase. Salford is a tough city, a dockside city, it had all the problems of a big city but in a small area, and it had its own police force. They had to be big guys to get into it, six feet tall or thereabouts, and they took no nonsense from anyone. They had a style of policing which was unique to Salford.

'There was evidence that Salford villains worked on the basis that if they came to Manchester, even if they got caught they wouldn't be treated as badly as they were in Salford by the police and especially by the courts. Salford Quarter Sessions and the Salford magistrates court were notorious for dealing with people fairly hard. There was a group of about twenty tough Glaswegians who had really been pushed out of Salford because of their behaviour. They were no longer welcome in Glasgow and they came down to Manchester – they lived in Salford but operated in Manchester – and they were in effect leaned on every minute of the day by a dedicated squad of detectives. It wouldn't be possible today, it would be regarded as socially undesirable, almost racist, but I have to say that it worked then and those who had any sense left. Those that stayed were arrested.'

The Glasgow men were apparently attracted by Manchester's swinging image as a club, drug and vice centre. The city's stipendiary magistrate even blamed them for a fifty per cent surge in violent attacks and robberies in a single year in 1969, while hitting out at the notion that Manchester was open house for villains. 'It is simply not true that Manchester is an Eldorado for every violent criminal,' said magistrate John Bamber. 'It is a false picture – a kind of commercial for a criminal's holiday resort.'[20] As they grew older, the young Salford lads looked up to some of the Scots, people like the McPhees, a family involved in armed robbery, counterfeiting and burglaries. They envied the wealth that crime could bring, at a time when legitimate work was drying up. Salford was an ailing city. The Quays was once the world's third busiest port, but in the seventies it was declared no longer viable. The docks were obliterated and families began to disperse from the area. The population fell as people left to look for jobs and Salford became one of the ten most deprived of the 366 urban districts in England and Wales.

Career options for working class lads with borstal backgrounds were severely limited. Crime was one, boxing another. Some of the lads started training at their local YMCA and within a few weeks Paul Doyle was having his first professional bout. He ran out of gas after a couple of rounds but his opponent simply couldn't hurt him; Doyle lost on points to Jonjo Greene, went on to become All-Ireland light-heavyweight champion. Paul Massey, meanwhile, continued his war with authority; clashing with the police when he went out to drown his sorrows after the tragic death of his mentor and older brother, Stephen.

Going out for a drink, grieving on my brother's death, and the copper come over and pulled me. I only hit him once and when he went down I lost my rag. I thought, *I'll give it this bastard. He's taking the piss. Because I'm getting charged anyway, I'll just boot the life out of him.* And then I remember another copper running over, so I booted him. He went flying over a car and I smacked his head on the police car and I booted him. And I got the cunt and I threw him. I had two of them on the floor and I said, 'Come on, get up now.' I was freaked out, my brother had just died, I'd had e-fucking-nough. And I had all my friends pulling me back. They said, 'Paul, get off before the police come.' And I said, 'No, I want a few more, I'm staying.' And I stayed.

About five more come. I just steamed into them all and about ten come, threw me in a van. Beat the life out of me, broke my nose. They had to take turns booting me in the police station . . . they had me over the counter, four had me there, one had me by the fucking neck and he just blatantly punched me in the face. And I remember standing there . . . and they's punching me in the face, punching all my nose, my eyes is out here, and I went, 'What you going to do, hurt me?' They couldn't hurt me. How could they hurt me, the way I had fucking been brought up? My brother's just died, I've got no life in me.

Went to court in the morning, I was pretty lucky really. I got six month. I got three month for the first copper I did in, three month for the other one and I was on a fifteen-month suspended sentence for breaking a copper's hand but the judge pushed that to one side because of the grief of my brother dying. Really I should have got four years for them two offences alone. But, you know, the magistrate worked in a reasonable manner, which was good of him.

★ ★ ★

Their constant fighting upset a main firm of bouncers with links to the Quality Street Gang. It was run by a renowned Salford hardman who'd had enough of these upstarts causing trouble. 'They were sick to death of us beating up their doormen,' said

Doyle. One of the pubs the lads drank in was the Druid's Home, in an old area of Salford where the street names reflected the textile trade history: Silk Street, Calico Close, Chiffon Way, Damask Avenue. They were in the Druid's on Royal Wedding Day 1981, the occasion of Prince Charles's marriage to Diana Spencer, when pubs had special dispensation to open all day and many celebrated by going on a bender. The atmosphere was convivial until the doors opened and a team of half a dozen burly men walked in.

'You're sitting in our seats,' said one of them.

A fight broke out and one of the men smashed a glass in the face of Massey's friend Matt Carr. The brawl was vicious and spilled into the street, where a man called Archie Waterhouse was kicked repeatedly in the head and left unconscious.

The next night, Massey went back in the Druid's.

'Get out the pub, get out,' said the frantic landlord. 'It's on top.'

'What do you mean, it's on top?' asked Massey.

'I've got a phone number there. When you come in I've got to phone these guys, they're going to come down and get you. And if I don't phone them, they're going to smash my pub up. So will you just leave the pub and don't come in again.'

'What guys?'

'About forty guys, big gorillas, doormen, all looking for you.'

'Looking for me? I'm barred out of no pub, fucking phone them. Fucking phone them, I ain't arsed about them.'

The young Salford crew refused to back down, but by now the police were also after them. Massey and two of his friends, including the one who had been glassed, were arrested and charged with attacking Waterhouse outside the pub. He had spent sixteen days in hospital and suffered brain damage. Paul Doyle, who had been fighting inside the pub, was not charged and became the main target for reprisals from the door firm. 'While the other lads were on remand, I had this firm after me. I would go to clubs and the doormen would say, "Paul, get the fuck out of here as fast as you can." As I left, I would see cars pulling up outside with guys jumping out, looking for me, and I was only a young lad at the time. I got a job on the doors myself but no-one wanted to work with me because of it. The other lads ended up getting jail.'

In July 1982, a jury at Manchester Crown Court listened as the prosecutor described how the fight had started in the pub and a glass was smashed in Carr's face. He and his friends believed Waterhouse had done it and later attacked him in the street, kicking him repeatedly in the head, said the prosecutor. Waterhouse's brain was shaken, he had trouble keeping his balance and needed help to dress. Paul Massey, Matt Carr and Mark Scott denied causing grievous bodily harm but were convicted and jailed for five years each.

The boxing ring was not violent enough for One-Punch. He fell into the football hooligan scene after travelling with friends to watch Manchester United at Newcastle; twenty of them were thrown out of the ground and had to battle hundreds of Geordies outside while the rest of the Manchester contingent was kept in at the final whistle. 'The violence was so exciting that, by the time we got back to the coaches, I was on a total high. That was it for me.' The 'casual' gangs were about to make their mark on the terraces and Doyle would be in the thick of it. Away matches provided not only the chance for trouble but could also provide easy pickings for thieves, and United had a large, ragtag contingent of jibbers, dippers, shoplifters and snatchers, with the Salford lads at the forefront. Doyle was arrested when United played Liverpool in the 1983 Milk Cup final, and was nicked again when the same teams were back at Wembley for the Charity Shield, this time for leading what the prosecutor called a 'disorderly rabble' in a charge across Euston Station to attack Liverpool supporters. He was jailed for three months for threatening behaviour.

* * *

Twenty years earlier, the London gangster Frankie Fraser had forged an unmatched reputation in the underworld by refusing to kowtow to prison authorities. Paul Massey adopted much the same stance and ended up in Wakefield, a high-security prison with a large proportion of sex offenders. He was not impressed.

> Wakefield Prison . . . it's like having a trip. There's nonces in there, there's rapists in there, there's fucking grasses in there. It's full of fucking scum. It crushes your head so much because of the scum and you're breathing the same air as them and you're outnumbered. I kicked quite a few arses, don't get me wrong. I've splattered a few of them. Oh, and enjoyed it. But what did they do? The screws and cons worked together to move me out the prison.

Other prisoners advised him to cool it but Massey was having none of it. 'The prison put me here, they'll take what I give out,' he replied. He was dragged down to the block and put on rule 43A, allegedly for organising demonstrations and a riot, and to protect some of the other prisoners from his assaults. At a meeting with the governor, he hit him with a chair – it was made of cardboard – and was thrown into the strip cell for five days, where he refused food and water. 'Of that two years, I bet I was on the block about fifteen months of it, locked up twenty-four hours a day on my own, solitary confinement,' he said.

Almost two years after Massey's conviction, three Appeal Court judges quashed his sentence and put aside his conviction on the grounds that it was 'unsafe and unsatisfactory'. Lord Justice May said the police had contended that Massey had admitted involvement in the attack on Archie Waterhouse and had been seen taking part by a woman police constable, but Massey had denied making any such admission at the trial, and the judge had not given the jury the usual warning about the danger of 'fleeting glance' identification. He was immediately released.

He came out of prison to nothing. By mid-1984, around half of all men in Ordsall, Lower Broughton and neighbouring Seedley and Trinity were drawing unemployment benefit, while almost half of all families in Salford claimed housing benefit. The lads had, however, learned a few lessons about making crime pay. 'What happened, we started hitting the fraud and deception in

Europe,' said Paul Doyle. 'We became more professional, knowing the odds are not in your favour doing robberies. You could earn large amounts of money in Europe [and] if you got caught, they'd just kick you out of the country. We ended up doing a big conspiracy.'

John McPhee, a Scot in his mid-thirties who was something of a mentor to the younger lads, said he knew a source for counterfeit banknotes in Amsterdam. McPhee, Massey, Doyle and Barry Gallimore raised £1,000 in a whipround to make the buy. They acquired a stockpile of forged £20 notes and also amassed stolen cheque and credit cards. A whole crowd of them went over to Amsterdam, buying designer clothes – Lacoste tee-shirts were popular – on the stolen plastic and sneak thieving from jewellery stores, with one of them distracting the staff while another grabbed trays of watches, rings and chains. They went wild, hitting the clubs at night, smoking dope and munching 'space cake', getting drunk and fighting with doormen. Two of them were even shot at after battering a couple of bouncers. They rounded off the night by kicking in some hotel room doors at 4 a.m., 'taxing' the startled occupants, then heading off to Brussels to do the same again. The lads made several similar trips, tearing it up in Belgium and Holland. In another scam, Massey secretly fitted a van with forty-five-gallon petrol containers and drove it from one petrol station to another, filling up on stolen credit cards. One card was presented seven times in a day, to buy petrol and goods worth nearly £500. He then sold the petrol for £1 a gallon.

This went on for at least two months in the autumn of 1984, and soon the Regional Crime Squad was onto them. They mounted Operation Twentyman and quickly rounded up some of the conspirators, including Massey. He was put in a cell in the Crescent police station in Salford, where he decided that he wouldn't see officers without his solicitor present. To make sure, he covered himself with his own excrement so they wouldn't come into his cell – 'to protect my freedom, my rights.' His friends were pulled out of bed in a series of dawn raids and most were charged with conspiring to defraud central clearing banks by passing off stolen cheques. The lads were banged up in

Strangeways, Britain's most overcrowded jail, with almost 500 prisoners just on remand. It contained some of the hardest men in the British prison system, in appalling conditions. Remand prisoners not convicted of any crime were allowed one fifteen-minute visit per day, one shower and one towel per week, and had to 'slop out' from overcrowded cells. Even the prison officers had been complaining for years about conditions in the Victorian jail.

Massey, as usual, refused to take things lying down. In June 1985, he and his cellmate Mark Harvey and a third man hid before evening lock-up, waited until everyone was asleep, cut through a bar in a fourth-floor cell with a smuggled saw and used knotted sheets to climb down to an exercise yard. Dog patrol wardens spotted them as they ran across the yard at 4 a.m. but they managed to climb onto a cellblock roof. Despite heavy rain, they clambered along the tiled rooftops, where they watched the sun come up. They remained there throughout the day and that evening were pictured on the front page of the *Manchester Evening News*, with Massey clambering up a sloping roof while the other two stood and watched in their prison clothes. The third man gave himself up but Harvey and Massey remained overnight. Another inmate supported them by going on hunger strike while others lit fires in their cells. Massey said they were protesting about conditions and the length of time it took to reach trial – he and Harvey had been in the jail for seven months.

Later that summer, Salford went up. Thirty youths, most in their teens, went on the rampage, surging down the road from Pendleton Green waving soft-drink bottles filled with inflammable liquid and stuffed with paper. They smashed windows, burned cars and hurled a petrol bomb at police. Dozens of officers were scrambled to the area under riot contingency plans and the gang dispersed without arrests. Senior officers were convinced it was a copycat incident following the Handsworth riots in Birmingham. Four nights later they were at it again when fifty teenagers 'went berserk', according to residents, and attacked shops and cars in Lower Broughton and Lower Kersal. More rioting followed in Regent Square, Ordsall, at roughly the same time that Cheetham Hill and Moss Side were first clashing on the streets.

It would be another year before the Operation Twentyman conspirators finally reached court. The prosecution said an investigation into forged £20 notes uncovered the plot to use stolen chequebooks and credit cards abroad. McPhee, thirty-six, from Eccles, knew where the snide notes could be obtained. Massey, McPhee and Doyle were convicted of being concerned in importing forged notes, while Barry Gallimore admitted the same offence and possessing 627 of the notes, worth £12,540 at face value. Gallimore said there had been four organised trips to Belgium and that the fraud 'might' be in the region of £100,000. Fifteen people had made one of the trips. 'We just went crazy, cashing cheques all over,' said Gallimore. He and Massey were said to be at the centre of 'a very considerable criminal enterprise' and also prime movers in getting the forged notes into Britain from Amsterdam. Five defendants were convicted of conspiring to defraud the clearing banks and three were convicted of passing forged notes. Gallimore was jailed for six tears, Massey for five, McPhee for three and Doyle for three years, nine months, with others getting shorter jail terms. In October, Massey and McPhee were back in court after being convicted of the petrol scam. Manchester Crown Court heard that they drove Massey's van around petrol stations filling up on the stolen cards until the mammoth tank was full. One card was used seven times in a day. There was evidence that the petrol was sold on for £1 a gallon and the fraud was 'on a substantial scale', the court heard. Massey and McPhee were both given one-year jail terms, to run consecutively to their other convictions.

Massey, once again, did hard time.

When the screws said, 'Do this, do that,' I did fuck all. I'm not bullshitting, I did nothing . . . They couldn't understand why they couldn't control me. I was in solitary confinement for maybe two years, maybe a bit over, when I'm doing my six years . . . So what happened then, I become very bitter against the system. They tried to break me . . . but instead of breaking me, they educated me. It made me stronger.

The lads were in their late twenties when they came out, hardened, street-smart and ready. They found that things had changed. There had been a nightlife revolution in their city, and suddenly opportunity lay there for anyone with the balls to seize it. 'When we come out, it was the drug scene, where if you're wise enough you can beat the system,' said Paul Doyle. 'The odds are in your favour to get away with it, rather than the robberies which are in the police's favour to get you. Everyone started asking for the "little things", which was the "Es". We seen what was happening.' Rave was emerging, and some of the Salford lads threw themselves into it without restraint.

CHAPTER FIVE

Madchester

IT ARRIVED WITH 'Hot'. On 13 July 1988, a different kind of club night was launched at the Hacienda in Manchester. There were palm trees indoors, a tiny pool by the dance floor, ice pops handed out to the crowd – and there was Ecstasy. For the next six weeks – the so-called Summer of Love – clubbers would arrive every Wednesday night in shorts and swimsuits, with whistles around their necks, to dance Ibiza-style, arms aloft, while the Happy Mondays and their cronies peddled small white pills that made you feel . . . ecstatic. Acid house had landed and British youth culture was changed forever.

The Hot night did not, of course, spring from nowhere. The Hacienda, a former yacht warehouse, had opened back in May 1982 as an experiment in club life, a 'space' to host both live bands and a disco. It was owned by the people behind Factory Records, the city's premier label, and its design was spare, modern and deliberately 'industrial'. They wanted an alternative to the city's jaded nightlife. Manchester's most popular clubs and discos were outdated and dull. There was little buzz about the city at weekends. It seemed an uneasy, joyless place, still mired in the economic decline of the early eighties and the Stanley knife mentality of the Perry Boys, the recordings of Factory both reflecting and defining the gloom. 'The Hacienda was looking for a direction in an era when the rock music scene was jaded, struggling in the shadow of punk and Joy Division . . . Manchester was living off the past, rundown, beset by bad drugs (heroin, cheap speed).'[21] Yet despite featuring artists such as Madonna, the Smiths and the Eurythmics, the Hacienda did not trade especially well – busy at weekends, dead in the week – until about 1986, when hip hop, techno and house music infiltrated from America, especially through DJ Mike Pickering, who was influenced by the ground-breaking Paradise Garage club in New York.

Acid house had been coming for a while, a culmination rather than an innovation. It had two essentials. The first was the music, a mix of sub-styles made possible by new technology and anchored by a pounding, incessant beat. House came from Chicago, techno from Detroit, blue-collar cities blighted by gangs. Techno pioneer Derrick May was himself in thrall to Factory figureheads New Order, who absorbed the sounds of the US clubs and then reinvented them, especially on their ground-breaking dance epic 'Blue Monday'. There was something unsettling about techno in particular and its sudden shifts of tempo: an urban soundtrack from the collapsed industrial sprawl of Detroit, once Motor City but now Murder City, USA. 'Six-year-olds carry guns and thousands of black people have stopped caring if they ever work again,' said May. 'If you make music in that environment, it can't be straight music. In Britain you have New Order. Well our music is the new disorder.'[22]

Another key musical ingredient came from the bizarre and extravagant clubs scene on the jet-set side of the Mediterranean holiday island of Ibiza, particularly Club Amnesia and its Argentinian DJ, Alfredo. Small numbers of Brits sampled the hedonistic delights of this al fresco disco, including a small group of south Londoners who tried to recreate the endless summer nights on their return to England. In the autumn of 1987, some of them gathered in Ziggy's club in Streatham, south London, after it had closed to relive the Ibiza experience. From that sprang the Shoom club and British acid house was born.

Ibiza also had its Manchester contingent, the kind of scallies found in most sunspots abroad – lads who live by handing out flyers, touting timeshare, occasional bar work. They were part of 'a large working-class enterprise culture that emerged in the mid-eighties and continues to thrive among the generation that took Thatcher at her word and decided simply to help themselves to a slice of the action,' according to Steve Redhead of Manchester's Institute for Popular Culture.[23] They brought a flavour of Ibiza's freewheeling nightlife back to Manchester and their amoral, do-it-yourself ethic was crucial in the events that would unfold.

The other essential of acid house was Ecstasy, a chemical first synthesised by German chemists in 1912 before its more important re-synthesis in the USA in the sixties. It is believed to work on chemical neurotransmitters in the brain such as serotonin which, when boosted, cause a short-term sensation of well-being and alertness. It also increases empathy, the experiencing of someone else's sensations as your own; indeed its first dealer wanted to call it Empathy. People who took a pill wanted to dance all night, to embrace, to love and feel wonderful about the world. Many claimed a life-changing experience. Ecstasy was classified as a non-addictive class A drug and made illegal in the UK in 1977, before it was popular. It started to appear in the early eighties, brought back to London by clubbers from New York and sold for £25 a pop. The first article about it was in *The Face* magazine in 1985, the year the first British seizures were made.

Under the influence of 'E', the music took on a new depth and resonance. 'To the unattuned ear, it can sound at best numbingly repetitive, and at worst mindless. It usually begins with a dissonant shudder and builds, often in the space of one ten-minute mix, into something relentlessly bombastic, a noise that is brutally technological and utterly primal. These records are designed purely for the dance-floor and, increasingly, seem structured to enhance the Ecstasy experience, becoming an integral part of the extrasensory overload that is the very essence of the rave experience.'[24] Or as writer Matthew Collin put it, 'Ecstasy plus house music equals mass euphoria.'[25]

Incredibly, Greater Manchester Police missed what was going on. In 1988, the year the pills took off, they made not a single arrest for either the supply or possession of Ecstasy. The following year, they made only five arrests for trafficking the drug. In 1990, by which time it was *the* recreational drug for young clubbers and rave was a well-established media panic, they made just four arrests for trafficking E, compared to 310 arrests for dealing cannabis. It was a dire failing. The media, too, largely missed the story, focussing instead on stern warnings about crack cocaine, even though crack was virtually non-existent in the UK at the time. Criminals were much quicker to pick up the new drug trend than either the police or the media.

It took a third ingredient, however, to turn Manchester into Madchester. The city's nightlife sounds were further transfused with a wave of indie bands – the Happy Mondays, the Stone Roses, the Inspiral Carpets, 808 State and others – who matched guitar or synth music with club beats and dressed in scally terrace chic. The look and sound gripped not just Mancunians but the immense student population of the city's four universities (including Salford). Previously, students and townies had rarely mixed; their night-time spaces were separate, their clothes, haircuts, accents and musical tastes often different. Now they came together, united by music, drugs and, most of all, by the Hacienda.

The Mondays were Hacienda regulars and became 'perhaps the quintessential rave generation group,' according to Steve Redhead of the Manchester Institute for Popular Culture. 'In many ways they represent and encapsulate a lot of the values of this new enterprise economy. They grew up immersed in a help-yourself ethic, actually working among drug dealers before they became successful as a pop group. There are also a lot of entrepreneurs involved in running the rave scene and they are anything but disorganised pleasure-seekers. The business ethic is straight free-market enterprise.'

Club culture took hold in Britain in a way it did nowhere else, and Ecstasy was soon the third most popular drug after cannabis and amphetamines. Almost subliminally, the street ethic and the central importance of E began to distort moral frameworks. Suddenly blagging was cool, theft was okay, drugs were rife and the scally was king.

* * *

Hot was a huge success and soon the queues snaked down Whitworth Street. Ecstasy keeps you going and the Hacienda clubbers did not want to be turfed onto the streets by the 2 a.m.

71

licensing restriction and told they had to go home. So they began to head off to an after-hours dance den called the Kitchen, two bare-walled flats knocked together in Charles Barry Crescent in Hulme. Towards the end of the Summer of Love, brothers Anthony and Chris Donnelly also began organising warehouse parties. They had the right street credentials: they were Wythenshawe faces and nephews of Quality Street Gang veteran Jimmy the Weed. Acid house hit them and others like an epiphany.

'The estate where we come from, drinking's the thing, get proper out of it and have a top chuckle with your pals,' said Anthony Donnelly. 'We had a base in Wythenshawe where every activity in the world was going on from. One hundred young lads in there on beer, but all of a sudden five or ten of them have gone wayward, they're coming in with fucking bandannas tied round their heads. From 1988 to the end of 1990 we didn't touch a drop of alcohol, not one fucking drink . . . for two years we went on a mission from God, we were like Jehovah's Witnesses going out promoting it.'[26]

The warehouse parties came to be known as raves, a term which gradually replaced acid house everywhere except in the newspapers. The most popular north-west location was Blackburn, a town with many disused industrial premises that could be broken into and transformed into makeshift clubs. During 1989 and 1990, thousands of ravers at a time descended on Blackburn for a series of illicit parties. They offered immediate pickings for the Salford lads who had just emerged from prison.

'The raves of course were illegal but it seemed that they were getting away with it in Blackburn,' said Paul Doyle. 'So we started to go up there, a gang of six or seven of us, and we'd ask who was running the rave. These big heavy doormen would be there and they'd be looking at us confused, thinking, *Who the fuck are these?* So they'd say, "Why? Who wants to know?" All of a sudden the guns would come out and we wanted the whole night's takings.'

Raves were made for violent young criminals. Older heavies were not interested; they didn't know what was going on, didn't understand the scene at all. It was wide open for the football hooligans, the robbery gangs, the bodybuilders and the scallies.

On one occasion, twenty Salford turned up at a Blackburn warehouse party to tax the door. 'The money's in the back room,' stammered a petrified doorman. One Salford lad went in and found the cash. He also saw a window in the room, and instead of going back to his mates to share the loot, climbed through the window and legged it. It took them weeks to track him down, by which time he had spent the lot. 'After we'd done that two or three times, they got sick of us and so they asked if we would do a deal and just take half the money on the night and leave them the other half,' said Doyle. 'They might have been big doormen but they soon realised that this was the late eighties and people don't fight with their fists down our neck of the woods no more. We got a big reputation over that.'

All over the country, rave organisers were hiring the handiest men they could to keep away both the gangs and the police, but in Greater Manchester there was no-one who could keep out Salford. The raves taught them a lesson some would use with a vengeance: control the security of an event and you controlled not only who came in and out but who sold the drugs inside. It was to have drastic consequences for nightlife in Manchester.

By now licensed premises were catching on too, and new dance clubs were beginning to appear, but the Hacienda remained the scene's home. 'Acid house, for a few brief moments, seemed to unite the city: the outcasts from the north side of town, the scammers and grafters and chancers and characters mixing with the pop stars and students and fashion-conscious club kids,' wrote Matthew Collin in his seminal *Altered State: The Story of Ecstasy Culture and Acid House.* Yet even as the scene was building to its exuberant, tranced-out peak, storm clouds were gathering. The problem was not so much the dealers but the gang members who were soon preying on them, taxing their money and taking their gear. They expected to get in without paying and refused to pay for their drinks at the bar.

The police, concerned at levels of drug taking and the activities of certain gang 'heads', already had the Hacienda under covert surveillance when, in May 1989, bar manager Leroy Richardson refused to let a Cheetham Hill mobster into the club without paying. The young thug – who, unusually for the Hillbillies, was white – threatened him.

'You know where I am,' said Richardson. 'I'll die before you'll be let in.'

'You'll most probably have to,' replied the mobster.

His name was Tony Johnson. They called him White Tony.[27]

* * *

The Hillbillies were at the height of their powers, feared throughout the city, their robberies ever more precise, more lucrative. As banks, post offices and security companies improved their security technology and procedures with time-lock devices, CCTV, explosive dye and other measures, so the robbers became more ferocious. In March 1989, guards were collecting foreign currency from a Manchester bank when an armed Hillbilly robbery team roared up and drove a stolen Audi straight into one of them, fracturing his skull. The gang escaped with £134,000 in foreign currency and £27,000 worth of travellers' cheques. No-one was ever charged with the robbery but two Hillbillies in their mid-twenties later went on a spree in Spain, Portugal and other Continental countries on some of the proceeds, and police officers found a holdall containing some of the stolen currency. The pair, described in court as 'professional criminals', were later jailed for eight and seven years each.

It was merely a foretaste of what was to come. Chinadu Iheagwara, aged twenty-two, and Steven Julien, twenty-six, both lived on Albert Fildes Walk in the heart of Cheetham territory. They were experienced bank robbers, and on an April morning a few weeks after the currency raid, they pulled on balaclavas, featureless clothing, and gloves to avoid fingerprints, and set off on a 'job'. They had scanners to monitor police frequencies, a driver and stolen getaway cars, and had carefully planned their routes.

Their target was Coin Controls, a currency depot in Royton, Oldham. They waited for a Security Express van to pull up outside, then watched the two middle-aged guards, William

Banham and Hayden Hooper, alight to collect cash. Iheagwara and Julien sprang from a silver Ford. Julien blasted the van door with both barrels of his shotgun, then re-loaded as the guards got out with their hands up. He demanded they open the cash chute, but when the electronically operated device jammed, 'they just went mad,' recalled Hooper. Iheagwara swung at Banham with a two-foot machete, knocking him to the ground and hacking his leg almost off. Julien then shot him three times in the groin and left thigh. Banham somehow managed to crawl under the security van for shelter but left his right leg sticking out. Julien fired again. 'I could see my leg was hanging off,' said Banham. 'I grabbed hold of it and curled up into a ball, waiting for the next blow to finish me off.'

Hooper ran, hoping the men would turn their attention from his colleague. He was shot in the back, shattering his pelvic bone, and fell. 'I went numb from the waist down,' he said. Julien then walked around picking up the spent cartridges so they couldn't be used as evidence, as pupils at a nearby school watched agog against a fence. The robbers had apparently believed that there was a third guard still in the van, and that he would open it for them. They were wrong – and had now injured the two guards so severely that they couldn't get into the vehicle to steal the money. They were driven away, leaving behind a bloodbath. Within days, Julien was on a beach in Trinidad, his parents' homeland. Iheagwara too had disappeared.

That kind of deadly violence was no longer the preserve of the Hillbillies. That summer, twenty-five-year-old Henderson Proverbs was drinking in the Spinners pub in Hulme when five men pulled up in a car outside. 'Several people walked in,' said Ron Gaffey, an experienced, phlegmatic Manchester detective with a passing resemblance to the former *Z Cars* actor Stratford Johns. 'One of them fired a shotgun and blew his head off. When I got there his head was everywhere. The pub was splattered with blood yet people were still playing pool. One of them looked up and said to me, "He's over there pal."' Proverbs died from massive injuries to this throat and neck. He had previously been involved in several skirmishes with a rival gang. This time the feud was over a woman, and a gang leader from Hulme was later jailed for life for the killing. Four other people were injured that month in two separate shooting incidents. The machete had been firmly relegated; arguments now ended in gunfire. 'There is no hope, no future,' said Hendy Proverbs's mother, Jasmine. 'In our generation, if there was an argument you just fought with your hands, but this generation now, they don't even want to use a knife, never mind fight with their hands. They just want to use a gun.'

The Hillbillies took their gunplay into the city. True to form, they became the first of the black gangs to cash in on rave, which was largely a white scene. This was especially noticeable at the Thunderdome, a new club located on Oldham Road in Miles Platting, perhaps the most desolate district of Manchester, a wasteland of rubble and ruined buildings dominated by a daunting clutch of decrepit high-rise towers. The club reflected both its surroundings and the way the scene was going: 'The Thunderdome was a very vicious sort of night, very hard-edged. You couldn't walk in there and be comfortable unless you were completely out of it. Heavy music, hard, dark. Cheaper drugs. Acid and speed.'[28]

The management employed a security firm from the Merseyside area, with doormen drawn from towns like Wigan and Haydock. They were burly lads, more than capable of handling the drunken louts encountered in their home towns, but Manchester was different. Their presence was resented, and when they turned away a Cheetham Hill drug dealer, their fate was sealed. In June 1989, a team of the Hillbillies' biggest hitters attacked the club as more than 300 punters danced inside. A masked man with a shotgun blasted three of the doormen in the legs. It was a stunning sign of Cheetham Hill spreading their power from armed robberies through drugs into clubs. Within days, police had taken into custody a number of men; seven were charged with conspiracy to kill but all would later see the charges dropped (one, a promising boxer, later won £60,000 in damages for wrongful arrest). It was the end of the line for the Thunderdome. Five months later it was wrecked by fire and the following year its licence was revoked.

The siege of the city's club scene was beginning. 'We have been threatened twice,' one club manager said at the time. '[They say] if you don't let us in, we are going to burn your club down, blow your legs off, whatever. Cheetham Hill seem to have a notorious name, gangwise, for instigating trouble in clubs and on doors. In Manchester it is far, far greater than people realise. There is about five or six or even [more] night clubs which have been threatened. They will take the door, put their own men on the door and whatever comes through that [they will] take a percentage or the whole take.'[29] Many doormen were unprepared for the impending whirlwind. 'It wasn't heavy on the drug scene in them days,' said a veteran Manchester bouncer. 'It was more drink. People would offer you out one-to-one, you'd take them out and have a fight. The other doormen would leave it unless any others joined in. So it was jacket off, dickie bow off, sometimes you'd take your shirt off, you'd be fighting bare-chested round the back.' Many of the doormen were ex-boxers and would put in gumshields to scare off challengers.

Those knuckleduster days were now passing. It quickly became essential for head doormen at the city's most popular clubs to know the top gangsters, the heads. The Hacienda employed Roger Kennedy, an athletic, powerfully built black man who had worked as a research chemist and won county titles as a sprinter. He had also worked as a doorman, knew many of the gang leaders and was prepared to visit and talk with them. 'I told the Hacienda management from the outset that I wanted a free hand to do it my way,' he told the *Manchester Evening News*. 'I said it might look shady at times, but it was for the best. The intelligent approach is the only answer.'

Despite his efforts, the new scene was so imbued with drugs that the clubs became awash with them. On 9 July 1989, sixteen-year-old Claire Leighton went to the Hacienda. At around 10pm, she took a tablet bought by one of her friends. Just after midnight she collapsed and died. The medical cause was generalised haemorrhage and disseminated intravascular coagulation; she had been killed by a relatively low dosage of Ecstasy. Claire Leighton was not the first person in Britain to die from taking Ecstasy, but she became the best-known. Media hostility towards rave grew stronger.

Two months later the Gallery, the melting pot for the city's black gangs, was closed for breaches of its licensing conditions. It unleashed the Furies. The next week, the Hillbillies arrived at the Hacienda, flashed guns at the doormen and marched in without paying. That Christmas, they turned up at Discotheque Royale, beat up one of the doormen, stormed the fire exits and mugged customers at gunpoint. The gang assault on Manchester's nightlife was underway.

* * *

Two rave organisers, Marino Morgan and DJ Chris Nelson, opened another club that November called Konspiracy, on the Fennel Street site of the old Pips. Workmen refurbishing the place found a sawn-off shotgun hidden in a secret compartment; it had been lying there for years, probably hidden by a robbery gang who had once used the club. It was a bad omen. Konspiracy was a subterranean labyrinth with six bars and five dance-floors. It was soon packed, particularly on Saturday nights. After a packed, breathless and heady half-year of success, it was clear that 'the lads' from both Cheetham Hill and Salford had moved in.

Other white gangs tended to give the black gangs a wide berth, part of a visceral racial fear that the black gangs played on. Salford, however, did not share it; they feared no-one, and the upstairs at Konspiracy became known as 'Salford's room'. They dominated the sale of dance drugs in the club, which were rife: one staircase was lined with dealers calling out their wares. The sale of drugs was also splitting along racial lines: black gangs were known for peddling heroin, white gangs Ecstasy and amphetamine, and both sold cocaine and cannabis. Salford soon got a reputation for being the main suppliers of 'E' and speed, demand for which was surging with the spread of the new dance culture.

Salford often sourced their wares in Amsterdam, a city that Dutch narcotics detectives described as the 'Colombia of Ecstasy'. The price there was £3.50 or less per tab if bought in bulk; the same tabs could be sold in the UK for up to £15. Cannabis was also readily available. Regular trips abroad soon brought the Salford lads to the attentions of Customs and Excise, who found they were using an ingenious method of importation. 'A high-level informant told us and some of them were going to Amsterdam to organise amphetamine deals,' said a senior Customs investigator. 'They would buy a kilo over there and then a couple of lads would look for two-door cars from Great Britain, belonging to people who were in Holland on holiday. They would break into the cars at night and hide the amphetamine in the rear door panels. Then they would take down the number plate of the car and use someone with access either to the Police National Computer or to DVLC in Swansea to trace the English address of the car owners. They would let them drive back with the drugs, then a week or so later they would go to that address, steal the car and recover the drugs. It meant they did not have to risk bringing them in themselves.

'The first load we picked up was in the car of a couple from down south who had gone away for a dirty weekend. People caught with drugs in a vehicle always claim they didn't know they were there but this couple genuinely didn't. The next load went to an address in Hampshire. The car was then nicked and we trailed it all the way back to Salford where, because of the gang's reputation, we had armed back-up. We seized a couple of loads but it was getting too dangerous for the informant and we had to stop.'

Salford not only dealt rave drugs at Konspiracy but also effectively controlled the door. They would stay on after hours, raiding the bar and smoking weed. Champagne was taken by the crate and bottles of spirits were wrenched from the optics. They were a law unto themselves and impossible to deal with. As an older club owner put it, 'They [the authorities] closed the night clubs in Salford and the drinking dens in Moss Side and drove the baddies into the city centre. Years ago, villains used to come into clubs in Crombie overcoats, with a girl on either arm, and they were welcomed because they spent money. That has all changed. This new lot have no respect for anyone.'

There also seemed to be a vacuum on the doors. According to Paul Massey, when he came out of prison in 1988 many older doormen had given up the job:

> They disappeared. Weeks before I got out, they had gone, just sacked the doors and got off . . . The doors were open. Whatever city you go in, new people will come in. So there is going to be a lot of fucking roughing around . . . Then the police are saying, 'Oh, there are these gang fights in Manchester since Massey got out and these doors are being attacked and shootings have been happening here and doormen have been stabbed up here.' And they are blaming me for it all, because there was a lot of incidents in Manchester town centre overnight when I came out of prison. What you have to remember is, the QSG, who had this control for fifteen to twenty years, are disbanded when we come out of jail. So now you have left all the doors for people to fight [over]. People are fighting for a fucking piece of it.

* * *

Something nasty was going on in clubland. In January 1990, fire and smoke damaged Rocky's nightclub and the adjacent Follies Club in Whitworth Street. In March, magistrates finally revoked the licences of the Thunderdome and the Apollo pub, a Hillbilly stronghold. In April, a suspicious blaze wrecked The Mall in Deansgate and in May a doorman was shot three times at close range outside Courts nightclub in High Street. Police even sought to close Hacienda, making a court application on four grounds: the premises were frequented by people who regularly and blatantly used and dealt in drugs; people arrested on the premises had been convicted of dealing in controlled drugs; the premises were ill-conducted; and licensee Paul Mason did not have proper control of the premises. The club hired the celebrated lawyer George Carman, enlisted letters of support from Manchester City Council and won a six-month reprieve.

The Kitchen in Hulme had no such backing and shut after

numerous problems. Stiff legal penalties introduced in 1990 threatened jail for promoters of any unlicensed events that made money; some responded by staging 'free' parties. Police pressure and gang terror brought an end to the Blackburn raves but clubbers could still find impromptu parties in the early hours, in country parks, private houses, even an Old Trafford church. The summer was long and hot and rave went massive. One door firm was even paid by motorway service stations to keep revellers off their car parks. 'When the raves were full up they started to have raves in the cafeteria areas at Knutsford Services and places like that,' said a Manchester doorman. 'We would get a phone call and we would go and clear 'em off, but first we used to tax them for their drugs and everything. There'd be six of us and three or four hundred in the car park but they were all right because they were only bits of kids. There was nobody heavy down there. All they wanted to do was pop their pills, listen to their music and dance themselves fucking silly. So we used to clear them off and make a few bob off the stuff we got off them. People on Ecstasy are totally out of it. You can't reason with them. Wide-eyed and staring. That's where the big money was being made.'

Konspiracy remained a focus for gang activity and the police sought to revoke its licence, citing a loss of control by management. Undercover officers had counted sixty-two people smoking dope inside. The clubs owners protested that they were trying their best and denied insinuations of gang control. 'We have never paid protection,' protested co-owner Marino Morgan. 'Konspiracy is ours. We run it – no-one else does. The gangs come in, but without Robocop on the door they are difficult to stop.'

They didn't have Robocop but they did have the underworld equivalent: Desmond 'Dessie' Noonan, who for a time was their head doorman. Noonan was a notorious enforcer who had emerged from a jail term for conspiring to pervert the course of justice by threatening to kill witnesses in a robbery trial – the witnesses were police officers. He came from a large and well-known Irish family, his numerous brothers and sisters all named with the letter 'D' for Dublin, their father's home city. His brother

Damian would later become head doorman of the Hacienda, while another brother, Dominic, was a convicted armed robber. Through his Irish connections, Dessie occasionally lent a hand to Anti-Fascist Action, a hardline group that fought neo-nazis on the streets. Some say he was partly responsible for the dearth of far-right activity in Manchester; he once punched a right-wing protestor so hard that the man literally flew through the air. 'He joined a march once and there was a big British National Party presence on the side,' said a police officer. 'Dessie walked up and I could hear these fascists saying, "For fuck's sake, it's Noonan." Half of them walked away.' In 1993, the BNP attempted to set up a branch in Manchester. The organiser was 'invited' to a meeting with Noonan in a Moss Side pub – and the branch folded immediately afterwards.

Noonan was typical of the new breed of doorman; he knew many of the villains and was someone whose own criminal record gave him massive credibility on the door. The police, however, were deeply antipathetic, arguing that employing such men was not conducive to respectability and good order. Konspiracy's case was not helped when a student was stabbed there in September 1990 and needed life-saving surgery. Police locked in 600 customers, spent four hours questioning them and found seven knives on the floor. That December, Konspiracy lost its licence, though it was allowed briefly to stay open pending an appeal. At the same time, the manager of the popular 21 Piccadilly club received live ammunition in the post after several turnaways on the door.

With clubland in turmoil, the gang war kicked off again. One man was in the thick of both.

CHAPTER SIX

White Tony

IF ALL THAT Greater Manchester Police believe is true, by the age of twenty-two Tony Johnson had murdered one person, been present at the killing of two others, pulled off a string of lucrative armed robberies, made the wearing of body armour *de rigueur* on the city's gang scene, and forced the closure of the most famous night club in Britain. A one-man maelstrom, he epitomised the new breed of young, urban gangbanger.

Johnson was raised in a home mired in tragedy. His mother was only fifteen when he was born and neither she nor his natural father spent much time with him; for most of his childhood he lived with his grandmother, Winnie Johnson, in her modest semi in Fallowfield, south Manchester. Winnie was a good woman with a tortured soul; in 1964, she had watched her own twelve-year-old son, Keith Bennett, head off down the street to his gran's; it was the last time she would see him. Somewhere along his route, little Keith was abducted by Ian Brady and Myra Hindley, the Moors Murderers. They took him to windswept Saddleworth Moor and killed him. His body has never been found. Winnie kept a small, morbid shrine to her dead son on her living room wall, around a framed print of the only photograph of him: Keith with his toothy grin, round glasses and shock of fair hair he had cheekily cropped himself with scissors. On each side of the picture was a cross and next to it were his spectacles, with one cracked lens. He wasn't wearing them when he vanished; he had broken them the day before.

Johnson was not big but was muscular in a wiry way, and he could fight. Once he was with a friend in the Arndale Centre when two black youths attacked them. 'Tony didn't hesitate; he just went straight into them, and the black lads backed off,' said the friend. 'He had no fear at all.' He left school at sixteen and began work as a window cleaner and glazier, but not for long. 'I knew he was into something shady because you don't claim dole and drive round in a flash car,' said his mother. When the police came round to search her house, Winnie knew he was heading in the wrong direction, and fast. One day she had had enough and asked him outright what he did.

'Mind your own bleeding business,' came the reply.

What she didn't know couldn't hurt her; it was better to be in the dark about Johnson's crazy life. Even so, he still returned home regularly with clothes for Winnie to wash. Johnson was obsessive about dress and would supervise the ironing to make sure the creases were sharp. He had a girlfriend, and soon a baby daughter. 'He loved his little daughter. But I don't think his girlfriend's parents wanted her to have anything to do with him,' said the relative.

Johnson had befriended Tony McKie, sometimes known as 'Black Tony', and the Adetoro brothers, all associates of Cheetham Hill, and was gradually accepted into the mob. The Hillbillies then were at their height, the most ruthless and systematic gang in the city. They had a number of leading figures with big reputations, yet Johnson was to impress even the most hard-bitten villains with his daring and cool. What he and others did was to take their private war outside the confines of a small area of south central Manchester and make it public. He may have murdered Scratch Gardener to prove himself to the older heads, but waiting calmly for his victim for half an hour in a ginnel was hard-core. Johnson bragged about it to friends and his rep was cemented when he became the driver and unofficial bodyguard for the Cheetham Hill leader, ferrying him around in a Ford Sierra Cosworth, a highly fashionable car at the time.

Others were not impressed. 'One person described White Tony Johnson to me as a trainee painter and decorator one day and a gun gangster the next,' said Anthony Stevens. 'One thing that the gun culture taught me was that you didn't have to be hard any more. All the years of me breaking my knuckles on people's faces, and getting my face battered all over the place, counted for nothing, because all you needed was some little sneak to walk up to you and go "bang" and you were dead. You didn't have to be hard to do that, all you had to have was the nerve and the bottle. It gave prominence to a lot of people who, let's take the guns and weapons out of it, would have been absolute nothings. These guys would have been postmen or whatever, but because they were game enough to pull out a firearm and use it to deadly effect, their reputations grew and this whole thing got completely out of hand. So there is this wannabe called Tony Johnson who wanted everything the others had and he was willing to commit any kind of madness to get himself a reputation, and that is what he did.'

★   ★   ★

In February 1990, two Pepperhill men stepped off the London train at Manchester's Piccadilly Station. Ian McIntosh and Maurice McPherson carried bags containing almost a kilo and a half of heroin, worth more than £225,000 on the street. It would have taken their firm to another level, but the police were waiting for them, and both were arrested. 'McPherson and McIntosh were quite intimidating people but were both out of the frame for a long time,' said detective Tony Brett. 'They were going to London to meet Turks, buying heroin in bulk, bringing it back to the estate, then distributing it. They could buy a kilo then for £30,000 and didn't even interfere with it, then sold it at £15 a hundred-mil bag. Ten bags per gram, you are talking a profit of £120,000. They built the supply line through a Manchester criminal living between here and London. He wasn't convicted. There was also intelligence that people were getting stuff from Liverpool. It was wherever they could get it at the time.'

The bust created a temporary heroin drought. It was also a double-edged sword for Delroy Brown. On one hand it weakened him, as he relied heavily for support on McPherson and on Ian McLeod, who was also in jail for robbery and possessing a firearm. The Pepperhill crew suddenly appeared vulnerable and their enemies, with Tony Johnson a prime mover, saw a chance. On the other hand, Brown was now able to assume the mantle of gang leader – and as one police officer who knew Brown very well asserted, 'He was absolutely fearless.' If there was going to be trouble, he was up for it. The third phase of the Moss Side-Cheetham Hill War was about to begin.

Ice T was one of the seminal figures in gangsta rap, a genre which both chronicled and celebrated street life, gang loyalty, guns, killings and cop hating, and portrayed women as bitches and whores. So when he came to Manchester to play at the International II Club in Longsight, an ugly, low-roofed building, it was a must-see gig for many of the city's black gang members. In fact just about the only white faces in the crowd were a small group from Blackpool. They found themselves watching a sporadic battle between Moss Side and Cheetham Hill youths. 'It kicked off all night, and it was bad,' said one of the Blackpool contingent. 'It was hard to tell who was who. There was blood everywhere: the floor, the stage, the stairs. Ice T came out and was shouting to the crowd, "Cool your posse, cool your posse," but it made no difference. We stayed at the back and kept our mouths shut. When we came out of the club at the end, every car along the road for about a quarter of a mile had had its windows put through.'

In March 1990, a hard-core crowd was again in attendance at the International to see the controversial rappers Two Live Crew, whose sexually explicit album *As Nasty As They Wanna Be* had caused outrage in the United States. It was another three-line whip for the gangbangers, though many 'civilians' were there too to check out a group that had earned reams of indignant Press coverage. Ten unsmiling young men arrived once the gig was underway. At their head, police were later told, was White Tony. They brushed past the doormen and into the club in a wedge, scanning in the dark for any Pepperhill. Their intelligence was good: Delroy Brown and friends were spotted across the club. With no compunction, the Hillbillies opened fire. Several hundred concert-goers ducked as someone fired back. Brown was hit in the back with a nine-millimetre bullet. Then the Hillbillies raided the box office and took £1,000.

'It was an Irish club,' said detective Ron Gaffey. 'There were something like four hundred people in there. Someone is firing at Delroy Brown, with four hundred dancers in between, and allegedly someone is firing back. Brown was wounded and those responsible escaped. One thing that still irritates me is that there were potentially four hundred witnesses yet not one of them came forward to tell us what they saw or, if they did, they weren't prepared to write it down. That included two young barristers who were there as revellers and who have supposedly taken an oath to uphold the law. I was flabbergasted. If we can't get people like that on our side, then what chance do we have? Then the very next day, we have got vehicles chasing each other and firing down the streets, like Chicago.'

Police announced the formation of a 'task force' to head off a repeat of the previous gang war, under the codename Operation Takeover, and set up a confidential telephone hotline for information. 'When we launched Takeover, we were also astonished to find the villains were wearing body armour,' said Gaffey. 'We were trying to find out where they got it, and also asking if we should have it ourselves. It was Johnson we clocked wearing it first. Suddenly there was a realisation of how big the weapons problem was. Several houses were raided and we recovered quite a lot of weapons. One guy was actually reaching for a gun in his bedroom as we were walking in. Does he know it's us? If he doesn't, what is he going to do? If he does, what is he gong to do? You felt vulnerable. It was very risky in those days.'

Gaffey was in no doubt about White Tony's status. 'Johnson was a killer. He was the hit man. He was a very nasty piece of work, very dangerous. He would swan around, go to the clubs, refuse to pay, just waltz in. People were so fearful of him.' His audacity saw him rise swiftly in the hierarchy of the Hillbillies. 'Cheetham Hill were quite well organised. All of them were intelligent in a streetwise sense and were acutely aware of police methods. I never found any of them to be unintelligent, though they weren't particularly pleasant. There was a bond in terms of the drug business. There were dangers in working in isolation, so it was much safer and more businesslike to operate in a group.'

The police targeted the Hillbillies in earnest but witnesses were loath to talk. Officers were also hampered by the failure to ensure a consistent flow of intelligence. The original card files put together in the mid-eighties during the first Cheetham Hill-Moss Side war seemed to have been thrown out, while many of the officers who had worked on phase one of the gang war had moved on. 'It was a new phenomenon, and our intelligence sources weren't good at that stage to infiltrate some of these gangs,' said Gaffey. 'We were a bit behind. We weren't properly focussed. They were very difficult to infiltrate anyway. It was difficult to know what had caused this but I think it was something very flimsy.'

While Delroy Brown recovered in hospital from his third serious attack in as many years, a young man was killed outside the Pepperhill. Egbert Williams, a nineteen-year-old partner in a Moss Side bakery, was stabbed through the heart in a fight in the car park and died as he lay on the ground. It followed an argument inside the pub and was not gang-related, but it added to the air of fear.

* * *

The annual Moss Side Caribbean carnival is Manchester's answer to Notting Hill, a noisy, colourful celebration of an exuberant culture. In May 1990, up to 40,000 people were out in shirt-sleeve weather, having fun, but the dealers were expecting trouble. 'This was a hot day [yet] all the Frontline had on long Macs and ski jackets,' recalled one. 'It means they're carrying.'[30] Then the Hillbillies arrived. Stone-faced and tooled-up, they marched into the throng, cutting a swathe. 'These guys were walking around with their hands in their coats and that was scary. That was really, really scary. They were armed,' said the dealer. 'There was a lot of rushing around, not knowing what was going on. People screaming. And then I don't know where they came from but I heard two shots. It didn't look as though they had found the person they were looking for but they had certainly found his car.' The Hillbillies had reached the Pepperhill pub and found Delroy Brown's red BMW outside. Some produced sledge-hammers from under their coats and proceeded to smash it up before turning it over onto its roof. 'That was just a blatant show of strength,' said the dealer. 'It was like, intimidating people, wanting people to know how strong they were.'

Among the crowd was Ian Brown, lead singer of the then-hugely popular Stone Roses. 'I watched the Cheetham Hill Gang walk through in army formation, eight-strong in rows, each man with a holster,' he later said. For Brown it was a turning point, the day the hedonism of Madchester turned sour. 'This is June '90, this is a different day. It's like America, the way the ghettoes of America were flooded with crack and coke, and so were the ghettoes of England, and the gangs and guns are going to come. Where there's drugs, there's money, and where there's money, anything goes.'[31] The Hillbillies' arrogance, even as some of them were under intense police investigation, was undiminished, with the swaggering Tony Johnson taking centre stage.

They even began to threaten the police. That summer the Operation Takeover detectives seized weapons, body armour and drugs including crack cocaine, and arrested two dozen people for offences ranging from possession of drugs to attempted murder. 'We started to recover a lot of firearms,' said Ron Gaffey. 'A picture of their weaponry began to emerge.' The result was death threats; one of the gangs said an officer would be lured into a trap and shot if the clampdown wasn't lifted. 'I got a couple of letters sent to the police station,' said Gaffey. 'They threatened to blow me up. That was happening to some of the other officers as well, but it didn't particularly bother us.'

However, one black constable was moved out of the area after threats to shoot him. The Pepperhill, mainly black or mixed-race themselves, had singled him out. He later returned but was advised not to patrol Alexandra Park. The threats were not idle. Two officers who stopped a car to check documents were surrounded by twenty youths outside the Pepperhill. One was butted and the other kicked before help arrived. A firearms team was moved into the area, mobilising every night at a base in Moss Side. Normally it would have been on standby elsewhere in the city and sent out only after a telephone request to an assistant chief constable. Now it could be sent out immediately. Talk of 'no-go' areas was robustly denied.

* * *

The West Indian Carnival in Chapeltown, Leeds, was another magnet for young black people that August. With its costumed masqueraders, soca and calypso, steel bands and garish floats, the noisy parade attracted 60,000 people. A contingent of young Cheetham Hill, including White Tony, also made the journey. As usual, they were armed.

The carnival officially finished in the early evening, but street dancing and loud music continued into the night. Even when a visitor from Birmingham was stabbed to death in Harehills Avenue in a row over a sound system, the bass thumped on. At 1.20 a.m., again in Harehills Avenue, another fight broke out, escalating from raised voices to pushing and shoving. One of the Cheetham crew, Gary Shearer, was attacked, and a twenty-eight-year-old Birmingham man, Sedley Sullivan, intervened to stop the scuffle. One of the Cheetham men responded by whipping out a gun and firing shots into the crowd. Sullivan and an innocent bystander, Rachel Soloman, aged eighteen and also from Birmingham, were both hit in the torso. 'Sedley and this girl were dancing by the sound system and they just shot at them,' Tresha Mitchell, a friend of Sullivan's, told the *Yorkshire Post*. Most of the crowd scattered. Then people began to shout that someone had been shot, and came back to help. 'There were no police on the scene and no ambulance after fifteen minutes. We had to shove him into a car to get him to St James's Hospital,' said Mitchell. The gunmen had left in a car. Both Rachel Soloman and Sedley Sullivan died from their wounds.

The police soon believed that Tony Johnson was involved. He was arrested and put on an identity parade, but wasn't picked out and denied any involvement. Instead two of his friends, Gary Shearer and nineteen-year-old James Walber, were arrested and charged with manslaughter.

Rachel Soloman's relatives issued a statement that summed up the feelings of many:

As each day goes by, the bitterness, disbelief and contempt
    it's hard to justify.
Why do innocent people who go out to enjoy themselves
    always suffer?
Why do the innocent suffer injuries and even deaths from
    trigger-happy hoodlums?
Why is it an innocent bystander is gunned down in cold
    blood without mercy?
What is the motive? Being in the wrong place at the wrong
    time.

* * *

Two innocent people were dead, yet there was no let-up in the
war. Someone tried to kill a drug-runner in Gooch Close, a small
cul-de-sac in the heart of the west side of the Alexandra Park
estate, firing three shotgun blasts from out of a Golf GTi. Another
man was in the Spinners pub in Hulme when a young gang in
masks walked in, shot him through the eye and leg with a small-
calibre handgun and him hit repeatedly about the head with a
hammer. He needed surgery to remove a slug from his brain.
Detective Ron Gaffey, whose previous visit to the Spinners had
been for the murder of Hendy Proverbs, returned there. 'You get
extremely frustrated. The guy had been shot in the mouth; a
fellow had walked up to him and fired and the bullet had exited
through the back of his throat. I spoke to him personally and he
told me to fuck off. He said he would sort it out himself.' At least
one of those suspected of the shooting was connected to a new
and, as yet, unnamed gang that would become known as 'the
Gooch'. A petrol bomb was hurled at police when they carried
out inquiries in Moss Side in the early hours of the next morning.
    The most notable police success came with the capture of
Steven Julien, who had staged the brutal Coin Controls robbery
and then fled to the West Indies, from where he could only be
extradited if he committed another offence. Local police put him
under surveillance and after nine months, he made the slip-up
they were waiting for, applying for a form of naturalisation using

a false identity. Officers picked him up as he lay sunbathing in brightly coloured shorts and baseball hat on a beach and flew him to Britain still wearing his shorts, to be met at the airport by detectives from Oldham and the news that his getaway driver, Mark Mann, had made a confession.

Julien and fellow robber Chinadu Iheagwara both admitted attempted robbery and two previous bank raids. They were described as part of a 'ruthless, determined and extremely dangerous group of men.' The machete-wielding Iheagwara was jailed for twenty years, while gunman Julien received twenty-two years. One of the guards had lost part of his leg, while the other had undergone sixteen operations on the wound in his back, which failed to heal. Judge Rhys Davies told Manchester Crown Court the offences were the most brutal and callous he had ever come across. Driver Mark Mann was jailed for eight years. He had been moved to six different prisons while on remand and each time had been threatened with death for confessing.

White Tony, however, was flying. His *forte* was also armed robbery, and that November he was the driver in a raid at Mumps Bridge in Oldham. Two gunmen forced guards to drive to another location and stole £362,000 in cash. Just over a month later, he was again believed to have been involved in a dramatic raid at the Bassett's sweet factory in Sheffield, in which three masked men chased payroll guards through the factory, firing a shotgun. They sped off in a cloud of £5 notes, dropping 200 as they made their getaway but escaping with £78,000. Johnson's fingerprints were later found in a flat the gang had hidden out in.

That Christmas, a series of events brought the crisis in clubland to a head. Konspiracy finally closed, ground down by the gangs. Its hardcore crowd moved over the Hacienda, only to find that the well-respected head doorman, Roger Kennedy, had quit. Kennedy had largely managed to keep the lid on trouble at the club. 'I employed diplomacy for two years with the gang leaders,' he told the *Manchester Evening News*. 'If I had opted for a violent approach, I'd have been shot – simple.' But he complained that because of this approach, some police officers seemed to believe he was a gangster himself, which was 'ridiculous'. A London door team was brought in, the management figuring that outsiders would not hold allegiance to any gang, and the police application to revoke the licence was withdrawn because of 'a positive change in direction at the club'. It even received a Best Venue in Britain award. Yet the relationship between the club scene and drugs had become indivisible. 'It wasn't the dealers that were the problem, really, it was the gangs against the dealers,' said Hacienda staffer Leroy Richardson. 'What the gangs thought was, here's a market where we don't have to do anything but threaten these people, who will give us their money. It wasn't the gangs dealing. They didn't have to. They let the dealers carry on and took their money.'[32]

The London door firm had not been working two weeks when Tony Johnson threatened one of them with a gun. That was it for Tony Wilson and his co-directors; they sat down on the Sunday night that January and agreed to close the club. 'With my trade union background, my idea was withdrawal of labour, going on strike,' said Wilson. 'Closing the club is actually going on strike. Everyone else agreed that was one way out of it, to re-group, re-design the entrance, and that's why we closed. It caused exactly what one wanted, it was a major statement. The police began to work very hard on the problems.'[33]

Once again the violence was displaced. Shots were fired at Peter Stringfellow's upmarket Millionaire Club in West Mosley Street, shattering the glass doors. On the same day, fired ravaged Wetherby's Club, which had been closed for refurbishment, on the eve of its re-opening. Bar staff complained that the Hillbillies had beaten up people in Dry, a cutting-edge bar opened by the Hacienda owners. Tony Johnson grabbed the microphone in a packed nightclub and declared he was top dog. He and a handful of street thugs were destroying the Madchester dream.

★ ★ ★

On 22 February 1991, Johnson and his friend 'Black Tony' McKie were in a Ford Cosworth when they were flagged down outside a Cheetham Hill pub by another vehicle. They knew the men in it, and approached for a discussion. Instead the men in the car opened fire with handguns. Johnson and McKie began to run, but within seconds both were hit and wounded. McKie managed to keep going. Looking back over his shoulder, he saw Johnson, already hit twice, struggling to escape as one of the men fired again. The shot brought Johnson to the ground; he could run no further. Two of the men approached him and one put a gun to his mouth. 'Finish him,' said someone. The gunman squeezed the trigger.

'As I stood there identifying Tony's body, my thoughts were about losing two sons,' said Winnie Johnson, who had raised Johnson as her own. 'I didn't know what he did, where he lived or who he mixed with but I always regarded him as my son. After suffering all these years over Keith, I can't believe I must cope with another murder. I brought Anthony up as my own. It's more than any mother should have to bear.' Tony McKie underwent major surgery and for days was too heavily sedated to be interviewed. When he did come round, he refused to co-operate with the investigation.

More than 200 mourners, including some of the most dangerous gangsters in Cheetham Hill, attended Johnson's funeral. They arrived in a thirty-strong motorcade and Johnson's family had to abandon plans to hold the service in a chapel and instead held it in the open at the graveside in Manchester's Southern Cemetery. The management of the Hacienda, on hearing the news, began making plans to re-open.

* * *

Four men sat in the dock at Manchester Crown Court in February 1993 for one of the biggest underworld trials in the city's history. Paul Flannery, Desmond Noonan, his younger brother Derek and Michael Sharples all denied murder of Tony Johnson. It was actually their second trial: the first, in the summer of 1992, ended with the jury unable to reach verdicts, and a retrial was ordered.

The police believed that Johnson's death stemmed from a £360,000 robbery he had carried out in Oldham with two brothers named Bulger. One of the Bulgers had allegedly left his £80,000 share of the loot with others for safe keeping, but when he asked for it, Dessie Noonan told him there was only £40,000 left. Bulger said he was going to complain to the volatile Johnson. The Crown alleged that Noonan then visited Paul Flannery, who was a patient in a hospital in Southport, and a plot was hatched to kill Johnson.

Flannery, born in 1959, was regarded as a serious criminal, having received his first conviction at the age of twelve for stealing a bus conductor's bag and assault causing actual bodily harm. A big, powerful man, he had numerous subsequent convictions for robbery, burglary and theft. A few months before Johnson's murder, he had been shot in the hand when his car came under heavy fire outside the PSV Club in Hulme. According to one source, Flannery had gone there to broker a truce between Cheetham Hill and the Pepperhill. The Moss Side men instead surrounded his car and holed it with bullets.

A few weeks later, the police launched an early-morning raid on Flannery's flat after he had allegedly threatened a traffic officer outside the Temple pub in Cheetham Hill (something Flannery denied). He was woken by the sound of the front door being smashed in, and fearing it was a Moss Side hit squad, he dived naked through a closed, first-floor bedroom window. 'I thought the first person to come through the door would be firing at me,' he told a court hearing some years later. 'I dived as I would into a pool, head-first with my arms straight in front.' Tactical Aid Group officers stationed at the back of the flat were astonished to see him crash through the window, land on a fence and bounce off. 'I came to rest face down. I felt like I'd been flattened by a bulldozer.' Flannery had broken his back. Police officers who found him then handcuffed him and dragged him naked along the ground. Flannery was rendered paraplegic by his injury, paralysed from the chest down.[34]

Flannery was still recovering in hospital when he was visited by Noonan. The Crown alleged that, despite his injuries, Flannery left hospital on weekend leave after the meeting and was in the taxi that flagged down Johnson and Tony McKie in the car park of the Penny Black. 'There were four people in it – Desmond Noonan in the back, Paul Flannery, Derek Noonan driving and Michael Sharples behind him,' testified McKie, who had become the chief prosecution witness. 'Tony got out and walked over to Dessie in the car park. They asked if we had guns but we said, "No," and Sharples and Derek got out of the car. I walked towards Paul in the car. He was looking over his shoulder and nodding towards Derek and Michael. I then saw he was holding a black automatic handgun and he fired a shot, which ripped the sleeve of my jacket. I turned and this time I felt as well as heard another shot and knew I'd been hit in the back. I started to run and heard another two or three shots fired. I stopped and looked back to see Tony struggling, trying to get away from Dessie. He got as far as the wall and Dessie fired a shot and Tony fell. The other two joined Dessie and Derek bent down. Somebody said, "Finish him," and I heard three shots.'

McKie said he had kept quiet for months about who had shot him because he wanted to make his own inquiries about how people he thought were friends could turn so violently against him, but his girlfriend was threatened when she went to visit him while he was in jail for another matter and soon afterwards he contacted police. 'That was the last straw,' he said. 'I was being put under a lot of pressure in Hull Prison to say that certain people were not involved. Then they threatened my common-law wife.' McKie admitted he was a criminal but refused to say how he earned his money. He said he thought his friend's killing would spark a bloodbath. 'I thought there was going to be a lot of guns on the streets. Tony Johnson had a lot of friends throughout England and a lot of people were very upset about his death.' He denied the existence of the Cheetham Hill gang though, claiming, 'It's just a media label.'

Another witness, Alexander McCormack, shared the ownership of a private hire car with Derek Noonan. He testified that Noonan told him his brother Dessie had been visited earlier that day by some men who 'tried to take him out.' Derek also said men had been shooting at him: 'They had shotguns. All I had was a poxy handgun,' he allegedly said. Noonan took the taxi on the night of the shootings, and afterwards McCormack met up with the Noonan brothers by arrangement. 'They were smiling and laughing and Derek said, "The body at the Penny – we did it."' He also told McCormack to have the taxi cleaned and its tyres changed, said McCormack.

The defendants all put forward alibi defences. Flannery said he was staying at the home of a friend on his first weekend away from the spinal injury unit. Dessie Noonan was drinking in Didsbury. Derek was inside the Penny Black, not outside; he was a partner in the pub and said he spent the whole evening working there before leaving at 11.30 p.m. by taxi. He did not hear about the shootings until the licensee phoned him at home some hours later. One defence counsel claimed McKie was trying to frame the defendants after 'doing a deal' with the real gang responsible, though they never said who this might be. They pointed out that though he claimed to earn £250 a week working for his father's building company, he had bought two Golf GTis and a £20,000 Porsche with the personal number plate MACAV.

The jury believed them. After a two-week trial, and many months spent in jail on remand, Flannery, the Noonans and Sharples were all cleared of Johnson's murder. They were free to go. 'Tony Johnson was a man I knew who had a heart of gold and was betrayed to his death by his friends,' said Flannery enigmatically, before being driven off to celebrate his freedom. No-one has been convicted for the murder of Tony Johnson.

White Tony subsequently became synonymous with Manchester's gangland, his life the kind of live-fast-die-young cliché celebrated in the testosterone lyrics of a thousand gangsta rappers. A blaze of headlines described him as a gang leader; he never was. In truth he was dupe, a young man impressed by older figures he saw as symbols of prestige and glamour, seduced by the champagne life and the respect that only fear could bring him. He was used and then killed. His death marked the end of one chapter and the start of another.

CHAPTER SEVEN

The Alexandra Park War

THE FIRST SERIOUS assault on the hard-drug traders of Moss Side was late in coming. For several years, Moss Side residents had been complaining that the drugs market around the precinct centre was effectively allowed to operate; they believed this was a deliberate, even racist ploy to keep the trade in one place, among the black community and away from white areas. For their part, the police were wary, perhaps too wary, of provoking a backlash. Memories of the riots were still fresh, while the more recent killing of PC Keith Blakelock during a disastrous intervention at Broadwater Farm in north London starkly showed the dangers of ill-planned operations.

By 1990, however, GMP was in possession of video technology that allowed for more discreet surveillance and evidence gathering. It also had sufficient numbers of trained undercover officers who looked the part and could make drug buys without arousing suspicion. The undercovers were used successfully in Operation Palace. 'After long intelligence gathering we identified sellers and customers in and around the Alexandra Park estate, which some dealers regarded as a police no-go area,' said Superintendent Paul Cook. 'Rather than go in mob-handed, as happened at Broadwater Farm, we picked offenders off over a six-week period and there was no trouble.'

Video cameras were used for the first time in an even more successful operation, codenamed Corkscrew, between September and early November 1990. A camera with a zoom lens was hidden in high-rise flats overlooking the Moss Side precinct and captured remarkable sequences of dealers trading openly. Twelve men, including two of the principal heroin dealers in the area, were jailed for between seven and ten years in what police hailed as a major success. Many were in their mid-to-late twenties or even their thirties, veterans in street dealing terms.

Yet while Corkscrew removed some of the most blatant drug dealers from around the precinct centre it could not deter the junkies who haunted the area. Moss Side had become the prime drugs market in the north of England and the remorseless demand for heroin and cocaine ensured that the sales pitches there would regenerate. In the four years to the end of 1990, the number of notified drug addicts in Greater Manchester alone more than doubled, and no-one knew the number of non-registered users. It was inevitable that more suppliers would emerge to meet the incessant demand.

These dealers would not operate so conspicuously. 'They realised that if they stood out in the open with no cover, the police were going to get them, particularly with film,' said Tony Brett. 'A lot then decided to move away from the shopping precinct because it was too public, and go into different methods. You had a split between those who had the nous to go into the mobile phone side, which remains the best method of selling drugs at street level, and those who were still prepared to stand on the street.' The main dealing area also crossed over the road to the Alexandra Park estate. 'There were still pockets to be found on the parade, because it is all about catching the customers, but eventually we started to get intelligence that it was happening on the estate, and this was the first time we saw the split of the two rival factions.'

The factions concerned came from either side of Alexandra Road, which divides the estate neatly down the middle. On the east side were the Pepperhill Mob, in their stronghold on Bedwell Close. On the west side was a group of young men who hung out around a shebeen in Gooch Close, a small cul-de-sac of semi-detached houses with an alley at one end. The shebeen brought in customers and the gang sold them drugs. Like the Pepperhill crew just a few hundred yards away, they had grown up together, could not find jobs, and turned to crime. Four of them had been sent to a detention centre for mugging a man in a churchyard in

1987; unluckily for them, a group of police officers was keeping watch from a clump of bushes. The police first noted their existence as a separate group when a car was shot up in Gooch Close in the summer of 1990, while at least one of the gang was involved in shooting Keith Erskine in the Spinners pub in Hulme at around the same time. Then, early in 1991, a gun was fired at a police officer in the close.

The Gooch lads looked like an American street gang: they had razor-cropped hair, athletic builds and wore bomber jackets, hooded sweats, baggy jeans and training shoes or baseball boots. Their affiliation was based on friendship and mutual reliance; there was little evidence of hierarchy. 'It wasn't a strict gang structure,' said Tony Brett. 'The Gooch all frequented the same area and realised there was strength in numbers, and they were prepared to enforce that strength if they had to. They were all born around there and had very strong links to that part of Moss Side. They were very proud of the fact that they were Mancunians, not yardies, whereas the other faction had a very significant person [Delroy Brown] who was an outsider.'

Their relationship with the Pepperhill lads was friendly, even as the two 'gangs' – they saw themselves simply as groups of mates – came to control much of the drug trade in the area, reining in the lone dealers and bringing order to a chaotic marketplace. 'In the whole of Moss Side you will have lots of independent dealers,' said a former gang member, 'but if they are making a lot, the Gooch or whoever will come along and say, "You are working for us now." Which makes sense.' It meant that 'for once somebody had got a grip of the dealing,' according to Brett. Independents found it unwise to compete.

In March 1991, the newly knighted Sir James Anderton announced his retirement at the age of fifty-eight. The colourful officer, who believed he might have been Oliver Cromwell in a previous life and declared he was moved by the spirit of God, was succeeded by his deputy, David Wilmot, a politically safer pair of hands credited with helping to rebuild police-community relations after the Toxteth riots as a Merseyside chief superintendent. Sir James went with a typically apocalyptic parting shot: 'I see around me a great sea of wrongdoing that seems not to lessen. I did have a kind of dream that I might, by example and protest, change the course of things so powerfully, and influence society and the country in the matter of rightful conduct, that they would turn away from crime and disorder and wilful criminal behaviour. Sadly, that has not happened.'

Yet to his officers, the death of Tony Johnson and the drug busts in Moss Side, the guns seized and the squeeze on Cheetham Hill, seemed to represent some kind of progress. No-one could predict what was around the corner.

*   *   *

The Gooch boys had no beef with Cheetham Hill. One of their leading figures was the cousin of a Cheetham Hill head, and the two groups often bought drugs from each other to re-sell. Delroy Brown, however, objected to the Gooch helping to enrich 'the enemy' and, in typically cavalier fashion, ordered them to stop. They told him where to go. 'As far as the Gooch were concerned, they were just getting on with what they were doing,' said Anthony Stevens, 'and they had some madman coming over there and saying, "You can't do anything in south Manchester and certainly not if you are dealing with people from north Manchester." The Gooch turned round and said, "Sod you, pal, we do what we want." You try to bully them, they are not having it.'

The chain reaction that became the Alex Park War began early in 1991 with a minor spat between a Gooch man and one of the Pepperhill crowd. Delroy Brown, recently released from remand after charges of gun possession had been dropped, became embroiled and shortly afterwards his car was stolen from outside the shebeen off Gooch Close. Brown blamed the Gooch lads. In a subsequent fight, Julian Stewart, a young lad who hung around on the east side of the estate, lost part of an ear. A car belonging to a Gooch man was torched in retaliation. Having been singled out by Cheetham Hill, Brown now became a hate figure to the Gooch too. He was also being informally identified as 'public enemy number one' by Greater Manchester Police. 'In my opinion, it was more about personalities than drug dealing,' said Brett. 'The Gooch had some very strong individuals who were not fearful and would have done him serious harm if they could.'

The mayhem that followed was remarkable because it was concentrated in such a small area: like two men fighting in a phone booth. Many young men who were to spend the following years trying to kill each other lived literally yards apart. They had grown up together, gone to the same schools, attended the same churches, played for the same football teams. Each side would draw members and allies from further afield – Longsight, Hulme, Chorlton, Rusholme, Whalley Range, Stretford, Old Trafford – but the battleground was invariably the Alexandra Park estate, with Alexandra Road its front line, dividing the two sides like no man's land. The estate became an eerie battleground of shifting no-go areas, unlit rat-runs, sudden ambushes and the crackle of gunfire after dark. Every hooded youth was eyed with caution, even fear.

At nine o'clock on a Wednesday night, 27 March 1991, a group of four boys were standing in Gooch Close talking about football. They included Junior Richards and his younger brother 'Darkie'. Around a dozen other youths were congregated nearby, some dealing drugs. 'The four of us were just talking when I saw a dark-coloured Cavalier come slowly down the close,' Junior later said. 'The front and back windows on the passenger side were wound down. I saw a flash of fire and then heard six loud bangs. We dived for cover and ran.'[35]

One fourteen-year-old took a bullet in the hip. Darkie was hit in the head, his left eye blasted out. Some children ran to get his mum, Maureen, who lived nearby. 'I found him at a house nearby,' she recalled. 'His eye seemed to have gone and he had a hole in his temple. He was holding his head and crying, saying, "Mum, am I going to die?" I just couldn't take in what had happened. I went in the ambulance with Darkie. He had an emergency operation. They took away what was left of his eye and fragments of a bullet from his head. The surgeons told me that a fraction the other way and the bullet would have instantly killed my son.'

The Gooch marshalled their forces. Within two hours, they closed in on the Pepperhill pub, charged through the doors, grabbed a twenty-year-old man and cleaved him with a machete. He was taken to hospital with head injuries, and from then on it was tit-for-tat. Shots were fired from a moving car in Whalley Range; a Gooch man was stabbed in the city centre. Each attack made things worse. Instead of focussing on the two or three people at the heart of their dispute, the Gooch retaliation was indiscriminate. 'They decided that everybody over that [east] side of the estate is our enemy,' said Anthony Stevens. 'So when the Gooch retaliated, they retaliated on everybody over there. They started troubling people who were innocent, and these people who were innocent had no choice but to defend themselves.'

Early on a Saturday evening, the Gooch again hit the Pepperhill pub. This time the attack was led by a man in a shiny home-made mask: he loosed a nine-millimetre handgun at a fleeing group, hitting one man in the leg while other bullets smashed through the dining room window of a house where a family were watching television. The next day, Che Cole was shot in the hand and arm by a man on a motorbike in Doddington Close, yet another dead-end street in a secluded position in the heart of Pepperhill territory. Minutes later, four Pepperhill men attacked Henri McMaster with a machete. Then they cornered some Gooch lads and poured fluid on them before setting them on fire; the Gooch escaped without serious injury.

The bloody picture was confused by an unrelated murder that same weekend of a junkie who regularly travelled from his home in Birmingham to buy heroin and crack; he made the trip three times a week and spent £1,000 a week on drugs. This time two men were waiting for him; he was 'taxed' and shot dead by a twenty-five-year-old gunman who was later jailed for life. Although unconnected to the gang wars, it added to the growing image of Moss Side as a war zone.

The savagery was making national headlines and local Labour MP Tony Lloyd appealed to the Home Secretary, Kenneth Baker, to raise the issue with the Prime Minister. 'If law-abiding residents of Moss Side are aware of people in possession of firearms, I urge them to tell the police,' responded Baker lamely. Moral choices on the Alex estate were not that simple. Few people dared speak out, as the tension became unbearable. Two council workmen who parked their van in the street were beaten up by a gang who mistook them for undercover cops. The police themselves asked for bulletproof vests to be standard issue for patrols in the area but were told they were too expensive and not practicable. One officer contacted a newspaper anonymously: 'We can buy our own body armour for more than a hundred pounds and wear it under our tunics without breaching regulations. Some are considering it. It is getting very ugly and is reaching the stage where we expect a shooting every time we come on duty.' Their bosses said they had a stock of equipment that could be issued 'when appropriate'.[36]

Police made a series of raids, smashing in doors and rousting gang members in their underwear. They found a stash of weapons near Gooch Close, including a Demon crossbow, a handgun, knives, a machete and a selection of full-face masks. Another cache, including a loaded shotgun, was recovered in the Pepperhill base of Bedwell Close. Detectives were also getting a clear picture of who was involved but had little evidence to use in court, even from victims.

Anthony Stevens saw his friends getting pulled into another needless war. 'If someone had stopped to think for a minute, they would have realised we all grew up together. In the past, they would come over to the Pepperhill and we would occasionally visit the Talbot, where they drank. Now, if you stepped across the border you were dead. It was ridiculous. I tried to explain to my lot that you can't make money if you are consistently caught up in violence.' They wouldn't listen. The Pepperhill shot at some Gooch men in a Golf GTi, the favourite car of the young black gangs. There were more attacks outside the Pepperhill pub. The *Manchester Evening News* ran a double-page spread under the headline 'Hell is a city' about Manchester's 'gun culture', and CID boss David James told the paper, 'There is a hard-core of people driving around in high-priced cars, dressed in designer clothing and wearing expensive jewellery. They don't have employment, so draw your own conclusions. Our information shows that the main players in the current problems are between nineteen and twenty-six. We know who they are, but people have to have the courage to give us evidence.'

As the paper hit the streets, the Gooch were out trying to kill one of their most feared rivals. Nineteen-year-old Winston Brownlow was one of a younger group on the east side of the estate who hung around on Doddington Close and had teamed up with the Pepperhill. Brownlow was walking from the Pepperhill pub when two men on a motorbike pulled up and the pillion passenger, wearing a helmet with the visor down, climbed off and fired a gun. He was a poor shot, and Brownlow was hit only in the hand. The gangsters' ineptitude as marksmen would prevent many fatalities. This time, however, the payback was lethal.

Carl Stapleton was seventeen, a slim youth with cropped hair. Like many recent school-leavers in the area, he was unemployed and tended to rise late and go to bed late. As a child of the estate he knew many of the young men involved and was friendly with some of the Gooch; one of his cousins was said to be a Goochie. Stapleton had been watching TV at his aunt's house one evening when he set off to walk the short distance home on the west side of the estate. He was seen talking to three black men and two white women in a walkway. Some time afterwards Junior Richards, whose brother had been shot at the start of the feud, was riding his mountain bike past an alley when he saw the body of a youth lying on his back in a pool of blood, with his hands held up towards his face. Yards away, music thumped out of a house party, the occupants oblivious to the horror outside. Richards ran for help, and an ambulance crew tried to revive the injured teenager, without success. Carl Stapleton died within twenty minutes. Fifteen stab wounds had lacerated his heart, lungs, liver and spleen. 'An innocent kid gets shot in the eye and now another innocent boy is stabbed for nothing,' said his father, Michael Bellamy. 'The killing has got to stop, but I just don't know how.'

The Gooch were once again out for vengeance. The following day a gang of them attacked Delroy Brown in the street, clubbing him over the head with a machete. Brown fled into the Big Western pub, with blood pouring from his head and the Gooch in hot pursuit. 'Call the police!' he yelled as he tried to get upstairs to the pub's living quarters. He managed to snatch one knife as it was thrust at him and vaulted over a stairwell before finding refuge in the cellar. The Gooch boys tried to break down the cellar door until they heard on a radio scanner that police were on their way. They fled seconds before the cops arrived. 'They were trying to kill me,' the bloodied Delroy told the officers. He was searched and a small amount of crack cocaine was found rolled up in a wad of cash in his back pocket; he'd had no time to ditch it in the life-or-death struggle with his enemies. Delroy was under arrest. First, though, he was taken under guard to Manchester Royal Infirmary – where treating gang members was becoming a nightly occurrence – while cops flooded the estate.

The huge police presence allowed national newspaper reporters to get out into an area they usually avoided. The *Daily Star* ran a 'news special on the most violent city in Britain'. A two-page spread appeared in the *Sun* under the banner headline 'THE BRONX OF BRITAIN'. *Sun* reporters visited the estate in an unmarked van: 'We came under attack as we drove an unmarked van down a deserted street which is home territory for the notorious Gooch Gang. A gang of youths, mainly black, emerged from a rubble-strewn alleyway adjoining Gooch Close. As we passed, they pelted us with bricks and stones and spat at the windscreen. One brick smashed through the passenger door window, showering our team with razor-sharp glass.'

Delroy Brown was remanded in custody charged with the murder of Carl Stapleton, the attempted murder of Henri McMaster, and possessing crack with intent to supply. Some of his friends were also rounded up, including the seventeen-year-old Julian 'Turbo' Stewart, but others remained at large. 'We have the guns and knives to hit back at the Gooch Close gang and we can do it, I promise you,' one told an *Observer* reporter. 'The scene has gone too far. Too many friends have been injured and I can see no solution.'

The suddenness and spontaneity of the violence presented a

big problem to the police. They never knew when the next attack was going to occur and by the time they arrived, any witnesses had vanished. They were desperate to maintain an air of normality on the estate. 'It is certainly not a no-go area,' said one officer. 'Milk and newspapers are still being delivered and houses being repaired.' But many people could not wait to leave the area. 'There is no real compromise among the gangs and I'm keeping well out of it,' admitted Larry Benji, a Jamaican-born local radio DJ and a regular in the Pepperhill pub. 'There is some really heavy shit going down at the moment.'[37]

* * *

In among all the violence, the drugs squad was trying to find out where the marketplace was. 'We eventually identified the busiest spot as Coleford Walk, just off Gooch Close,' said Tony Brett. 'That was an area within the estate that was being controlled by the Gooch.' Though this war was not specifically about drugs, they provided the backdrop, and officers like Brett realised they might be the best way of disrupting the gangs. They had a useful new tool. Someone had brought a camera to show criminal intelligence officers: it was tiny but had the capacity to microwave pictures away from a scene and could be controlled remotely from a distance. Chief Constable Wilmot agreed to buy it.

GMP launched Operation China that May. They were helped by some excellent inside intelligence. One resourceful and tenacious young police officer – who had previously helped to locate the first-ever 'crack house' in Manchester, just off Pepperhill walk – had succeeded in 'turning' several key gang members and was able to get accurate information on what was going on. His highest-level informant was none other than Delroy Brown, but he also spoke regularly to a key Gooch figure. It was the first time anyone had properly penetrated the inner workings of the young black gangs. The officer went by the codename Delta.

'I found out they were very well organised,' he said, speaking on condition of anonymity. 'They had safehouses, girlfriends they briefed to carry out jobs or hold weapons for them, fleets of cars, used codenames for different parts of the estate, streetnames for each other, and used TKs [telephone kiosks] instead of mobile phones to prevent interception. I would get paged by my informants and we would speak from TKs or I would meet them in out of the way places like builders' huts or in the middle of the night sitting on the swings in the park. I heard their life stories. I found out that they loved the money, the clothes, the champagne and the pick of the women, but most of all it was ego that drove them. They loved the respect.'

A hand-picked team of around a dozen male and female officers, led by Tony Brett and aided by Delta's flow of information, prepared to bring down the Gooch using video surveillance pioneered the previous year in Operation Corkscrew, this time with their new microwave camera. They had the danger of working in a war zone. The Gooch had frightened away many tenants around their dealing area and had wrecked flats to prevent re-occupancy, deterring prying eyes and providing stash points for their guns and drugs.

Undercover officers managed to occupy a flat with a view of the area by posing as squatters and set up their surveillance equipment inside. Others posed as buyers. Over a five-week period in May and June, they filmed scores of transactions and made thirty-seven buys – all of heroin except for one purchase of crack. 'The main players in Gooch Close would share the dealing,' said Brett. 'If someone was a bit short of money that day, he might deal for a couple of hours. That made it better for us because it meant lots of them implicated themselves. We couldn't penetrate a gang like that and we couldn't follow the abusers away because they went into walkways, so we had to go in undercover, with dramatic effect. Going in and doing buys had never been done before. It was a very, very intimidating situation: twenty to thirty people there with pit bull terriers.'

A lull in the feud, lasting a few weeks, helped. Then in June a five-man hit team tried to kill a leading Cheetham Hill face who had upset one of the Moss Side gangs. There was a car chase and shooting in Hulme and an attempted ambush on the Alex estate. A young Gooch soldier was hit in the mouth with a shotgun pellet on the eve of Carl Stapleton's funeral. Police again raided the Pepperhill pub, with customers dropping drugs on the floor as they fled. Chief Constable Wilmot announced the setting up of an airborne armed response unit, with an armed response vehicle (a specially adapted Range Rover) on twenty-four-hour standby. It was the first time the city would have a dedicated firearms team available around the clock. Wilmot's biggest concern was the use of guns by drug suppliers in inter-gang rivalries, and on August 8 he met community leaders to discuss policing Moss Side. He listened to concerns about the gang conflict, promised new co-operation and said he would change policing methods if necessary. It appeared to be a welcome *rapprochement* from the Anderton era.

Just a few hours after the meeting, it was still light when Howard Swarray was shot through the lower arm in the enemy territory of Doddington Close, which had become a focal point for the east side faction since the closure of the Pepperhill pub. Police, who regarded Swarray as one of the main heads in the Gooch, traced him to Manchester Royal Infirmary an hour later but he refused to make a complaint. Within twenty-four hours, Kevin Lewis, aged twenty, of Doddington Close, had been shot in the shoulder in retaliation.

The Pepperhill had been depleted by arrests and shootings, and some leading members now left the area temporarily. Delroy Brown, Maurice McPherson and Ian McLeod – the latter faced charges of kidnap, assault and blackmail and would be jailed for three years – were all in custody. The war was far from over, however. In August, shots were exchanged in a residential Moss Side street between youths in two cars at tea-time. People on the street heard one youth shouting, 'You're dead, you bastard,' before the cars burned rubber. There was another gunfight at a gig in Longsight by the Jamaican MC Papa San.

★ ★ ★

In the pre-dawn gloom of Tuesday, August 20, a lone police motorcyclist appeared on Princess Parkway, heading south along the deserted thoroughfare towards Moss Side. A few seconds behind him emerged a convoy of vans, cars and outriders, trailing in military style through the deserted streets. The line stretched back for a quarter of a mile. It was an eerie, disconcerting sight. Tucked inside the vehicles were almost 200 officers, clad in dark blue nylon jackets with the logo 'POLICE' on the breast. They had all been briefed that morning. Some were armed.

As it neared the Alex Park estate, the convoy split into splinter groups, with fourteen separate teams heading for forty specific addresses. The officers were out and into action as soon as they had parked.

'We are the drugs squad! Open up!'

Doors went in across the estate, most on the west side around Gooch Close. Pumped-up officers burst through hallways and ran upstairs to catch the occupants in bed. A stream of young men were handcuffed and marched out to the vans. 'What are you doing here again?' protested one mother. 'You searched our house two weeks ago.' Twenty-one people appeared briefly in court the next day to face charges in the culmination of Operation China, aimed at the Gooch Close drug market. They included several men who were regarded as the inner circle of the gang.

Simultaneously, the police applied to revoke the licence of the Pepperhill pub, held by Winston Purcell, a Bible-reading Rastafarian who had taken over from his brother Louis. It had become probably the most notorious public house in the country. Manchester licensing justices heard that police had seized cannabis and heroin five times between February 1990 and July 1991. Weapons associated with incidents there included revolvers, a machete and a Roman candle fired at a police car. There had been eight 'incidents' in 1990, including the killing of Eggy Williams, three assaults, possession of a firearm and disorder by a crowd preventing an arrest. In 1991 the police had dealt with another eight incidents involving firearms, assault and drugs, and a customer being chased through the pub by a masked gang. 'On several occasions, there was deliberate and wilful obstruction on the part of certain customers of the police when arrests were about to take place on the premises,' said Guy Robson, representing the police.

Louis Purcell tried manfully to help his brother, testifying that there were no such gangs as the Pepperhill and the Gooch. He said that many youths began using the pub only after the shopping precinct had been cleaned up. The hearing was also not without moments of farce, particularly when Helen Meadows, a blind pensioner who lived near the pub, told the magistrates she had been a regular for a number of years. Although she couldn't see, she said, she had never *heard* any fights. The licence was revoked and the pub shut its doors.

★ ★ ★

The Gooch were badly dented but not destroyed. Not all of their senior figures were arrested in Operation China – indeed according to the police officer called Delta, most of those picked up were 'lieutenants and foot soldiers' – and in the eyes of those who remained at liberty, there was still a death to avenge.

Darren 'Dabs' Samuel was a young-looking nineteen, worked as a mechanic and was the father of a four-month-old son, Keaton. Though not from Moss Side, he was mixed up with the Pepperhill, was out on bail for attempting to murder someone in a stabbing in Hulme and had reportedly exchanged fire with the Gooch in the past. That October, he was standing outside the Cottage Bakery in the precinct centre with two friends, waiting to buy a meat pie, when he saw three Gooch riding through on mountain bikes. They didn't even bother to hide their faces as one drew a silenced nine-millimetre pistol. Dabs fled into the shop and vaulted the counter, followed by two of the men, one in a baseball cap with a Vikings logo. They fired ten shots from two guns, hitting the teenager in the head. He died in the arms of Brenda Brownlow, whose son Winston was one of his closest friends.

Dabs's girlfriend was in no doubt who had shot him. 'The Gooch Close gang did this,' she said. 'They wanted Darren dead because he had a nice car, plenty of money and me. They were jealous.' Within hours, police had the names of two chief suspects, and both were remanded in custody charged with murder. Police escorted the cortege at his funeral in December. Youth leader Hartley Hanley told a full congregation at Our Lady's Church on the Alexandra Park estate that the time had come to ensure that the killers were caught. 'Keeping silent gives our consent to monsters,' he said. 'Monsters that can kill callously and as easily as if they were changing a pair of shoes.'

* * *

A volley of shots aimed at a moving car heralded the New Year of 1992 on the Alexandra Park estate. Within a fortnight, a man had been shot in the eye, another had been stabbed and forced to jump for his life from a flat window in Pepperhill Walk, and bullets had been fired at a car by a man emerging from a house. Manchester Ambulance Service became the first in the country to try out bulletproof vests capable of stopping nine-millimetre shells, shotgun blasts and knives. Any hopes in south central Manchester that the terror of the previous year might subside were blown away.

The gunfights and drug busts took their toll on the estate. One in three houses in Gooch Close stood empty; some tenants had been forced out so their homes could be used to hide or sell drugs. In all, about 200 of the 1,400 homes on the estate were vacant. Yet things should have been getting better. In March 1992, twenty members of the Gooch Close Gang were jailed or sent to detention centres for a total of 109 years for running their drugs bazaar. So strong was the video evidence that only three of twenty-two defendants denied the charges. The *Manchester Evening News* identified three 'ringleaders' as Howard Swarray, Jason Bennett and David Fullerton. Swarray, two of whose brothers were also sentenced, had been seen making more than twenty-five heroin deals in one day. Another gang member was ordered to forfeit the £20,000 he claimed to have made. Others operated on a much lower level: Junior Richards said he sold heroin to buy a pair of trainers. The judge praised the 'bravery and fortitude' of those officers who had carried out the dangerous buys and surveillance and commended Sergeant Tony Brett. 'The gang thought that what we did was cheeky and outrageous, and to a degree respected us,' said Brett. 'They had tried to make the area a police-free zone but hadn't succeeded. The community were quite pleased and it was good for morale in the force.'

The Gooch were in jail. The Pepperhill pub was shut. Delroy Brown and some of his closest allies were in custody facing serious charges. Cheetham Hill was in disarray after the death of Tony Johnson and the investigation into the Leeds carnival murders (for which Gary Shearer and James Walber would be jailed for seven years each for manslaughter). Officers who had been waging a losing campaign against the gangs for several years were entitled to feel that at last they were making headway.

'China had a massive impact,' said Tony Brett, 'but the void was filled very quickly.' Detectives knew that while the operation had helped to stop overt daytime street dealing, other means would be found. The Pepperhill regrouped around Doddington Close as some of the older east side heads deserted the scene. Their most deadly young gunman vowed to avenge Dabs's death. 'There was quite a few people saying, "This is getting ridiculous, we are out here to make money, not to die,"' said Anthony Stevens. 'What you were left with was the hardened kind of criminal element who, this was all they wanted to do. This is the life they loved.'

CHAPTER EIGHT

Young Guns

THE NEXT WAVE of south Manchester gangbangers was even more dangerous than the twenty-five-year-old 'veterans' of the streets. Seduced by the glamour, money and status of the gangsta life, they were the first generation to move into existing gang structures, to adopt pre-ordained roles. 'Those criminal elements which exist in Moss Side . . . seem to be influenced by, or be modelling themselves on, the posse type seen particularly in America,' said Detective Superintendent David Brennan, then head of Greater Manchester Police drugs squad. 'Quarrels can begin over women, over cars or over territory, in that these gangs tend to dominate an area for no other reason than that it is *theirs*. They have no fear of anything: arrest, prison, injury, even death. They actually enjoy the buzz that comes from the fear of being shot at, or the sense of power when carrying a gun. They love walking around with a gun on them. They revel in the respect that goes with having money, access to drugs and a gun. Their sense of well-being comes from "status".' That status was often achieved by violence. 'For them, violence *works*. The more extreme the violence, the more status it brings.'[38]

Julian Stewart was typical of the younger element. He came from Old Trafford and had been an active, sporty boy with a gregarious personality. 'When he was a child, he was very loving,' said his mother Sonia. 'He made friends very easily and he was very outgoing, very generous and very popular. He played a bit of rugby in the early years, he also did a bit of boxing as he grew older but didn't keep that up for very long. He was interested in computers.' Julian changed, however, when his parents' marriage broke down. 'He wasn't very happy about that and children

114

react to breakdowns in different ways. Some can cope and some can't. Unfortunately he was one of those who can't. He began to become a bit disruptive in his relationship towards me. He wanted to live with his dad, so there were a few problems there. It unsettled him at school at one point and he began to become quite disruptive.'[39]

Julian found the allure of the Moss Side gangs attractive. In his mid-teens, he joined bad company, just at the time when the Gooch-Pepperhill War was kicking off. He soon had the mountain bike, the stoney stare and the streetname: Turbo. 'Julian was a youngster, and he was a bit misguided with his loyalties,' said Anthony Stevens. 'There were older people above him who should have known better. These kids were at a very impressionable age and I don't think they realised what they were getting into. It is like accepting the devil's shilling: once your face is known, that's it, you're one of them. They were just little runners who took the pressure off the big guys.' Stewart was also driven by a sense of revenge: the Gooch had cut off part of one of his ears in a fight. They were said to keep it pickled in a jar as a trophy.

In the spring of 1992, Stewart appeared with Delroy Brown and two others at Preston Crown Court, charged with the brutal murder of Carl Stapleton. The case collapsed: a young female witness vanished after the judge refused to allow her to give evidence from behind a screen, and the Crown was forced to offer no evidence. 'I was told that he was basically dragged into that matter,' said Sonia Stewart. 'He didn't give certain information about other people, that's my understanding of it. He didn't tell me about what he might or might not have been doing, because it wasn't that type of relationship.'

It was the first in a line of gang trials in which the prosecution case fell apart through fear or reluctance. A month later, masked men tracked a teenage witness in a kidnap case to a house on the Alex Park estate; they burst in and pistol-whipped him, causing severe injuries. In July, three of the Pepperhill hierarchy – Delroy Brown, Ian McLeod and Julian Stewart – and a fourth man faced trial charged with wounding and attempting to murder Henri McMaster, one of the first attacks in the Alex Park War. The case was moved to Liverpool Crown Court to avoid jury intimidation, but key witnesses still turned hostile, leaving the prosecution without a case. McMaster and a man called Andrew Yankey originally had made statements saying McMaster had been attacked with machetes by the four men in Whalley Range. At trial, however, McMaster said his injuries might have happened in a car crash. Yankey disclaimed ever seeing an attack, and when handed his previous statement in the dock, he denied having made it. Two other witnesses could not be produced. The defendants were cleared but kept in custody facing further charges.

Other important cases went the same way. One Young Gooch hothead faced serious charges including kidnap and violence but his alleged victim refused to give evidence and was himself jailed for twenty-eight days for contempt of court. December of that year saw the trial collapse of two men charged with the murder of Darren Samuel. The chief witness, an eighteen-year-old woman who had been with Dabs when he was shot, took an overdose rather than turn up at court. Police found her on a hospital ward, where she refused to talk to them. 'She is only just eighteen and a kid really,' said her mother. 'I understand the police problems and I am not complaining about their conduct, but surely they understand the pressure she has been under? She was just about conscious when I saw her and I think she is going to recover, but she has lost a lot of weight and is having psychiatric care.'[40] With no reasonable prospect of her testifying, the prosecution was forced to offer no evidence, and the two men were formally cleared. 'We were locked up on the say-so of a girl I don't even know,' said one of them, Kevin Reid, outside court. 'We were innocent.' (Reid would later attain a certain comic notoriety when he was found hiding in a wheelie bin after a robbery and shouted, 'Squatter's rights, I've been living in the bin!')

The rule of silence had been established. No-one has ever been convicted for the murders of Anthony Gardener, Carl Stapleton or Darren Samuels

* * *

Nicholas 'Sailor' Murphy was another young man from Old Trafford who associated with the Doddington gang. He came from a large, close family and he was smart. 'I knew him when I was a detective in Old Trafford,' said Tony Brett. 'I next saw him at the shopping precinct during Operation Corkscrew but he left; he had the sense to move away.' According to Brett, Sailor knew that it was safer to sell drugs by mobile phone than standing on a street corner, allowing the seller anonymously to control when and where the gear was delivered and so avoid video surveillance. A young runner on a mountain bike would be sent with the wraps so the dealer would not even touch them. 'Your punter ... can phone you from wherever he likes and if he wants to talk to you personally, they've got no money and need a lay-on or whatever, they can speak to you over the phone without getting embarrassed,' explained one dealer. 'It's not so much sophisti-cated, it's just an easier way to do business. The aim is to make as much money as quick as possible, as easy as possible.'[41] The drugs would usually be kept at a safehouse, sometimes with a diary to record transactions in crude code, a wall safe, snapseal bags, scales and radio scanners. The scanners were a useful tool in the days before digital trunk systems allowed all police messages to be encoded. The gangs were still ahead of the police, with their ageing handheld and in-car radios.

Tony Brett said Murphy was so prominent in one dial-a-drug ring that the police actually named it after him. 'It was suggested that Nicholas Murphy controlled a lucrative network called the Sailor System.' Other dealers used similar trading names: Queen, Sunshine, Slim, Jasmine. Drugs squad officers were especially concerned because they believed it was being used to sell crack, and Manchester had been waiting for a cocaine epidemic. As early as 1984, James Anderton had declared, 'We are virtually waiting for an explosion in the incidence of cocaine in this area and in the country as a whole. Production is expanding. New markets are being sought and this country is a prime target.' Crack, which came to public consciousness when it ravaged America's cities in the late eighties, was seen as the harbinger, and became the *bete noire* of drug enforcement, despite its relative scarcity in the UK. Operation Miracle was conceived both to smash the phone network and to head off a predicted crack explosion.

'We bought all over Moss Side, at various locations,' said Brett. 'There were lots of independents, and in Operation Miracle there were people not gang-related at all. These were people who had seen that the market existed and decided they were having it, with a system that made it harder for the police to deal with them. They were all quite tasty individuals in their own right. And with that came crack as well. We heard of one-to-one, a bag of heroin and crack. People will take crack with heroin to calm down. I was very sceptical but we asked for it and got it wherever we went.'

Another senior detective on the operation was Ron Clarke, who later went on to write a drugs strategy for GMP. 'We were given information by informants that crack was being sold,' said Clarke. 'One hundred and thirty drug dealers were targeted. We had all of their pictures on a wall in the incident room and sent undercover officers in to buy crack.' According to Clarke, however, they didn't find it. 'We went in to buy crack but found brown-powder heroin dealers. They said words to the effect that they didn't have crack but they knew how to get it. We arrested thirty-five people and stopped because we couldn't handle it any more.

'They were actually selling heroin but we got them to go and buy crack. The crack house couldn't handle it and got out the demand elsewhere. By insensitive policing and targeting an area rather than individuals, you can make the matter worse.' Though he wouldn't say it explicitly, Clarke implied that the operation inadvertently encouraged the manufacture and supply of crack in the Moss Side area. Other evidence would appear to back up this view. There certainly was no cocaine glut at the time; on the contrary, a huge Customs bust that January had uncovered nearly a tonne of Colombian powder imported by a Liverpool gang and led to a temporary 'drought' in the north-west. Within a couple of years of Operation Miracle, however, genuine crack rings were operating in the area, including one in Bedwell Close that used a very similar system of cellphones and hire cars to make drops, selling crack at £25 a rock.

In terms of arrests and convictions, Miracle had been a success – but had it unwittingly helped to propagate crack cocaine in south Manchester?

* * *

Nicholas Murphy somehow escaped arrest in Operation Miracle but was attracting the attention of dangerous people. Three armed men bundled him into the boot of his own black Golf GTi outside a snooker hall in Old Trafford; he was found twenty-four hours later with minor injuries. Cheetham Hill were suspected, possibly on a taxing mission, though Murphy wasn't saying. Two months later, he and a friend were driving through Moss Side in Murphy's 140mph VW Corrado when another car pulled alongside. The two vehicles raced as shots were fired. Murphy was hit in the head but managed to keep the car under control; his passenger was hit in the shoulder. Their car eventually crashed and they ran off. The Corrado was later found with all its windows smashed in a Moss Side close. Murphy needed surgery to remove the bullet from his skull and surgeons fitted a steel plate over the wound.

The summer of '92 saw a spate of shootings involving soldiers from the Gooch, the Doddington and Cheetham Hill, who had re-entered the fray. One Doddington man was shot in the chest while driving his GTi. Another needed thirty stitches in a head wound after he was macheted; he acquired the nickname 'Peanut' because of the long scar on his head. A well-known door boss from Moss Side was badly hurt by the Gooch outside the Phoenix club on Oxford Road. August saw a daytime clash between Doddington and the Hillbillies in the Moss Side precinct, leaving a convicted armed robber from Cheetham with bullet wounds to his shoulder and chest.

The precinct had become a virtual no-go area for the law-abiding, deserted by shops and businesses, waiting for the inevitable bulldozers. Even junkies were scared to go in. 'The precinct was hell on earth,' said an officer who served in the area at this time. 'There were quite a few battles there. The worst one was between the drug dealers and the old Operational Support

119

Unit – they were animals, a motley crew of officers, a couple of them former marines, who really wanted to annihilate the gangs. They did a job on that precinct. The centre had a police room in it but whoever was on duty just locked the doors and pulled down the blinds and got on with paperwork for a month. It was a form of punishment; you had your radio on but otherwise you didn't go out.'

More shootings followed, in Hulme, Moss Side, Stretford, Longsight: drive-bys, car chases, attempted hits at pop concerts, shootings in pubs and at houses. So many young men were cruising the streets with guns that it was impossible to keep up. Even ambulance crews were at risk. A man from Doddington Close was shot in the side outside a reggae evening in Trafford Park. 'I started to dress the wound with help from my colleague,' said an ambulance paramedic. 'About forty people were gathered round the vehicle. Suddenly it started to rock and a side window was smashed by someone using their fist.'[42] The crew had to drive away to continue treating their patient. In six weeks during August and September 1992, police dealt with 110 reports of gunfire in the Moss Side area alone.

November saw another blaze of gunfire, beginning with a fight between two gangs at the PSV Club in which a man was shot in the leg and a teenager was hit with a machete. Someone fired at least five shots in yet another afternoon attack at the Moss Side precinct. A man being taxed for £30,000 by four youths in bandanas leapt to freedom through a plate-glass window at a derelict house in Moss Side. In December, the Doddington's top shooter, hell-bent on revenge for the death of his friend Darren Samuel, came across eighteen-year-old Marlon Jones, one of the leading Young Gooch, and two friends using a telephone in a shop on the Alex estate. Jones was high on the Doddington's hit list and the gunman drew a semi-automatic weapon and fired at least three shots through the shop window. Two bullets hit Jones in the chest. They were later removed by surgeons, the glass having reduced some of their velocity.

A dozen people had been shot in three months, and at least three more would be wounded that December. It was hard to know exact figures; many injuries went unreported. Chief Constable David Wilmot asked for detailed CID reports on the shootings as a report to the Police Authority showed serious woundings up by two-fifths year-on-year on the C division, covering Moss Side, Whalley Range, Hulme, Rusholme and Fallowfield. Two Manchester drugs squad officers were sent to Miami, Florida, to see how police there dealt with drug-related gang conflict. Wilmot's most important reform, however, was the formation of a dedicated armed crime unit to deal with the escalating violence. The police continued to make arrests and weapons seizures, but many of the younger elements now affiliated to the gangs were unknown to them. One detective opined that at least half a dozen of the hoodlums involved were aged seventeen or under, and almost all were under twenty-one. They wore bullet wounds as badges of honour.

In the early hours of New Year's Day, police officers raided a party at the Nia Centre, a music venue and theatre for black artists. As they entered the building, a boy of fifteen fired two bullets over their heads. There was instant panic, with people being crushed in the melee. The boy was Thomas Pitt, one of a family of brothers from Longsight who were making a name for themselves in the Doddington Gang. He was later given twelve months' detention, the maximum allowed given his age. 'Menace of Gunchester' declared the headline in the *Manchester Evening News*, reprising a sardonic but memorable nickname for the city. It had been another bad year.

* * *

On 2 January 1993, two teenage boys were queuing in Alvino's Pattie and Dumplin' Shop for something to eat. John Benjamin Stanley, fourteen, was with his pal Neville Gunning, fifteen. 'Benji' Stanley had been adopted at twenty-two months and lived with his adoptive mother, stepfather and two older brothers barely a hundred yards away in Cadogan Street, one of the old Moss Side terraced streets. Benji was an average student at school; his friends thought he was 'a good laugh'. It was 8 p.m. on a Saturday night.

A gunman in a camouflage combat jacket and balaclava with a single-barrelled shotgun jumped out of a silver car and fired through the glass front door of the shop. His first shot missed the boys, so he entered and shot Benji in the chest at close range before walking out. The fourteen-year-old collapsed, and died later in hospital. It seemed Benji had been singled out. Gunning had been hit by a few stray pellets and was in 'serious shock', according to the police, but was otherwise unhurt.

The Press coverage of Benji Stanley's murder outstripped that for any of the previous Manchester murders. Horrific as the murder of a schoolboy is, it also came in a traditionally quiet 'news time' and the papers, TV and radio went to town on the story. Benji's age, his innocence, the shockingly public manner of his execution and above all the emotional impact of his smiling photograph in school uniform brought the media circus to Moss Side in a way not seen before. According to a cynical piece in the *Independent on Sunday*, 'The area became "Baby Beirut", "Britain's Bronx". Television cameras turned up, pointed in the wrong direction and filmed reporters speaking in breathless tones of a lawless underclass. Youths posed for Sunday supplement colour magazines sporting Second World War revolvers, clad in bulletproof vests and bandanas tied round their faces. Moss Side became the essence of lawless Britain.'

Benji Stanley swiftly became a martyr, his name a rallying call for those prepared publicly to oppose the violence. Hundreds of cards and sympathy messages arrived in sacks. It was the fervent hope of many in the community that his murder would be some kind of watershed. Detective Chief Superintendent Ron Astles called it 'probably a new dimension in Moss Side violence' and said, 'The incident has got to be the catalyst that persuades the public to come forward and give us the information we need. We don't want it to be the first of many – it should be the last.' Despite a huge police investigation, the inquest into Benji Stanley's death recorded an open verdict, and the murder file remains open. The most likely explanation for his killing is that he was mistaken for a member of the Doddington Gang and was shot by a Cheetham Hill hit team paid by the Gooch.

Liberal Democrat leader Paddy Ashdown visited Moss Side after Benji's death. He was on a fact-finding tour to study the UK and its people, an experience he later wrote about in his book *Beyond Westminster*. Ashdown was taken to the shopping precinct with a local man acting as guide. By now, the precinct was ghostly, with most shops gone. Ashdown observed 'car loads of addicts, mostly white, and all with a dreadful pallor and haunted, searching eyes, cruise the estate to "score a hit".' He walked on. 'As we wander through the Moss Side shopping precinct, a youngster comes up to me and says, "What the hell are you doing here – if you are not dealing, fuck off!" As he does so, he pulls his bomber jacket back to reveal the butt of a sub-machine gun.'

Ten years earlier, it would have been unthinkable for one of the country's most senior politicians to be threatened with a gun while touring a metropolitan shopping centre. Now, no-one seemed surprised. The unacceptable had become mundane. Ashdown also spoke to police officers on the Alex estate. 'We don't know anything about what goes on here – we all live away from the area,' confided one. 'We don't have any regular beat officers on the ground; we've no intelligence and no community contact. It's virtually impossible to police. Everyone carries guns but at least they haven't used them on us yet. They just use them on each other.'

They were using them with growing indifference. A seventy-three-year-old man was shot by mistake in the hip by a youth on a bike in the precinct. A shootout in Old Trafford injured an eighteen-year-old woman when bullets zipped through her bedroom window. Andrea Mairs was hit an inch above her heart as she watched two gangs fire at each other in the street. 'There was a gang of young people firing across the street,' said her father Daniel. 'Everything happened in slow motion. I shouted at my wife to keep down but Andrea was already at the window. Andrea just fell to the floor like a rag doll.'[43] More bad headlines, more bad news.

★　★　★

123

In May 1993, Detective Superintendent David Brennan of Greater Manchester Police drugs squad drove up the M6 to Preston to address the annual drugs conference of the Association of Chief Police Officers, the influential body that represents the views of Britain's most senior policemen and women. Brennan had prepared an unusually candid paper on the Manchester gang scene.

He spoke for half an hour, playing his audience video extracts from some of the successful police actions, including Operation China against the Gooch in 1991. A dealer was shown waiting being approached by punters, with his stash of drugs hidden under a stone in a garden. 'Within a short time of this incident a police van went past and was stoned by those same youths.' His next clip, from 1992, showed a man known as Cannibal selling a bag of heroin. 'You will have noticed already his up-rated transport system in the form of a mountain bike and his distinctive baseball cap and leather jacket. When you see him reach into his inside pocket it is not yet a gun he is reaching for, it is his Vodaphone. These trappings of the trade mark the elevation of the young kid . . . after he has got his streetname, his Vodaphone, his mountain bike and his street cred. The next step is the Golf GTi and the gun; that is if he survives as a sole trader in an area increasingly dominated by gangs.'

He then turned to those gangs. 'There is the Moss Side situation in which there are two rival gangs, the Doddington and Gooch, both consisting of somewhere around thirty identified members, with the Doddington's ages averaging at approximately eighteen and the Gooch's about twenty. When we look at the Cheetham Hill Gang, which operates just north of the city centre some two miles from Moss Side, the numbers are considerably larger, approximately sixty having been identified, with an average age of over twenty-six years. Apart from the fact that Moss Side's gangs are weaker by division, Cheetham Hill have always been stronger and more sophisticated in that they are organised almost on military lines. They are beginning to wear standard uniforms of boiler suits and balaclavas on their taxation excursions and they are almost militarily precise when it comes to achieving their objectives. The Moss Side gangs are at present limited to different-coloured bandannas as an identifying feature.

'The euphemistically termed Salford Lads tend to be involved in the supply of the "clean" drugs amphetamines, ecstasy, etcetera, mainly to the rave scene in the city centre, but they are not averse to dealing in any other drugs . . . if there is money to be made. There is also a tendency to become increasingly involved in the supply of weapons. Their numbers appear round about the forty mark, with the average age similar to the Cheetham Hill Gang's.'

Salford. The word was being heard more and more among police officers, journalists, club owners, promoters, DJs, doormen, bar staff, always in the context of a brooding menace. Rave had shown the Salford Lads how to cash in on the scene; Konspiracy had shown them how they could control a door by intimidation. They now had the notion to run doors rather than merely steam in without paying, not just at one club, but at all of them. 'Something happened, and I don't know what it was,' said ex-cop John Stalker, 'but probably it was a realisation amongst a group of Salford-born tough guys that they were going to see how far they could push things. They started to stray into Manchester and came up against black, and indeed other, Manchester gangs and there was a fight about who should run doors. You had almost two armies girding themselves for a type of war, a war that actually didn't involve the police, in that the police were not the enemy, the other side were the enemy. Salford has traditionally bred some very tough guys. It is a tough city, a dockland city, and they decided that they were not going to blink first.'

CHAPTER NINE

The Firm

THE 'SALFORD LADS', like 'Quality Street Gang' twenty years earlier, was a loose description, encompassing a broad alliance of young criminals from Ordsall, Lower Broughton, Higher Broughton, Pendleton, Weaste, Seedley, Charlestown, Trinity and other benighted areas of the inner-city. These shock troops could be called out by the main heads – numbering less than half a dozen – when the occasion demanded. A few of them had been part of the 'proper rum outfit' that had coalesced in inner Salford ten years earlier. Some had since gone their own way, others had fallen by the wayside, but those that remained were older, cannier and more hardened.

They announced themselves, dramatically, at the Hacienda, the flagship of Manchester's pop-cultural renaissance. Having closed the club in January 1991, the Hacienda owners began moves to re-open after the death of White Tony Johnson a month later. This time they had a new strategy: they were going to try to reach an accommodation with the gangs. 'The Hacienda has held secret negotiations with gang leaders to prevent trouble when it re-opens,' reported the *Manchester Evening News*. 'They have been offered complimentary tickets as peace offerings.' The club's bosses also met the police to discuss security improvements, though they received little help. Staff were to have radio pagers so they could be warned if certain faces were about, but when the owners pleaded for uniformed officers to stand on their doors, in the same way they policed soccer matches, the police chief chairing the meeting flatly refused. He did say that 'city centre task groups' would do the rounds at night to monitor known troublemakers.

One woman had already complained to the Press that she had been refused entry by police and doormen to a club in Hanging Ditch, in the city centre, because of her boyfriend. 'They also said it was because I was from Salford,' said Louise Lydiate. 'There were loads of police around and two uniformed officers on the door.'[44] The story didn't identify her boyfriend – Paul Massey.

The Hacienda re-opened in May 1991 with an event dubbed 'The Healing'. It had airport-style metal detectors at the door and enhanced video surveillance. People known to cause problems, management told the media, would not get in. The *Sunday Mirror*, however, reported:

> A drug gang gatecrashed the grand reopening of Britain's trendiest club, despite tough security.
>
> Thirty thugs barged past bouncers at Manchester's Hacienda nightspot, closed three months ago after violence between warring gangs.
>
> Sixty police officers backed by a riot vehicle were called to throw out the smartly dressed 'Cheetham Hill Mob' after they refused management pleas to leave.

The gangs were not going to accept any control at 'their' club, but it would be Salford, not Cheetham Hill, who seized the moment. 'As Cheetham Hill faded as a force in the town, police clampdown and internal whacking doing their bit to silence them, Salford rose again. Like a phoenix. Salford rose like a great big fucking bird, from the flames of rubbish burning on the Ordsall estate, a great big fucking bird with wild, staring eyes and a beak that would peck your fucking head off if you dared to return its stare,' wrote Hacienda co-owner Tony Wilson. 'The designer bars followed the clubs, the cool shops followed the designer bars, and the heads and young fuckers who sheltered under the head's protection followed all.'[45]

They waited a few weeks for the media hype and police presence to subside, then moved in. A large firm arrived at the Hacienda one night, some armed. The entrance was closed, but one of the club staff opened a side door to let them in. In the ensuing chaos, six of the doormen were stabbed. One was clubbed across the head with a bottle, then jibbed four times in the thigh. Another was saved from serious injury when a rib blocked a knife blade. Police arrived quickly and sealed the building, while a force helicopter with spotlight hovered overhead. Ten customers, aged between eighteen and twenty-five, were questioned the next day.

Having closed down their business once, the Hacienda owners were not prepared to do so again. They beefed up security even further, with video cameras monitored on four screens near the entrance, two rottweiler dogs on standby and plans to issue doormen with chain-mail vests. Customers were told to hand in weapons on their way in – and were given them back on the way out. Perhaps sensitive to the club's pivotal role in the city's nightlife, and its national image, the police withdrew an application to have its licence withdrawn. 'This is a marvellous moment for the Hacienda,' said Tony Wilson. 'The club is now playing a full role in the cultural life of the city.' Striking a deal with the gangsters was not mentioned but that is what they had done. 'The management employed a door firm controlled from Salford, some of whose employees were alleged to have taken part in the violence, and charged, though cleared, with matters relating to the killing of Tony Johnson, Wilson reasoning that the only effective security firm was one unafraid of anybody or anything,' wrote DJ Pete Haslam. 'The doormen maintained a hard reputation but believed in giving leeway to certain characters in order to keep the peace; there were one or two untouchables. The bad vibes hung around.'[46]

Three men were charged with affray for the attack on the Hacienda bouncers. They were all from Ordsall.

*　*　*

Ordsall, pronounced *odd-sel* by locals, sits like a lost island by the basin of the Manchester Ship Canal, in an area once known as the Barbary Coast. A triangle bounded by Trafford Road, Regent

Road and Orsdall Lane, it is a former dockside community that has seen its traditional employment disappear. The ships, cranes and dockers departed, eventually to be replaced by the waterside flats, businesses and suits of the modern Salford Quays development: close in geography but a world away in outlook. Ordsall too was re-developed, its semi-derelict maisonettes and council blocks replaced by single-storey bungalows with gardens and tall fences, and millions of pounds more would be spent in the nineties to upgrade the housing stock and amenities. Compared to the wastelands of east Manchester, it was neat, tidy and unforbidding, but its social and economic problems were acute. It remained an introverted community held together by strong family ties, similar in size to Alexandra Park and equally scourged by unemployment. The 1991 census showed that a third of young people were jobless and less than a quarter of residents owned their own homes. The north of the estate was seen as particularly problematical, with those living in the south end sometimes referred to as 'lemons' because they were 'softer'.

Ordsall and neighbouring Pendleton, with its intimidating high-rise blocks, were heartlands of the Salford Lads, their numbers bolstered in particular by a Higher Broughton mob run by a family of brothers of Irish descent. Locally they were known not as the Salford Lads but as 'the Firm' or 'the Young Firm'. Armed robbery, burglary, ram-raiding and car and computer theft were specialities of their acolytes. Their grip was first evinced on the Ordsall estate around 1989 in a series of confrontations with Salford Police. The area had been on a slow burn for most of the decade, with street disturbances flaring sporadically. Now they grew fiercer. In November 1989, a police van was lured to a block of flats in Ordsall by a bogus call and then wrecked by a firebomb. A gang attacked another bobby on the estate after he stopped a joyrider. The Firm saw the 'dibble' as their natural enemy; a few even began to dabble with the bash-the-rich anti-capitalist group Class War.

January 1990 saw a major stand-off after a shooting at a club. Paul Massey's cousin held a surprise thirtieth birthday party for him at Valentine's in Higher Broughton, and among the guests was Paul Doyle's brother Bradley, who was standing at the bar when a masked man strode up and shot him in the leg. He staggered out to a cab firm where his fifty-four-year-old mother Lillian worked. 'He was very pale and his tracksuit bottoms were covered in blood,' she recalled. 'He said, "Don't worry, I'm okay." He was in shock and I wanted him to go straight to hospital but he kept saying he was fine and wanted to go home.'[47] Doyle took a cab home; he was later treated in hospital for a flesh wound. Meanwhile scores of officers had arrived outside Valentine's, some with guns and dogs, and sealed off surrounding roads. A helicopter hovered overhead. Instead of leaving, the customers barricaded themselves inside and there was a long, tense face-off until eventually they trailed out. Massey later denied all knowledge of the incident. 'I came in an hour later,' he said. 'Everyone was dancing, there were six hundred people enjoying themselves. Someone said that someone had got shot but I looked around and everything just looked like a normal night, so I thought it was a wind-up. People were there, like myself, for a party and the police tried to spoil it.'

Armed police descended on the estate the following week in a hunt for the gunman. In response, a crowd of about 100 protesters besieged the Crescent police station in Salford. Some wore balaclavas and paraded pit bull terriers. One, in a full-face mask, emerged from the crowd and walked along the line of police officers, pointing his finger as though it was a gun. A couple of weeks later, Paul Massey was charged with intimidating the officers. The charges were later dropped. In June 1990, there were further serious disturbances in Pendleton after police arrested youths who crashed in a stolen car. Missiles were thrown at the police and fire brigade and twelve people arrested.

The distancing between Salford Police and sections of the Ordsall community gave the Firm an opportunity to put them-selves forward as alternative authority figures, meting out their own summary justice to transgressors and spraying the names of alleged 'grasses' on the estate in prominent positions. They also began to have a disturbing effect on grassroots democracy. Both the Liberal Democrats and the Conservatives announced they

Chief Constable James Anderton with weapons seized during the 1981 Moss Side riots. The riots marked a nadir in police/community relations, while Anderton's crackdown on top-level armed robbers created opportunities for the newly-emerging gangs.

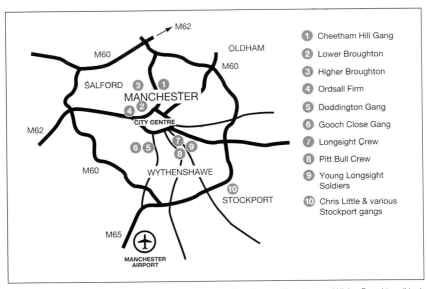

1. Cheetham Hill Gang
2. Lower Broughton
3. Higher Broughton
4. Ordsall Firm
5. Doddington Gang
6. Gooch Close Gang
7. Longsight Crew
8. Pitt Bull Crew
9. Young Longsight Soldiers
10. Chris Little & various Stockport gangs

The gang map of Manchester as it developed through the 1990s. Ordsall, Lower Broughton and Higher Broughton all had their own 'firms' but were often lumped together as the 'Salford Lads'. Some smaller crews are not shown.

Darren Samuel was shot dead in a bakery in the Moss Side shopping precinct by members of the Gooch Close Gang, possibly as a reprisal for Carl Stapleton's death.

The first death in the Alexandra Park War: Carl Stapleton was only seventeen when he was hacked down with machetes in a Moss Side street late at night by members of the Pepperhill Mob. He had fifteen separate wounds.

John 'Benji' Stanley became perhaps the best-known victim of the gangs when he was shot dead in January 1993 at the age of fourteen while queuing for food in a Moss Side shop.

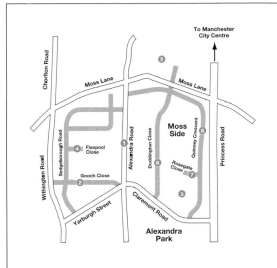

① Alexandra Road marked the dividing line between the two gangs, east and west.

② Gooch Close, home of the gang which bore its name.

③ The Pepperhill pub, HQ of the Pepperhill mob.

④ Carl Stapleton was the first fatality in the Alexandra Park war.

⑤ Moss Side Shopping Precinct, which became a drug-dealing centre and the scene of Darren Samuel's murder.

⑥ The Doddington Gang ran their drugs market here until it was smashed in Operation Balboa.

⑦ Nicky Murphy was gunned down in Rosegate Close in 1995 as the Doddington began to implode

⑧ Quinney Crescent saw numerous shooting incidents throughout the Alexandra Park war and beyond.

The Alexandra Park estate in Moss side was the battleground for an extraordinary conflict between the Gooch and the Pepperhill/Doddington gangs, two factions that existed just a few hundred yards apart. The estate witnessed numerous violent incidents between them; some of the more serious are listed above.

Operation China, in which microwave video cameras were used to secretly film a drugs market, saw twenty-two Gooch members jailed and was hailed as marking the destruction of the gang, as in this cutting from the *Manchester Evening News*. But the gang would soon be replenished by fresh recruits known as the Young Gooch.

Julian 'Turbo' Stewart was wearing a bulletproof vest when he was shot dead in January 1994. Media reports described him as "second lieutenant" in the Doddington.

"Put it away buddy. This is Chicago not Manchester!"

This cartoon in the satirical magazine *Private Eye* showed how the gang wars had blighted the image of Manchester by the mid 1990s.

3 shot in Chicago-style raid

THE BRONX OF BRITAIN

THE WEAPONS — THE VICTIMS — THE INNOCENTS

GANG

Manchester disunited

Gun gangs call a halt to war in the streets

Headline writers cast the city as "The Bronx Of Britain", "Gangchester" and "Gunchester". The agreement of a ceasefire between the gangs in the summer of 1994 saw a welcome fall in shootings in the Moss Side and Hulme area and offered hope that the undesirable image would fade. Unfortunately the truce would not last.

would not contest certain Salford wards in the local government elections of May 1990. 'We are not standing in Ordsall, Blackfriars or Pendleton,' said a LibDem spokesman. 'It is an indictment on these areas but we regard them as unsafe. We would not put any of our candidates and party workers at risk by sending them into high-rise flats in areas which are known to be a target for criminals.' The Tories could not find anyone at all willing to stand in Ordsall, Blackfriars or Lower Broughton.

Members of the Firm also arrived at Seedley Labour Club in an attempt to intimidate Labour MP Stan Orme. 'A group of them were trying to organise a meeting, ostensibly about police activity in the area,' said Salford councillor John Merry. 'We smelt a rat fairly quickly and said the MP wasn't prepared to attend. Then things got rather unpleasant. Myself and the other staff working for me were threatened. They implied that we would find ourselves in severe trouble if the MP didn't turn up. There were three or four of them. One advanced towards me in a very intimidating manner and the others pulled him off.'

The civil unrest was one indicator of how the rule of law had broken down in the area. Another was a sudden increase in firearms incidents, including the shootings of a couple of 'old school' hard men. Guns were much in demand for the area's young blaggers or armed robbers, a crime that had become a Salford speciality. One batch of eight weapons was stolen from a safe at the flat of an ex-police officer and gun enthusiast who had held them legally. They would be used to kill three people and injure two others. One of the batch, a Magnum revolver, found its way into the hands of Ian Spiers, a young man who lived on the Ordsall estate. In January 1992, Spiers shot his girlfriend Donna Maloney, who was only seventeen, after a row, and then turned the gun on himself. Both died.[48]

Ian Spiers's wake saw yet another large-scale disturbance. About eighty mourners had gathered at the Brass Tally pub near Liverpool Street when a passing beat bobby saw a man outside who was suspected of burglary and tried to arrest him. The man was one of the pallbearers. Mourners poured out of the pub and in the ensuing fight several officers were hurt. A senior officer tried to defuse the situation by entering the pub to talk to the ringleaders. He was warned that there were firearms in the area, and if there was any attempt to storm the pub, they would be used. Police sealed off the street. They returned in force four hours later and the mourners dispersed. 'The whole family is furious,' said the dead man's mother, Mary. 'One of the pallbearers got out of the car and, the next minute, police were diving at him, and then everyone else got involved.'

It was becoming clear that law and order were breaking down among sections of the Ordsall community. There were persistent rumours that some tenants were paying protection money so they wouldn't be burgled, something that was eventually confirmed by the city's housing chief. Shopkeepers were also being leaned on to pay a few pounds a week to avoid being robbed or torched. That wasn't enough; the Firm wanted more. They had the numbers and now they had the guns.

* * *

When a *Coronation Street* scriptwriter Tony Warren invented the Rovers Return, he had a thousand role models. Salford, locals say, was built on pubs, with Regent Road often described as the best pub crawl in Europe. But as economic blight bit and the city's population fell (by eleven per cent between 1981 and 1991), the pub stock started to deteriorate and many began to close. Those that remained were vulnerable, especially in the rougher areas – which, in inner Salford, was most of it. Pubs are a cash business and licensees are isolated. Robbery, especially late at night when the customers have gone and staff are cashing up, is a constant threat, while the danger of extortion is never far away.

The first sketchy reports of an organised protection racket emerged in the *Manchester Evening News* in February 1990, with a story that a dozen men were trawling pubs demanding money to 'stop trouble'. Typically a gang of young thugs would be sent into a premises to start a fight, then a day or so later the landlord would receive a visit from one of the heads offering to prevent any further aggro, even to put bouncers on the door – for a price. Non-compliance meant the threat of violence or the destruction of the pub. It was hard, very hard, to say no.

In July 1991, the landlord of a Salford pub called the Bowling Green lost an eye in a beating. A month later, the Lowry in Pendleton, named after one of Salford's most famous sons, closed its doors after repeated attacks by gangs. In September, Spats in Swinton closed after constant intimidation; three different teams of doormen had quit after hoods threatened their families and a bouncer who asked a youth to drink-up after closing time had a revolver pulled on him. In January 1992, four firebombs were thrown through a window of the Weaste Hotel. The Salford Arms in Chapel Street was petrol-bombed. Twenty-five men smashed up the popular Inn of Good Hope in Eccles.

The essence of 'protection' was fear, and that extended to customers and witnesses as well as licensees and their staff. One rare prosecution saw three men jailed for a pub attack but only after the police had been forced to apply for arrest warrants compelling *witnesses* to turn up. A manager at the Langworthy Hotel was so terrified by racketeers that he even faked a robbery to pay off his tormentors. He was found on the floor of the pub with cuts to his arms and claimed robbers had taken £1,100 from the safe. Later he confessed to stunting the theft himself; his barrister told a court that he had been beaten up twice and received threats over the telephone.

He was replaced by a new licensee, who did not have long to wait for his own initiation into the ways of Salford gangland. On a busy Sunday night, a short, stocky man entered the building with a sawn-off shotgun. 'This chap came into the pub, first going into the vault, and then pointed the gun at one of the staff,' said the assistant manager. 'Then he came into the lounge, where I was sat at the bar having a drink. He put the gun in my face. I was really scared. He was jumping up and down, wanting to know where the licensee was, then he fired a shot into the ceiling.' The licensee was not on the premises and the gunman left. 'Despite the pub being packed we have not had a single call from anyone with information,' rued a detective two days later. 'The public have got to ask themselves whether they want the bully boys to get away with acts like this or are they going to give us some help.'[49] But no-one was talking. Two arson attacks later and the pub was closed, its front door heavily bolted and steel grilles placed over the windows.

Others followed with depressing speed: the Kings Arms, closed after the landlord was threatened; the Rovers Return, razed; the Hobson's Choice, torched; the Sabre, burnt out; the Brass Tally, torched and its licence revoked; the Unicorn, severely damaged by fire; Poet's Corner, destroyed by arsonists; the Pen and Wig, razed; the Butchers Arms, smashed up after the landlord appeared in a local paper discussing his improved security measures; the Grosvenor, burnt out; the Regent, forced to close by the strongarm tactics of a 'security company' and then burned; the Castle, torched after the landlord quit; Summerfields, burnt out; the Winston, smashed up and robbed by seven men in balaclavas.

Perhaps the worst loss was the Tallow Tub, which was damaged by fire and later bulldozed. 'It had a unique Victorian interior, wonderful tiling, a curved bar and stained glass screens, the kind you see in old films,' said Peter Barnes of the Campaign for Real Ale (CAMRA) pressure group. 'If it had been in Chester, York or London, it would have been cherished, but it happened to be in Salford, so we lost it.' Others were part of the city's heritage: the Three Crowns, a 200-year-old building on Blackfriars Road, had seen the birth of the Manchester and Salford Trades Council, the forerunner of the TUC. It formulated its 'grand and noble principles of Arbitration, Mediation and Conciliation' on the premises. None of these principles was in evidence when the pub, renamed Buskers, was smashed up in a fight, then gutted by fire.

Salford's licensed trade was in the grip of a wave of intimidation not seen before or since. Some of the damaged pubs did re-open after repair but many closed for good as the big chains began to pull out. In less than twenty years, Grand Metropolitan shed almost all of its thirty-nine premises in the city, Greenalls was left with just ten out of twenty-six, and

Whitbread sold, closed or demolished two-thirds of its thirty-one. By the early nineties, the big brewers had disposed of almost eighty per cent of their Salford houses, and the local independent brewers, twenty per cent. Some were demolished to make way for road schemes, particularly on Regent Road, some closed because of declining custom and some were sold to comply with Monopolies and Mergers Commission rules, but in many other cases the malign effects of racketeering made the pubs untenable. The city topped a league table of 'pub dereliction' compiled by CAMRA.

Salford had never been well-served by nightclubs but now they, too, had all gone. Even late-licence café bars, like Sangsters in Eccles, were forced to close amid police claims of drug use, fights and demands for money. 'I was involved with clubs from 1986 but nothing like this existed until the 1992–3 period,' said one former club boss. 'It often starts with mild intimidation on the door. Then it escalates. If they get the door they can tell the management how much their doormen get paid, they can control the drugs inside and they can control who goes in and out. I was never asked for and never paid any protection money but I was asked for a "loan". The protection started with shops and the landlords in little pubs. The trouble was, there were so many of them. And for about three years, the police response seemed to be that there were no protection rackets in Salford. That just allowed one person in particular to build a mini-empire. Then one or two others started catching on.' Those pubs that remained often seemed to open and close mysteriously, at short notice, as landlords quit suddenly or brawls caused damage. One was the Jubilee in Ordsall, a hangout for the Salford Lads, where the licensee, rugby league player Phil Ford, quit after a nasty fracas. Many of those that did stay open were rumoured to belong to 'the boys', though their names didn't appear over the door. How many pubs paid protection is impossible to know, but easy to guess.

The Firm used some of the money to move into legitimate business. They set up a taxi firm using proxy operators, though it was quickly closed down by the police and Salford Council.

They also moved into the property market. Operation Wangle, run by a small team of officers at Salford police station working with the Inland Revenue and housing benefit officers, was set up to investigate a particular series of mortgage frauds with links to some Ordsall lads. The conspirators selected rundown terraced houses or homes repossessed by building societies. These were bought for knockdown prices by a Swinton property speculator. The homes were then re-valued at vastly inflated prices by a bent chartered surveyor and would be bought by a member of the gang, who would apply for a mortgage using false details supported by forged employment references and fake MIRAS applications. One terraced house was bought for £17,000 and 'sold' for £29,500 the same day. Not only would the difference be pocketed, but tenants were then put into the properties to pay the rent with housing benefit; effectively, the tax-payer was paying the inflated mortgage. It was a no-lose situation for the crooks and a good way to launder money. Officers believed the fraud had been active for at least two years, between June 1990 and August 1992 – at the height of the early nineties house price boom – and the amounts involved totalled more than £500,000. An insurance agent who acted as the linkman was eventually jailed, as was the property speculator, the surveyor and a Salford man who admitting obtaining a mortgage by deception. Seven other conspirators were given community service.

In 1994, Central Television's *The Cook Report* took over the Staff of Life pub in Prestwich, between Salford and Bury, fitted hidden cameras and drafted in a landlord from the Midlands, with the intention of exposing the Salford protection rackets. Within hours of opening, a fight broke out in the pub and was caught on film. Presenter Roger Cook suggested it had been deliberately staged. Soon after, a large man turned up at the bar asking for £200 a month for 'security'. Another interviewee, his face obscured, told the programme he was paid £40 every time he smashed up a pub: 'The gaffer, he'd say, "Go to such a place and cause a bit of a rumpus." If people were there that got involved, then tools were used – knives, machetes and sometimes a gun would be pulled out, just to keep the public away. Then the landlord would be approached by another lad. He would state the terms – how it could be stopped. If he agreed to the terms, it would be all right. If he didn't, it ended up shut because it would be burnt. Eventually they all pay and they get peace of mind.' One prosecution resulted from the material supplied to police by the programme makers, against a man who openly bragged about attacking a landlady.[50]

★　★　★

Residents began to complain at public meetings that a criminal hard core was effectively running Salford. One of those to speak out most strongly was a former head of Salford Police, Jim Tumner, who led a Home Office-backed project called Salford Safer Cities. 'We have got to stand together against these evil creatures,' he said. 'They are preying on respectable people. The villains think they are local heroes when they should be viewed as the dregs, absolute scum. They operate like hyenas, hunting in pack. They don't have the intelligence to do it alone, only by force of numbers. There are probably not more than two hundred and twenty real villains in the city [but] look what they are doing to us. Salford has more crime than all of Warwickshire.' City councillors backed him up. 'The impression I am getting from community leaders is that there is some organisation behind it,' said one. 'What worries me is that there is some intelligent mind connected with it.'[51]

One of the few bodies to speak out publicly was, oddly, the Campaign for Real Ale, a group more usually associated with beer festivals and discussions about hop varieties and kegs. Its Manchester magazine, *What's Doing*, regularly listed pubs that had been forced to close and warned that 'thug rule' was destroying an important part of the region's social fabric.

Perhaps the most worrying aspect of all this is the inability or unwillingness of police to do anything about it. They either know what's going on and haven't tackled it or they are in ignorance. It's extremely difficult for the victims. They've got nowhere to go. ... Vast tracts of the inner city have become virtually publess. So what? you might think. It only affects rundown pubs in grotty areas. That's no longer true. As pubs disappear in those grotty ghettos, the villains are seeking new pastures for their criminal activities. Your friendly neighbourhood local could be next.

When a senior officer told Greater Manchester Police Authority that there was 'no cause for alarm', councillors were distinctly unimpressed. 'There is a general feeling that there is a protection racket taking place, otherwise why on earth are so many pubs closing their doors?' asked Bill Eccles, leader of the Tory group on Salford Council. 'I'm sure it's not solely because of a lack of commercial opportunities.' John Gaffney, the chairman of Salford South police panel, said police denials of protection racketeering at the notorious Langworthy Hotel were 'diabolical'.[52]

Incredibly, Salford Police continued to deny publicly that there was any evidence of organised crime at work in the city. This was either a cackhanded attempt at spin or an extraordinary failure to grasp what was going on. In a single year in the early nineties, robberies rose by forty-three per cent and serious woundings by fifty-six per cent. Recorded crime was fifty-seven per cent higher than the national average in 1992, most of it thefts and burglaries. The city's chief superintendent was now Frank Halligan, whose detectives had blown the whistle on the war between the black gangs ten years earlier. 'There are individuals who make a great deal of money out of drugs and are involved in serious crime,' Halligan admitted. 'But I would not call it organised. We are persistently arresting these people for serious offences.' There seemed to be a terror of acknowledging any degree of organisation. The six-foot Salford beat bobbies of John Stalker's day would have handled the problem with a nightstick behind a closed cell door. Now the boot was on the other foot.

★ ★ ★

In the first week of July 1992, Ordsall went up in flames. Fires were set to lure police and fire crews into the estate, where someone fired live ammunition at them. Two police dog handlers were slightly injured by a bullet that ricocheted around their van. The nearby McDonald's restaurant was fire-bombed. A security guard was beaten up in Salford precinct. The giant Carpetworld warehouse was burned down. 'Battle of Ordsall,' blazed the headlines. 'This isn't like the Moss Side riots ten years ago,' a community worker told the *Observer*. 'It's much more sinister and organised.' Apparently it was an orchestrated response to police attempts to crack down on the serious car theft and joy-riding on the estate. The rioting went on sporadically for two weeks. Some wag christened the area 'Confrontation Street'.

Observer reporter Peter Beaumont, who visited the estate in the aftermath of the riot, found that everywhere he went, one man's named cropped up.

> Thirty years old, lithe, muscular and intelligent, this man is accused by residents, police and press of being the focus for the growing conflict between the police and the estate's young men. He has achieved a status of almost mythic invulner- ability in the hardbitten estates of Salford, a 'hero' for the roughneck minority of youths on the fringe of his world, who – according to his myth – has cocked a snook at 30 detectives who have been on his case for the last two years.
>
> His reputation – true or false – is that of a young gangster in the old style, flash and hard, a lover of fast cars, quick to anger, who commands the respect of local youths with his own version of morality, which forbids hard drugs and petty crime against his own community.

An angry city councillor soon made the man's name public. Joe Burrows, chairman of Salford social services committee, spoke out at a full council debate on the disturbances. 'Massey, Mr Big, why don't the Press print his name?' he challenged. They duly did, to which Paul Massey responded, 'This is not the first time I've been accused of things when I've nothing to do with them.'

He said he had been arrested ten times since being released from prison in 1988 but had not been charged with any crime.

According to Massey, the police viewed him as a threat to the success of Salford Quays, the multi-million-pound renewal of the Ship Canal basin, and offered one of his friends £55,000, a new house and a new identity to help put Massey away. The attempt failed, though detectives privately claim that they did develop a key informant who was very close to him. An intelligence officer also visited Massey's girlfriend Louise in an unsuccessful bid to persuade her to 'turn'. The same officer had received threats that he would be abducted and tortured because of his success in building up an informer network in Salford and this in turn brought Massey to the attentions of D7, the branch of MI5 that liaises with police and Customs to penetrate organised crime. Massey was put under MI5 surveillance. 'They helped us out with Massey because he was believed to be threatening a police officer,' said a senior detective. 'D7 are very good, very professional, but we found that they didn't like the criminals coming back at them. When terrorists realise they are being surveilled, they will try to get away; criminals will come up to your car and have a go. They got very nervous about that. They are from the dark side and are great for distant surveillance from five miles away but they are not used to confrontations.'

Massey knew he was under constant surveillance and kept a bug detector and a radio scanner at his home. At the same time, he denied any involvement in both serious crime and the disturbances on the estate. Prove it, was his response – and neither the police nor their Intelligence Service friends could. Some even began to suspect they had overplayed his influence. 'We made the mistake of thinking he was bigger than he really was,' said one officer. Yet his name was never out of the frame, even when he was personally blameless. When an off-duty police officer bumped into Massey in Discotheque Royale, a popular city centre club, they began to argue, and a friend of Massey's stepped in and hit the officer, who later needed a dozen stitches in head wounds. Robert Macer, a father of three, 'totally misread' the situation, his solicitor later said. 'It was a gross error of judgment but no weapon was involved,' he told a court. 'Mister Massey was a close friend and Macer regrets his reaction.' Macer received a year's probation and had to pay £250 compensation to the officer.

Once again Massey's name had cropped up when an officer was hurt, and the 'Get Massey' campaign inside Salford Police grew stronger.

CHAPTER TEN

Door Wars

NINETEEN NINETY-THREE was a pivotal year for the gangland takeover of the clubs and pubs of Manchester and Salford. It saw a key alliance between the Salford Firm and other Manchester villains, including some who had strong links with Cheetham Hill. This alliance would be so strong, and involve such dangerous people, that few could stand up to them. The prize was the city's expanding nightlife.

A clubland revolution was underway in the UK, with Manchester at the forefront. The warehouse parties had eventually succumbed to a government clampdown with the Entertainments (Increased Penalties) Act, but had also forced a re-think of licensing laws, which led to clubs being allowed to open later. Raves moved indoors to the big nightclubs and leisure centres. Outdoor raves were increasingly unsafe; Legendary 3, a gigantic bank holiday bash at Warrington in 1992 saw marauding gangs robbing dancers and more than 100 reports of cars being broken into. 'It was absolute chaos,' recalled one policeman. 'It got to the stage where people would turn up to report an armed robbery and all we could say was, "Please take a seat."'

As rave moved mainstream and became 'clubbing', the emphasis shifted to the legitimate licensed trade rather than illicit parties. 'Clubs took over old buildings in rundown areas (often attracted by the low rents and rates, occasional refurbishment grants, and a lack of local residents and businesses likely to lodge planning objections) and thus achieved a trailblazing position at the forefront of city centre regeneration; the Hacienda on Whitworth Street, Sankey's Soap in Ancoats, the Boardwalk in Knott Mill.'[53] An equally exciting expansion began of modernist

142

chrome bars with cool names and minimalist décor, something again pioneered by the Factory crowd with their Dry Bar on Oldham Street.

All of this meant a buoyant market for dance drugs, and more doors to take over. The gangs had already shown how little respect they had for Manchester's existing door firms. Cheetham Hill had shot the bouncers at the Thunderdome. Salford had stabbed the doormen at the Hacienda and ploughed a stolen car into the doorway of the Wiggly Worm after being refused entry to its successful Balearic night 'Most Excellent'. The Gooch had forced the closure of the hugely popular Solstice 91 nights at the Academy, a venue attached to Manchester University, and had attacked a door boss at the nearby Phoenix. They had also shut the Limit, a small, gang-infested club in Lloyd Street, firing shots at the club after some of their soldiers lost a violent confrontation with the bouncers. When officers visited the club they found bullet holes in the walls and a weapons stash including a machete, truncheons, spade handles, crowbars and a chair leg, all used for protection by the doormen. The police obtained an injunction ordering the Limit to shut, the first time they had taken such action against a club rather than a rave.

Much of the previous violence had occurred when gang members insisted on entering venues without paying. Now things changed; they began to show a clear desire to organise and control the doors themselves. This was no longer young men crudely asserting their masculinity with a punch-up at the end of the night. It was orchestrated intimidation with a purpose – and the opportunities seemed boundless.

21 Piccadilly was perhaps the Hacienda's main rival as the most popular club in the city. It catered for an older, middle-of-the-road market, with a red-carpeted entrance, stricter dress code and door supervisors in long black coats with red carnations in their lapels, organised by square-jawed head doorman Stuart Schofield. That did not stop it coming under pressure. When one of its bouncers was arrested for having a machete in his car, his solicitor pleaded it was for protection: 'He often received threats from members of vicious and violent gangs.' Drug dealers began

brazenly to operate inside, despite the best efforts of the management and door staff. In July 1993, Salford launched a full-on assault inside the club. The doormen were attacked, customers were chased and punched and two innocent bystanders were stabbed. It was chaos, and thirty-five police were needed to quell the violence.

Police believed that this was merely the most visible example yet of an organised attempt to take over club doors; to show managers that their existing doormen could not keep order. It had happened at the Hacienda, Konspiracy and elsewhere; at one smaller club, CS gas was let off in the premises and the doormen were then battered as they ran outside, gasping for air. But then it had seemed ad hoc, opportunist; now there seemed to be an impetus, a direction. There was talk of a new company that was going to employ doormen: P-4 Security took its name from a Nokia mobile phone but police intelligence indicated it represented 'the four Pauls', four well-known hard men on the city's club scene. In fact it never traded and was eventually struck off the companies' register.

Manchester was one target; Salford was the other. While the protection racketeers and extortionists had cut through Salford's licensed premises like a scythe, there were still some pickings to be had there. This time, however, they found some serious opposition.

* * *

The roots of the Salford Door War went back to the shooting of Bradley Doyle at Valentine's club, which caused a rift between people who had previously been friends. Doyle's brother Paul branched off and started running pub doors in Salford. He was asked to mind the Griffin in Lower Broughton Road, on condition that he barred a crew including some of his former friends. Doyle duly told them they could not come in. One of his men was shot in the leg in reprisal. 'That started the warfare,' said one source.

On one side were elements of the Ordsall Firm and allies from Manchester, including some renowned doormen who helped the Firm to exercise control at certain venues. Ranged against them was a powerful team led by Doyle and Graeme Boardman, a blond-haired, sixteen-stone fitness fanatic who boxed and pumped weights. Boardman was a legend even by the violent standards of Manchester's senior bouncers. 'He was impossible to fight,' said a friend. 'He would just explode on to you from all angles and you couldn't do a thing about it.' Though well-spoken and from a respectable middle-class background, he had an unsurpassed reputation for hair-trigger ferocity. 'I think he was schizophrenic,' said Doyle. 'He just loved violence.'

On one occasion, Boardman single-handedly took out eight Manchester City football hooligans on the door of a club. 'I also saw him knock out a fifteen-stone man standing behind him with a punch he threw over his shoulder,' said another friend. Boardman's favourite weapon was a small hammer kept hidden in his jacket sleeve. In a fight, he would jerk his forearm down to propel the head of the hammer into his palm and would deliver several crushing blows before flipping the shaft into his hand to wield in the more conventional manner. By that time, his opponent was usually finished. When Boardman used his hammer on a Hillbilly head one night outside Rockworld on Oxford Road, the battered gangster returned with a mob including a world-class Manchester boxer and they stormed the doors wielding bats and knives and gassing the bouncers. One doorman was so scared that he tried to run through a large mirror to escape. Boardman was smuggled out of the club unscathed but was unable to work in Manchester city centre after that.

Following their work at the Griffin, he and Doyle were asked to run the door at the Inn of Good Hope, a popular pub in Eccles which had previously been wrecked by a mob. The head doorman there had banned one of the Firm and was expecting trouble, so Boardman and Doyle were brought in to sort it out. On the first night, carloads of Salford turned up and one of them came to the door. 'He said to me that I shouldn't bar him because I was his mate,' said Doyle. 'I said he wouldn't come in if he was a mate.' One of the Salford crew challenged the head doorman to a straightener – a one-to-one fistfight – for £5,000, an offer he wisely rejected.

Matters came to a head in August 1993 when Boardman and Doyle accepted another contract to run the door at a Bolton nightclub called Kiss. This was too much for their rivals, who considered the door to be theirs. A small, elite contingent of Salford and Manchester hoods pulled up in a car at the Inn of Good Hope and Boardman and Doyle went out to speak to them. The men in the car said they had been promised the door at Kiss.

'We've got it,' replied Boardman.

'Well, you know how it is,' said a large Manchester man with a very scary reputation. 'You can have a door one week and not the next.'

The short fuse inside Boardman ignited. He slapped his own face hard and roared, 'That sounds like a challenge. Come on then. Get out of the fucking car, now!'

There were no takers. No-one wanted a streetfight with Boardman.

The next night, Doyle was sitting upstairs at the Inn of Good Hope reading his Saturday football *Pink*. Leaning on the stairs were several of his henchmen, while in the bar were several well-known professionals from Salford Rugby League Club. Two of the doormen, Jimmy Mythen and Alan Maloney, stood behind the glass door at the front of the pub. A black Vauxhall Astra pulled up, at around 11:20 p.m., and a figure in the passenger seat let loose with a rapid-fire handgun, blasting eleven large-calibre bullets through the glass doors and windows and hitting Mythen and Maloney in the legs and lower body. It took just six seconds.

A day later, regulars were enjoying a Sunday night drink in the Devonshire Arms, another Boardman-Doyle pub in Liverpool Road, when again a black Astra pulled up. A masked man got out, levelled a pistol and fired four times at the two doormen, who dived for cover. A nine-millimetre bullet hit a twenty-three-year-old customer on the elbow, ricocheted through his stomach and exited from his back. He survived after two operations.

The breweries that owned the pubs clubbed together to put up a £10,000 reward to help capture the gunmen. 'The group have done a good clean job for us,' said one club boss. 'Now they are coming under fire from a so-called security firm who are simply trying to gain control of all lucrative nightspots. They are carrying out attacks in Manchester as well as the Salford area. They have also moved in on two major construction sites in Salford. It's old-fashioned protection but with very up-to-date weaponry.' Boardman and Doyle knew who their rivals were but refused to co-operate with the law. The police, however, already had a strong theory about who was behind the carnage. Two separate teams of detectives were working on the pub shootings and the attack at 21 Piccadilly, which they believed had been carried out by the same crowd. Ten days after the shooting at the Devonshire Arms, armed police arrested eight men in the optimistically named Operation Finale, while another six men were sought.

★ ★ ★

Both the dock and the public gallery were packed at Manchester Magistrates Court in March 1994 for what should have been committal proceedings against nine Salford men accused of violent disorder at 21 Piccadilly. Prosecutor Peter McNaught gave a rough outline of the Crown's case and named Paul Massey as the alleged ringleader. 'The evidence against Mister Massey was that he was the person who organised a group of people to go to the club and cause violence.' However, said McNaught, he was unable to proceed with the case. Witnesses either had not turned up at court, or had turned up but were too frightened to give evidence.

Head doorman Stuart Schofield, a crucial witness in the case against Massey, had retracted a statement through his solicitor and police had tried but failed to serve a witness summons on him over the previous six weeks. He had 'gone on holiday' and could not be located. Another witness who had originally made an identification had apparently absented himself from work so police could not see him. Summonses had been issued against all twelve witnesses to compel them to attend but only five turned up, all expressing reluctance. Mr McNaught said there had been a threat against one young woman who had produced a doctor's note to say she was not fit to give evidence.

'They are all reluctant to give evidence primarily because of fear,' said Mr McNaught. 'Witnesses have been approached directly or indirectly by intermediaries and have been told why they should not attend court.' They included two complainants who had been injured in the attack. The prosecutor said it meant he could not proceed against five defendants but could carry on against the other four, although that would mean compelling the two wounded men and two young women to give evidence reluctantly and there was little point. The stipendiary magistrate formally acquitted the defendants, to loud cheering. 'This is a court of law, not a cabaret,' rapped the magistrate.

Outside, on the court steps, Massey and his jubilant friends posed for photographs, fists punching the air. 'This was a blatant case of the police fitting me up,' said Massey. 'This stems from the riots in Salford a couple of years ago. The police have had a vendetta against me ever since.' His bow-tied solicitor, Gareth Hughes, joined in the 'victory' pose, and said any suggestion that his client had brought about the collapse of the case was 'vigorously repudiated'.

No-one was ever convicted for the 21 Piccadilly brawl, or for the gun attacks on the Salford pubs. Boardman and Doyle lost the seven or eight door contracts they had, largely because they refused to co-operate with the police. The door wars had highlighted a problem extant in other cities but more acute in Manchester, with its peculiar gang culture. Where did the security stop and the protection start? Clubs and pubs had to employ doormen to stop fights and keep undesirables out, but what was to stop those same undesirables from setting up their own proxy security firms? This problem was to reach alarming dimensions for two reasons: a sudden, swift expansion in the licensed trade, and a failure to monitor and control the industry.

Few politicians were interested in attempting to regulate a youth-oriented industry they cared little about. One who was was Ian McCartney, the five-foot one-inch, Scottish-born Labour MP for Makerfield, on the edge of Greater Manchester. Despite his diminutive stature and owlish glasses, McCartney was made of stern stuff: he had played scrum-half in Scottish club rugby and led a Glasgow paper boys' strike at fifteen. He first noticed in the mid-eighties that some firms of doormen were operating protection rackets in all but name, selling drugs and intimidating rivals, club staff and customers alike.

'Up to the late 1970s, criminals who wanted to raise for funds for major activities such as drug buys would turn to armed robbery, but that carried the risk of long jail sentences,' said McCartney. 'They realised, with the change in attitudes among the licensing authorities and the strategic decision by the brewing and entertaining industries to expand the pub and club scene, that there was an opening for them. Hundreds of thousands of pounds was spent to encourage young people into a drinking environment and there was an explosion of the industry. There was also an explosion of private security and the criminals sussed out that here were rich pickings. They formed companies over-night. In the Thatcherite ethos of the mid-eighties, you could get a suit and a mobile phone and suddenly you were a company director. Before the police realised it, they had in some areas lost control.'

McCartney began compiling a dossier of incidents in Wigan, where he suspected one company was attempting to wipe out its rivals by force. In a single year, he and Wigan MP Roger Stott recorded eighty-two assaults by bouncers – many on customers but others on rival doormen or witnesses. McCartney provided the Home Office with a dossier of grievous bodily harm, arson, intimidation and racketeering. 'There was a network of bouncers using body-enhancing drugs and mixing that with profuse drinking on duty. That led to a very unstable killing machine on our streets. They can control the sale of drugs on the premises, they can control prostitution, they can even sometimes control the taxi companies used to take people home.'

McCartney eventually led a small political lobby pushing for tighter regulation of security firms, which he likened to private armies. He was equally scathing of the leisure companies and big brewers, which he believed, had a vested in interest in keeping down the wages and standards of door staff. They certainly did not want bouncers to join trade unions. 'The brewing industry has got a lot to answer for. Not only were they complacent and dishonest in not accepting the problem, but their accounting procedures to control the black economy were nil. Pub managers could hire and fire as they wished, paying cash out of the till to bouncers who gave names like Donald Duck, with no accounts, no tax, no insurance.' Eventually Ian McCartney managed to sway the British Entertainment and Discotheque Association, a group of mainly blue-chip companies that owns many of Britain's clubs. 'They were prepared to co-operate with registration schemes and to pay for them and to recruit legitimate bigger companies or have their own in-house training.' Or so they said. A Commons debate in the mid-nineties, led by Labour's Jack Straw, failed to persuade the then-Tory Government to legislate for the licensing and regulation of security companies. Deregulation was an article of faith for the Tories.

Manchester did introduce its own scheme in May 1994 to regulate club doormen, though not the firms that employed them. Doorsafe stipulated that all security staff working in premises holding public entertainment licences had to be registered and trained in first aid, fire procedures, licensing legislation and drug awareness. Registration was initially for life and individuals could be refused their 'green badge' if the police or licensing authorities had good cause, though in practice this was rare. It was hoped that the scheme would 'weed out' the more criminally inclined elements but this turned out to be wishful thinking. There was even an attempt by the giant GMB union to organise the region's doormen. 'Several firms contacted us from Manchester, Wythenshawe and Macclesfield,' said a GMB official. 'At first we thought it was a bit of a hoax, because it was unusual for doormen to do this. We held a conference at our college in Whalley Range and invited all the door agencies from around the area. They came from Liverpool, Salford and Cheetham Hill. We had these different factions under the same roof without World War Two.

We even had jackets made for them; they said, "Unity is Strength", with black and white hands shaking. They started to pop up everywhere.' The unity, however, was illusory.

Ian McCartney's brave public stance earned him and his wife a series of menacing late-night phone calls. Wreaths and bereavement cards arrived on their doorstep and their children were threatened. McCartney was even head-butted by a drunken off-duty doorman when he went for a quiet drink in a social club. His attacker had read about McCartney's opinions and took exception to them.

* * *

Not just door security was being squeezed; any street-level commercial activity was fair game. Jimmy Carr and Marcel Williams were partners in Manchester's dominant fly-posting business, accepting contracts to paste up adverts at various sites around the city. Carr, a tough customer with a conviction for blackmail, had effectively gained control of the twilight profession in Manchester, running a crude monopoly with his Streetwise Publicity and Display. Lately, however, he had been coming under assault by rivals wanting to take a slice of his business. Some of his workers had been attacked with baseball bats, and a couple of his vans had been set alight. He strongly suspected that someone close to him was siding with the opposition.

In May 1994, a rush job came in: film posters for the new movie *Four Weddings and a Funeral*. Carr and a student called Chris Horrox were feverishly putting up posters near UMIST university when they were approached by a man with a gun. A few words were exchanged and the man raised his arm and cold-bloodedly shot Carr four times. Horrox, who had no idea what was going on, said words to the effect that what the gunman had done was a bit drastic. The shooter turned to him, said, 'Who the fuck are you?' and shot him. Carr somehow survived, but Chris Horrox was killed.

The media portrayed the murder as part of a flyposter war, a battle for control of a business worth hundreds of thousands of pounds a year in Manchester. Marcel Williams, a dreadlocked former American Football player who was Carr's erstwhile partner, was eventually arrested and charged with murder. His two trials at Liverpool Crown Court would produce sensational claims of gun-running, drug dealing and protection racketeering, and provide an intriguing peek into the workings of the city's black economy.

It was alleged in court that a group headed by Manchester doormen Paul Carroll and Dessie Noonan wanted to move into the flyposting business, and were not particular about how they did it. Carroll was then head doorman at the Hacienda, while Noonan was well-known across the city. It was said that they had a 'showdown' meeting with Carr in a McDonald's restaurant. 'We talked to Mister Carroll and it was all sorted out,' Carr later testified. However, he suspected that one of his employees had been giving information to 'the other side', so he sacked him. 'A week later, my van was burned out in an arson attack and two days later another van was set on fire. We were told who'd done it by Carroll. It was the person wanting to show allegiance to his new masters,' said Carr. Three of Carr's workers were attacked with baseball bats on Oxford Road, a prime posting site because of its huge student population.

Carr believed that his partner, Williams, had betrayed him. He testified that Williams was the man who approached him as he and Horrox were putting up the film posters: 'I said jokingly, "Are you following me?" He didn't reply. He raised his hand and shot me. Initially, I thought I was shot in the mouth. I fell down. I was on my elbows. I recall saying, "Why, Marcel?" and he said, "You know why." Then he shot me again. I think the second went into my shoulder and into my neck. I pretended it had killed me. I lay flat on the floor and thought, *Christ, just stop*. I felt two more bullets hit me, one in my back and one in my shoulder.' Then Chris Horrox was killed.

Williams's version of events was markedly different. He claimed to have been at the home of his student girlfriend at the time of the shooting and she backed up his story, saying they had watched the end of a Dusty Springfield documentary together.

The trial, however, did not appear to be going well for him. Carr's testimony was powerful.

Enter Paul Flannery. The wheelchair-bound former robber, who had broken his back escaping from what he thought was a Moss Side hit squad, now contacted Williams's legal team and said he had information vital to the defence. The jury was discharged to allow the defence to investigate this information, and a re-trial was ordered three months later. This time Flannery appeared as a witness. He testified that he, Paul Carroll and Dessie Noonan had met Jimmy Carr in September or October 1993 opposite a mobile phone shop. Carr had been having trouble with Carroll, who was then head doorman at the Hacienda, and with Tommy Morgan, head doorman at the popular Sankey's Soap nightclub in Ancoats. Carr gave Carroll, Noonan and Flannery £10,000 and some guns for their assistance in 'sorting out' the problem, testified Flannery. But the situation 'seriously deteriorated' and Morgan went to people in Salford to get them involved in a rival fly-posting venture. According to Flannery, Carr subsequently attended two meetings with the Salford faction at the McDonald's burger bar beside the Ordsall estate. At the second of these, said Flannery, the Salford faction included Paul Massey and his friend Bobby Spiers. They wanted a share of Carr's business, told him he was 'blinding them with science' about how it worked and insisted there was more money to be made than he was making out. Carr refused to back down and the Salford people angrily left, saying, 'Something's going to go down.' Soon after, Carr and Mr Horrox were shot. Flannery claimed the shooting had been ordered by the Salford gang and that Carr had named his former business partner only because he believed he had betrayed him. 'He thought Marcel had put him on a plate and sold him down the river,' said Flannery.

Flannery denied suggestions from the prosecution that he ran a protection racket in Manchester or was involved in any door security business. 'All I do is get money through involvement,' he said. 'People come to me to make sure there is no trouble.' He would not admit to any particular association with the Hacienda nightclub or drug dealing there. 'I'm not trying to say I'm not involved in illegal activities,' he told the jury. 'All I'm trying to say is I'm not trying to incriminate myself.' He denied that he'd had someone observing the previous trial. For his part, Carr denied he had ever met Flannery or Massey, or that he had admitted at one meeting the name of the 'real' gunman.

Yet clearly Flannery's evidence swayed the jurors. They took just eight minutes to acquit Williams of murder and attempted murder.

* * *

In the late summer of 1994, a team of researchers from Salford University visited the Ordsall estate to explore the way people live in a high-crime inner-city area. A previous survey into witness intimidation had been aborted after threats to a researcher and abusive behaviour towards residents who had cooperated, but this time more than 300 door-to-door interviews were successfully conducted. The academic team gave the area the fictional name 'Oldtown'.

Their findings, contained in the report *Whom can you trust? The politics of 'grassing' on an inner city council estate*,[54] backed up what residents had been saying for years: that a criminal gang had sought to replace the police as the voice of authority on the estate. The so-called Salford Firm oversaw criminal activity, carried out punishment beatings and advised young law-breakers on how to avoid getting caught. It implemented its own street justice to intimidate witnesses and to punish those who committed unsanctioned crimes. The gang even had its own 'public shaming area' in the central shopping precinct, where the names of 'grasses' were written in graffiti. As the only place with any local amenities – a supermarket, chemist, betting shop, job shop, pub, hardware store, and so on – it was the one place the names would be seen.

Family ties were extensive and strong and meant everyone was aware of who the local criminals were. Paradoxically, this lack of secrecy was a good way of ensuring silence; the more people knew about the gang the more they lived in fear of it. In the words of a community worker:

Everyone knows who this group is and what they are into at any particular time. This creates the fear – nothing is kept secret really and the grapevine is very active. The gang's exploits are known throughout the estate very quickly after any incident has occurred. People then become wary of walking past this gang – they may be challenged – because everyone knows what is happening. Then everyone is a potential grass.

Ken Keating, a wild-looking man who acted as unofficial spokesman for the Firm, even took to driving around the estate in his 'Grasswatch' vehicle, a white van with a message printed on the side: 'Do the Police and DSS give YOU money for informing on your neighbour? Is your neighbour informing on YOU?' Leaflets circulating in the area asked, 'Are you an informer? Warning: informing can seriously damage your health. It is a major cause of smashed kneecaps and regular visit to hospital.' The Firm did claim to have its own code of conduct. 'They do not believe in old people being robbed, sex attacks and the poor being robbed,' said Keating. Giving information to the police about rape, mugging old ladies or interfering with children was not deemed to be grassing, but the Firm still preferred to dispense its own justice to such offenders in the form of a 'smacking'. It was unacceptable to inform about a ram-raid or a robbery. Even schoolchildren told the researchers that reporting something to a teacher was grassing and could result in 'getting your head battered'.

The Firm also claimed not to attack women. A senior police officer told the researchers of one case where a woman was persuaded to go to court as a witness on two very serious assaults against a gang member.

We did our best but they kept intimidating this woman. They kept shouting at her and calling her names, making threats towards her, but when they did something physical they didn't do it to her, they did it to her son. They caught him, he was nineteen, and they stuck a screwdriver up his bottom, which caused all sorts of terrible internal injuries, which is one of the traditional techniques of dealing with what they call a grass.

On another occasion when three young girls were knocked down by youths in a stolen car, the Firm's leader, elsewhere referred to as 'Mr M', intervened and ordered the car thieves to pay them £650 to prevent them from going to the police.

The report said that those held responsible were commonly referred to as the 'Salford Firm' and probably comprised 'twenty to thirty "full-time" members involved in criminal activity at varying levels of seriousness.' Two commonly expressed beliefs among the interviewees were that 'you're all right if you're local' and 'people round here don't rob off their own'. Whether either was true was hard to say. The researchers suggested that social cohesion and trust on the estate, where the normal influence of official agencies and the Government was weak, had more in common with pre-industrial rural and tribal communities. 'People won't talk to the police,' admitted Syd Turner, a former Mayor of Salford who had lived in the estate for over fifty years. 'We have had to ask the police not to visit the homes of people but to take details over the phone. Once the police are seen knocking on someone's door, that person is accused of being a grass.'

The Mobil petrol station beside the estate became nationally infamous as Britain's most hazardous. Child robbers smashed car windows and stole from vehicles on a daily basis. After more than 150 such attacks in a year, a BBC TV documentary called *Lost Boys* explored the lives of some of the miscreants. The film-makers found feral youngsters living 'a semi-wild and criminal existence in the streets and alleyways of their home town.' Their youth meant they were often repeatedly released from arrest only to commit more crimes: one youth had been caught thirteen times attempting robbery at the petrol station. A local bus company stopped running through Ordsall because of attacks on its drivers and vehicles.

Orsdall was not alone; inner-city Salford generally was suffering enormous levels of crime. Old people deserted Lower

Broughton because of persistent intimidation by youths. Thieves ransacked more than twenty empty homes on the Wheater's Field estate, using wheelie bins to cart away roof slates and metal piping. When a group of councillors visited the area to have a look, their minibus was stoned. A council-commissioned report said Lower Broughton had 'deteriorated alarmingly . . . mainly due to crime, fear of crime and extensive levels of vandalism . . . Intimidation and harassment of tenants is resulting in an escalating number of void properties which have been heavily vandalised.' Parts of Salford were like 'Beirut without the sunshine,' said one MP.'

Much of Higher Broughton was as bad; residents talked of the area being 'under siege'.[55] One in three Salford residents was living in poverty, according to the pressure group Church Action on Poverty, despite millions being spent on improving Ordsall, Trinity and Greengate. A third of children were entitled to free school meals. Health indicators such as the rate of strokes and heart attacks were appalling. The police admitted they were overwhelmed; Chief Inspector Stuart Nelson even urged Salford residents to write to his own chief constable asking for more bobbies. 'The scale of the problem in this city is such that it is like having ten fires and four firemen,' he said. The *Guinness Guide to Finding the Best Places to Live in the UK* rated Salford as the second worst (after Barnsley; Rochdale was third from bottom). It scored abysmally in categories such as education spending, truancy, qualifications, crime rates and culture – there was one cinema in the whole city and no concert hall or theatre.

By 1995, panic buttons were being handed out to witnesses in court cases in Salford. The alarms could be carried in a pocket and sent a signal direct to the police when triggered. A secure waiting room was allocated at Salford Magistrates Court so that prosecution witnesses did not have to wait with defendants' friends and relatives. The council also belatedly appointed a witness liaison officer to support people giving evidence. 'Intimidation is endemic in Salford,' said councillor Jim King, himself a victim of it after reporting a crime. 'People constantly tell me they are frightened to report crime and are threatened if they agree to be witnesses.'

Gang and crime culture in Salford had grown so insidious that it seemed to reach into almost every area of life, even to threaten the economic future of the city itself. 'There is widespread evidence that one of the major threats to Salford's ability to attract new industry or commerce into the city – and then retain it – is the level of crime that is experienced by many of the companies already there,' said one report.[56] Crime was a direct threat to the 'new era' promised by Salford Quays and its surrounding enterprise zone, which had attracted investment of around £350 million by 1991 and created an estimated 4,000 jobs. The businesses of the Quays were so plagued by burglaries, particularly of computers, that one company director described the area as 'like a beautifully iced cake but with poison seeping out of it.'

CHAPTER ELEVEN

Ragamuffin Tearaways

ONE RULE OF a successful drugs pitch is that you never rip off your customers. It was a rule the young Doddington broke without hesitation. 'I watched somebody serve a punter and before the guy returned to his car, he grabbed him, punched him, took the drugs back off him and the rest of his money, his watch, his bracelet and rings and his car keys and told him to get off the estate,' said Anthony Stevens. 'What is the sense in that – beating up your source of income? This seemed to be the order of the day; they were all doing it for a laugh.'

Typical was an incident outside the West Indian Sports and Social Club in Moss Side, where the Doddies sometimes hung out. Drug-user Sidney Reynolds and a female companion had driven to Moss Side to make a buy. The woman went into the club while Reynolds, who was already smacked up, stayed slumped in the back seat. Sixteen-year-old Dean Laycock followed her back to the car to steal her money and Reynolds, a big, powerful man, jumped out and grabbed him in a headlock. They fell to the floor

'Where's my t'ing?' shouted Laycock. T'ing was slang for a gun.

Another youth appeared. 'Where shall I pop him?' he shouted.

'Pop him in the leg,' said Laycock.

A bullet tore through Reynolds's thigh and into his heel, smashing the bone to pieces. Laycock was later convicted of assault with intent to rob, and wounding with intent. The jury chose not to believe his alibi that he was at home looking after his pet chinchillas, nor his assertion that the Doddington was a football club and bandanas were worn to keep warm in Moss

Side. Tommy Pitt, also sixteen, was cleared of being the gunman. He was however, incarcerated for a year – the maximum allowed for his age – for affray and possessing a loaded firearm in a public place for shooting above the crowd in a night club.

Another Doddie, Tony McElroy, shot at two customers with a Luger when they complained about the poor quality of his heroin. 'It was not for lack of trying that you failed to kill both addicts,' Mr Justice Morison told him at Manchester Crown Court, pointing out that there were 207 gun-related crimes in the Hulme and Moss Side areas in the final six months of 1993. 'The problem is made worse by the difficulty of persuading witnesses to give evidence,' he added. 'I saw for myself the way you sat in the dock staring at the witnesses in this case, no doubt hoping they would be frightened to give evidence against you.' He jailed the arrogant, moustachioed young gunman for eighteen years.

'They didn't seem to understand that while they were doing that, the amount of people who had the nerve to come back was dwindling by the day,' said Anthony Stevens. 'These punters thought, why on earth should I go down there just to get taxed? A lot then started to think, what they are doing isn't so hard, why don't I just buy drugs in a big quantity for myself and certain mates and become a dealer myself in my little estate, miles away. This is what happened. So all these groups of guys who used to stand about are now fighting over an ever-decreasing market and it has become more and more desperate. All of a sudden it is not a laugh any more. So people have decided, right, what we will do now is, we will take money from people who have made it illicitly, because they can't exactly go to the police.' There was a sharp rise in taxing.

The Gooch were now the most powerful of the Moss Side gangs. 'There is no one leader,' said a gangland figure at the time. 'They are quite well organised in terms of drug distribution. They make the Doddies look like ragamuffin tearaways, which they are. They are just guns for hire now. The Gooch are that bit more organised and the people in charge are a bit better at communication. The Doddies are basically just responsible for taxing.'

The young guns got even younger. A police dog sniffed a bag of crack cocaine and heroin dropped by one dealer and managed to follow the scent for half a mile through a maze of alleyways to the house where a fourteen-year-old was watching TV with his mum. The boy had recently been given bail charged with eleven offences, including threatening to shoot someone, burglary and possession of heroin. When previously arrested at a house in Moss Side, he had been sleeping in a bulletproof vest. His thirteen-year-old accomplice had been charged with armed robbery and had been on the run from a local authority secure home for five months. He had been bailed ten times by juvenile courts.

'I feel like King Canute trying to hold back the tide of drugs,' admitted Chief Constable David Wilmot. 'Police alone cannot tackle this problem. We have poured resources into fighting drugs and the problem has not diminished, it has increased.' He cited the case of a fourteen-year-old boy on the city's Monsall estate who made £2,000 a week selling drugs. The boy had recently been convicted but freed by the court – and had gone straight back to work. 'For every dealer we arrest, there are at least another ten people willing to take their place,' he added.[57]

★ ★ ★

While Salford and Cheetham Hill forged an unholy alliance in their push into the city centre, the Gooch-Doddington war raged unabated. Old wounds would not heal.

In May 1993, Doddington elder Ian McLeod and a young buck were driving through Moss Side in rush-hour when a VW Golf pulled alongside them at a junction. A gunman leaned out and fired several large-calibre bullets into McLeod's vehicle. McLeod drove off but hit a tree, and a minute later was seen to get out of the car with blood pouring from his neck, and head towards the precinct. McLeod later had a steel plate inserted in his shattered skull.

Two hours later, the gang wars claimed an innocent victim. An innocent dad called Brian Byrne was crossing a road in

Fallowfield when he was fatally struck by a stolen car that was involved in a chase after a shootout. As Mr Byrne lay dying in the road, a second car pulled up and its occupants threatened witnesses. The dead man left a ten-year-old son orphaned, as the boy's mother had died when he was a baby. The car had been stolen from Cheetham Hill, had been seen earlier cruising the Moss Side-Fallowfield area, and was later found burned out.

In June 1993, there was a car chase and shootout at evening rush hour between two gangs in cars in Old Trafford; eight spent cartridges were recovered. Then a Doddington posse on mountain bikes surrounded nineteen-year-old Warren Williams in his black BMW on Claremont Road, and a hitman dressed in black opened fire. Williams escaped by ducking under the dashboard, then crawling out of the passenger door and jumping onto a passing bus. His car was later found wrecked, with two bulletholes in a door, covered in Doddington graffiti.

The Gooch who had escaped Operation China were using as their base the Sports pub, a modern, ugly building in Whalley Range, a fading Victorian enclave that was once the leafy preserve of the old cotton classes but now blighted by prostitution. The Doddington had made occasional sorties against the Sports, but nothing to match the terror of 25 June 1993. Three men, wearing what witnesses described as paramilitary uniforms, burst into the pub just before closing time on a Friday night. They had a sub-machine gun – possibly a Thompson – and two automatic handguns. Their targets were among a group of about forty people on a raised section of the busy lounge. One was Adrian Stapleton, whose cousin Carl had been hacked to death by the Doddington two years earlier and who had himself been cleared of the murder of Darren Samuel.

The gunmen stood on seats so they could take level aim, and opened fire. 'It was like the Saint Valentine's Day Massacre,' said a witness. 'Bullets smacked into walls all over the place, carnage everywhere.' Stapleton crumpled as bullets hit him in the mouth, chest, arms and legs. Philip Marshall, aged twenty-seven, took a bullet in the mouth and another in the body. Winston Fisher, twenty-seven, was also shot. The hit squad fired at least thirty rounds; a massacre was avoided only by chance. The blood-soaked victims were taken to Manchester Royal Infirmary, where armed police stood guard as they underwent emergency surgery. Only close family were allowed in to see them. They would survive, though Stapleton would carry the facial scars for the rest of his life. It was clear that the Doddington now had access to at least two machine guns: a different one had been used in an earlier gun battle in Old Trafford.

*   *   *

Three ingredients were making the Manchester underworld uniquely violent. 'Whenever we talk drugs now,' said Detective Superintendent David Brennan, 'we are also talking guns and gangs.' Gun crime in Greater Manchester rose by almost a third in 1993. C division, which included Moss Side and Rusholme, saw 295 firearms incidents, including 237 armed robberies, a year-on-year increase of ninety-four per cent. Early in 1994, the police found four AK 47 rifles and three submachine guns in the boot of a car near Chorlton Street bus station. 'The guns were coming from numerous sources and they were plentiful,' said Anthony Stevens. 'I could understand some people who owned a firearm for their own protection, just in case. What really frightened me was the people who carried firearms not for protection but because they wanted the respect that it gave. People saw them walking around with a long Mac like they used to ten years ago. There were people who weren't under any kind of threat but would walk around with a gun because they knew the street would part like a sea because you would know that he was one of those gunmen.'

Three hundred miles from Manchester, three men burst into the Gun Room in Ivybridge, near Plymouth, and bludgeoned the owner unconscious, fracturing his skull. They tied him up, locked him in a lavatory and stole forty-one handguns. Their car was found abandoned, its engine running and its doors flung open, in Moss Side, and two of the guns were recovered from a drug dealer's house in Sale. Two Manchester men were later jailed for twelve years for the raid; though they were white, it was believed they had quickly sold the weapons to the warring black gangs.

Another source was Alan Ratcliffe, a balding, bearded, forty-six-year-old former engineer who had converted the cellar of his modest semi in Farnworth, Bolton, into a legal gun shop with more than 100 weapons, including assault rifles, on display. The house was securely alarmed and locked, but the tweed-jacketed Ratcliffe was also selling guns illegally. He had an extra licence to buy machine guns on condition that he turned them into blank firers to be used only as theatrical props; instead he bought a full-firing Thompson from a Manchester supplier for £140 and sold it illegally for a reputed £450. It was believed to have ended up in the hands of Moss Side mobsters. Another weapon was used to shoot a gangster in Moss Side in summer 1992 and it was after that that a police raid uncovered a pistol hidden in a child's wardrobe. It led to Ratcliffe, who admitted passing it on without a certificate. The majority of the weapons he sold illegally – seventeen, according to his admissions – were never traced. Gun dealers' buying and selling records were reviewed twice a year but who they sold to was not thoroughly checked. In July 1994, he was jailed for three years after admitting offences of unlawfully transferring firearms.

Police were also concerned about legally sold de-activated guns, which were being re-activated for full use. A 'de-act' was not classed as a weapon because the barrel had been blocked and ring pin removed, and so they could be sold openly or by mail order, but it was easy for a halfway competent engineer to restore them to working order. De-acts could be bought in surplus stores, at fairs and through specialist gun magazines. The price was as low as £60, yet once restored they would sell to criminals for up to £1,000.

*   *   *

Delroy Brown had been absent from the most recent gang clashes, locked in jail on remand. His police handler, for whom Brown was a vital source of up-to-date information, had assured him that the charges against him would almost certainly be lessened or dropped, but much to the surprise of both of them the Crown Prosecution Service pressed ahead with the case. In July 1993, Brown was convicted of possession of crack cocaine with intent to supply. 'JAIL FOR PUBLIC ENEMY DELROY,' crowed the *Manchester Evening News*:

> A gang boss regarded by police as Moss Side's public enemy No 1 was finally behind bars today after a series of court dramas.
>
> One battle too many with a rival drugs-and-guns gang sent him into the grateful arms of the law.
>
> Today Delroy Brown, 29, of Greysham Court, Whalley Range, leader of the Pepperhill mob, was beginning a six-year jail term – and cursing his Gooch gang enemies.
>
> Lady Luck, which had seen Delroy survive various attempts on his life, finally deserted him in a clash with the Gooch boys.

Brown would not be heard from again. Having 'dropped down the rankings,' in the words of one officer, he dropped out of sight: he seemed to have come from nowhere, a man with a mystery past, and now he disappeared again. One source claims he returned to the Alexandra Park estate on his release from prison and tried to reassert his authority, only to be beaten up and told to disappear for good. He fled back to Birmingham, leaving a legacy of irreconcilable hatred.

In August one of Brown's protégés, Winston Brownlow, was cleared of attempted murder when the victim told a court he was no longer certain Brownlow was the man who shot him because he had bad eyesight and was not wearing his glasses at the time of the attack. 'I can't definitely say it was Winston who shot me,' testified Carl Ricketts. 'I have changed my mind – no-one has threatened me.' The collapse of gang trials had become the norm. In the same month, Ray Pitt of the Doddington was jailed for contempt of court for refusing to testify against a man accused of shooting him.

The kind of intimidation witnesses could face was revealed in another trial. A young man called John Mack had been shot three times in Longsight; one of his former schoolfriends was charged. Mack himself was later arrested for robbery, only to find himself in a cell in Hindley remand centre near to his alleged attacker. He was assaulted just before he was due to leave for court to give evidence and was given messages by his assailant's friends that he and his family would be shot dead if he testified. 'I have been assaulted twice,' he told the court. Masked men had also attacked the home where his pregnant girlfriend lived with their baby daughter. The judge accepted that, because of the duress, Mack could not be jailed for contempt, and the man accused of shooting him walked free.

October 1993 saw a pitched gun battle in Alexandra Road, a drug buyer mugged and shot on the Alex estate, a kneecapping outside a Stretford snooker hall, a Doddington soldier shot in the leg in Longsight, and three people shot as they sat in a car in Chorlton. Recorder Rhys Davies, Manchester's leading judge, warned of having to impose deterrent sentences to curb the massive rise in firearms-related offences. He said ten years ago there had been 107 such offences; in 1993 they were expected to top 1,400. A Manchester police officer wrote to *Police Review* magazine demanding that he and his colleagues be armed.

Four days after the judge's comments, the Young Gooch trapped two men at a Bonfire Night party. Their victims had been part of a crowd of several hundred at the Guy Fawkes evening laid on by a local youth project in Quinney Crescent when a gang of four young men let off at least four shots from a shotgun. One of their victims was Doddington member Kevin Lewis, twenty-two, who had already been shot at least once before. A few days later, another attack was made on a Doddington redoubt. A gunman hiding behind bushes opened fire with a shotgun on a group of young friends. They were chased into a house and one fourteen-year-old was hit in the head and legs by pellets and shattered glass from the door panel he hid behind. They hit the lights and lay in the dark for fifteen minutes until the coast was clear.

Yet for all the recent shootings and terrible injuries, no-one had been killed since Darren Samuel. It was testament to the bad shooting skills of the gangbangers and the skills of the trauma staff at Manchester Royal Infirmary, by now inured to wounded young men arriving in 'GTi taxis' and being offloaded before their friends sped off.

* * *

Doddington youth Julian 'Turbo' Stewart had survived one attempt on his life when his body armour deflected a bullet. He had walked free from charges of murder, attempted murder and wounding. Lately, Turbo had been upsetting some of the Gooch. He spoke with Anthony Stevens, an intelligent and level-headed older man who had been through similar experiences, and expressed confusion at his inability to escape the world he was in. The Gooch were still after him, he wore a vest all the time and was constantly looking over his shoulder. Yet he had not reached that crucial decision to get out.

On a cold January day in 1994, Stewart and a friend, Terence Wilson, were chased across Princess Parkway by two mixed-race men, one shouting, 'You're dead.' Later, they were in Radley Walk, off the notorious Quinney Crescent, a loop around the east side of the estate that marked the edge of Doddington home turf. A black man approached them, asking for drugs. He wore dated clothes, suggesting he might recently have left prison. 'He started to get friendly by referring to someone he knew who was also a friend of mine,' Wilson later told an inquest. 'But I was cautious about him because I didn't know who he was or what he really wanted.'

The man asked them their names. Stewart said his was Turbo, and the three shook hands. Wilson said he was just about to walk away when he heard a bang. 'I saw the flash and Turbo fell to the ground. It looked like an automatic handgun but things happened so fast. A car screeched up a passageway and I ran because I felt it was connected.' Stewart had taken a single shot to the left side of his head. He died within seconds, wearing his bulletproof vest and carrying £4,000 in cash. The shooter left a pair of spectacles at the scene, made of plain glass and worn as a disguise.

Sonia Stewart was told of her son's death by a relative and was taken to the scene. Due to a delay in forensic experts reaching the scene, his body lay in the street for several hours, only partially covered. 'Obviously I was very distressed, but even more so because of the fact that he was left lying there, which I thought was totally unnecessary, very disrespectful. There was a lot of feeling in the community that that shouldn't have been so. He wasn't removed and he wasn't covered. It was very distressing because I could see part of his body.'[58]

The investigating superintendent called it 'a cold-blooded assassination, one of the worst I have seen.' The newspapers described Stewart as a 'second lieutenant' in the Doddington Gang. The Police Authority offered a £10,000 reward for information. More than 1600 people were interviewed in the subsequent enquiry, and 131 made detailed statements. Yet no-one was able, or willing, to identify the gunman, believed to be a hitman brought in by the Gooch to take care of Turbo.

Sonia Stewart was a dignified lady who worked for the city council. Like many of the mothers who would lose sons to the gang war, her son had kept her in the dark about his life, even when he had once before been shot. 'I only knew quite a while after it, actually. Someone told me about it. I didn't know why it had happened. Julian wasn't living with me and hadn't for some time so I didn't know what his business was. I tried through other family members to keep a track of whether he was okay or not but, that is basically it.'

She did not believe that the street gangs were heavily organised. 'I think that is just dramatics by the media to get a good story. I think they are young men who need a lot of help. A lot of them don't see a future for themselves either educationally or in terms of employment but I don't think they are listened to. They are not taken seriously. And then it is a case of, well, why bother? It is very sad. A lot of them are just young boys with nothing better to do. The way they are described sometimes, as if they are the mafia, is very unfair. A lot of them need help with their education, with employment. Julian as far as I'm concerned was very naïve, like a lot of other young men today who think they know everything but don't. He might have just got caught up in something that he didn't expect.

'I would like the media to be fairer in how they portray Moss Side, fairer in how they portray young black men in general. The way it is all dramatised in the Press, it gives a very, very bad impression and it won't help the people in the area. Crime isn't just young black people. This sort of incident can happen to anyone's son. You don't have to be from a certain background or certain colour for it to happen to you. I don't blame myself. Julian was disciplined, in fact to the point where he thought I was too strict and he often said that to me. He was brought up properly.'

Several men would be arrested but no-one was ever tried for his death. 'He was one of an early wave of youngsters who died unnecessarily [because of] unscrupulous people above them who used them as cannon fodder,' said Anthony Stevens. There would be many more to come.

★   ★   ★

February 1994 saw builders move in to start demolishing parts of the Alex Park estate. Fifty houses would be knocked down, to be replaced by new homes built by a housing association, and ninety-eight others substantially renovated. The narrow and secluded walkways and isolated open spaces would go; play and recreational areas were to be improved. The changes were intended partly to 'design out' the crime that made domestic life so unbearable.

The effects of the work – and of the deliberate movement of certain families off the estate, some for good – were not immediately noticeable. Indeed the Gooch were planning their most brazen act yet: to kill a police officer. Certain key figures in the gang had become exasperated by the success of the officer codenamed Delta, whose work in cultivating top-level informants was yielding excellent inside intelligence. So one of the Gooch leaders hatched a plot to pass on to Delta bogus information that a large amount of ammunition could be found in a disused house in Moss Side. Delta had received similar tips before, and the gang anticipated he would probably check out the house alone at first. The Gooch's main gunman would be waiting with a revolver obtained from a source in London, and would shoot Delta dead.

Delta's sources were so good that he learned of the plot in advance. He immediately told his boss, and a meeting was arranged with the firearms department. It was agreed that Delta should go along with the plan, with firearms support, and turn the tables on the waiting gunman. The GMP top brass, however, refused to sanction such a risky operation, and instead, pulled Delta out of Moss Side. He was ordered not to set foot in the district again. They may have acted with the best of motives but 'the decision not only compromised his informant, but also allowed the Gooch's plan to work,' wrote one of his former colleagues. 'Unwittingly, and without firing a shot, they had hamstrung Delta – he had become ineffective.'

It's impossible to assess what the impact of Delta's withdrawal was, but there would be a firearms incident every two days in the Moss Side area in 1994. One of the most serious was an attempt to kill eighteen-year-old Laurence Brown, who had previously been cleared of attempted murder charges after the Bonfire Night shooting of two Doddington men. Brown was chased in a Golf in Moss Side and took a bullet; he crashed the car and was found in a doorway by an ambulance crew. Drug dealing had been driven from the Alex estate by the constant warfare; Claremont Road was now the Frontline. A police observation point on the first floor of a building overlooking the street was sussed out and attacked by a mob, some armed with sticks. There seemed to be no end, no purpose, just a mad whirlwind of taxing, shooting, intimidating, dealing, spending. The older heads were losing influence, losing face.

In August 1994, at the Moss Side carnival weekend, some young Hillbillies took potshots at two Doddington bosses, including Ian McLeod. They missed but the atmosphere became evil. 'Bullets were flying over kids' heads,' said one eye-witness. 'The Cheetham Hill who did it were just the young idiots who wanted to hook into it. They wanted their bit of fun.' A short while later, thirty-three-year-old Ray Odoha was getting into his car on Claremont Road when Ray Pitt of the Doddington tried to shoot him in the head. Instead the bullet hit his arm, breaking it. Pitt fired again but his gun jammed, saving Odoha's life.

Odoha was a man with many friends in Cheetham Hill, Now some of them decided to call time.

CHAPTER TWELVE

The Truce

ONE FRIDAY MORNING, the telephone rang on the cluttered desk of Andy Nott, crime reporter for the *Manchester Evening News*. The caller was a main player in the city's gangland, a contact Nott had made while covering a sensational murder case. He had something to say. Nott listened, asked the occasional question and took notes. Then he ran the story past a police intelligence contact to see if it was true. The contact came back and said it was.

The next day, Saturday, 13 August 1994, Nott's exclusive appeared on page two of the *Manchester Evening News*. 'Gun Gangs Call a Halt to War in the Streets,' announced the headline.

> Murdering gangsters who have brought bloodshed and death to the streets of Manchester have been having secret 'truce' talks.
>
> The violence in the inner-city gun war has reached such ferocity that influential gang members have decided 'enough is enough.'
>
> Now members of the two Moss Side factions, the Gooch and the Doddington, have met with the Cheetham Hill mob to try to call a halt to the tit-for-tat shootings which have left a trail of misery over the past decade.

The catalyst had been the shooting on carnival day of Ray Odoha. 'We had to decide how to respond and it was such a serious business it would need a lot of bullets for a suitable reply,' Nott's source told him. 'Then we considered that another option was no bullets at all. It seemed to make sense.'

The story was a genuine scoop, revealing a degree of organisation by the gangs that had not been apparent before. The Gladiator was a prime mover, phoning influential figures on all sides. Backing him up was Paul Massey, with the considerable weight of Salford behind him. Mobile phones had been buzzing for days, but there was a huge amount of suspicion among the factions. The first summit meeting had been held at the Whalley, a large pub in Whalley Range. Members of all four of the gangs attended but it was an uneasy meeting and many wore bulletproof vests. The Doddington stayed in the car park. A second meeting followed at Cheerleaders pub in Castlefield. 'It is very delicate because it only takes a small thing to wreck all that has been done, but so far the peace seems to be holding,' said the source. 'Our lives were becoming hardly worth living because of the constant threat of what might happen around the next corner. It got to the stage where it wasn't worth it.' Cheetham Hill, always the most disciplined of the black gangs, were readily on board. Some of the original Gooch, having served their time for the Operation China busts, prevailed on their younger hotheads to cool it and signed up too. The tearaways of the Doddington were the unknown quantity – but they warily agreed as well.

A few days after the story broke, the gangsters hijacked a big music event, featuring the likes of Mica Paris, at the Ritz ballroom in central Manchester. The gang head who had phoned the *MEN* had flyers printed up and distributed in pubs saying, 'Cheetham Hill, Gooch, Moss Side, Salford, everyone is invited to the Truce Soul Night.' He neglected, however, to tell the promoter – former Pepperhill man Anthony Stevens, now a successful businessman. Stevens soon found out that what he had planned as a great summer night out was going to be invaded by just about every gangster in the city. Then someone started spreading rumours that Cheetham Hill, the Gooch and Salford planned to lure the Doddington there to wipe them out. 'It was my worst nightmare,' said Stevens. But it got even worse.

One the day before the event, Stevens was summoned to Longsight police station for a meeting with the leader of the police 'C10 squad'. He had no idea what C10 was until he was told it was a section of the serious crime squad developed to deal with drug and gun crimes. DCI Tony Cook, an expert on the south Manchester gang scene, wanted to know what was going on. Stevens said he was going to cancel the show. No, he was forcefully told; the show had to go on. Sickened by attempts by the gangsters to present themselves as some kind of community police force, C10 also intended to make this a show of power – their own.

Caught between a rock and a hard place, Stevens decided to press ahead. 'I thought, the only thing we can do is make the event as much fun as possible. We went to a warehouse and bought a thousand whistles and horns and streamers and turned it into a cheesy, birthday party-type place.' At 2 pm, he received a phone call: the security firm he had booked were pulling out. 'I'm calling all these security firms but there was not one in town that would touch it. Then all the bar staff had been called to tell them not to turn up because they might be killed, so we had to get agency bar staff.' With no-one else to turn to, Stevens spoke to 'two complete headcases' in the Gooch and offered to pay them extravagantly to do the door. They agreed.

He then spoke to the Doddington, who had been planning to boycott the event because they suspected it was a set-up. They had changed their minds. 'Fuck it,' said one of them. 'If they are that bad they think they can set us up, we will either all go or none of us, and we have had a meeting with everyone on the estate and we are all going, and anyone who doesn't is dead.' It was going to be a long night.

There was an early flashpoint when a couple of muscle-bound doormen from another club turned up early and demanded to be let in free. The Gooch 'security team' simply put guns to their heads – end of discussion. In the event, the venue was crammed and there was no hint of trouble. Then the Doddington arrived. 'I saw a massive gap open up in the crowd and all of a sudden they walked in,' said Stevens. 'There must have been a hundred of them. I have never seen anything like it. They saw me in the DJ box and all walked over and started shaking my hand, saying, "Are you all right, T?" Every gangster known to me in Manchester was there, three to four hundred of them, all stood at the back in clumps so they could enjoy themselves but watch the opposition at the same time. And do you know what? That was the second best night I ever did.'

Despite an enormous police presence outside, the harmony held.

★　★　★

One of the architects of the truce was Paul Massey. He was an ally of the man who placed the phone call to the *Evening News*, and had used similar friendships forged over the previous few years to help pull the warring sides together, having met some of the leaders from all sides while in prison.

> I have had a talk with [them all] and we decided a truce was there and needed to be done. But you have got to have had enough. For ten years, a lot of people had died unnecessarily and a lot of people were being dragged into a situation which didn't really concern them. It was just getting out of hand. We got the communication between them all and it turned out pretty well.

Massey saw himself as the middleman, the guarantor, and wasn't prepared to let his reputation be trampled if the deal broke down. With his street radar working overtime, he was all too aware that one faction might use the ceasefire to build up strength for renewed conflict.

> We just say as we're leaving, 'If one stabs the other in the back, we'll back the one who gets stabbed. So I hope we're not going to waste our time being here and I hope we can get this lot sorted out today.' You've got to be careful, because the one who's calling the truce could be calling the truce because they're weak at the time. And in four months [or] two years time, they get more powerful, because they've got the money and got more new boys in the time, they move in against

other people. Which can't be accepted, because . . . I've put a shield against these people who could have walked all over them. You've got to put it over, this is the end, this is the end. People know that I'm not going to jackal on any side. I'm not going to start moving any goalposts. Because once you make an agreement . . . and then you stab them in the back and everyone else gets to hear, your reputation's no good. Your credibility's no good.

Two months after the initial summit, Moss Side was visited by 'Juan' and 'Twilight', previously deadly rivals from the Crip and Blood gangs in Los Angeles, on a so-called peace mission organised by Panther UK, a left-wing organisation for black youth. The Crips and Bloods – whose red and blue bandannas had once been copied by the Gooch and the Doddington – had themselves agreed a ceasefire, and the two emissaries extolled its virtues at a public meeting. A collective of prisoners in Strangeways under the name Project X recorded a CD; *The Summit* contained a track about the armistice and others about gang life in the city. It seemed to set the seal. (As early as early 1993, pop mogul Peter Waterman had released a mini-album with a track on it called 'Gunchester' by Manchester group Family Foundation which described how gangsters were ruining the nightlife in the city.)

The truce was a coup for those who brokered it. It boosted their stock, already high. It also, whether by coincidence or design, trapped the city in a pincer movement. 'The gangs are very happy with the mutual stuff,' said a well-informed local journalist. 'They don't want to shoot each other; there's money to be made if they have it carved up.' No longer at war, the gangs could move freely. They would use that licence to tighten their choking grip on the city's nightlife.

★   ★   ★

Not every door security firm was aligned to one of the four gangs, and those that weren't were no pushovers. One was Loc-

19 Security, run from a steel-doored office in Ardwick by Steve Bryan and Mickey Francis, two men both respected and feared in the after-dark door world. Bryan was a formidable-looking ex-doorman who bore the scars of countless battles, while Francis carried a bullet-hole in his forearm and had served time for leading the Guvnors soccer hooligan gang that followed Manchester City. Both men were personable and chatty but had run the doors at some wild places, including notorious Limit club, and knew the city's gang heads on first-name terms. They employed dozens of doormen and were building a decent portfolio of pubs and clubs.

Inevitably, one or two of their venues suffered problems with Salford elements, not always in a concerted way. Some of the younger gangs were acting independently, flexing their muscles, emboldened by the way the older heads seemed to have such a hold on the city. At Christmas 1994, there was an altercation at BarKay when the Loc-19 bouncers knocked back several members of a young Salford mob that had caused trouble in there previously. In the confrontation that followed, two of the Salford gang were shot. A doorman was later jailed for four years for possessing a pistol; he said he had been handed the weapon to look after by men from Moss Side who had carried out the shooting.

Some older Salford faces seem to have then used this incident to get backing for their own determined attempt to take over the door at the popular Home nightclub. Home, 'the Hacienda's first big purpose-built competitor',[59] had opened behind Piccadilly train station in 1993 and was soon attracting a trendy crowd. Its management had refused to have a Salford-sanctioned firm on the door and instead employed Loc-19. Salford responded with threats and drive-by shootings outside the club.

The big assault came one evening in mid-March, 1995. A call-out saw a number of tough-looking young men begin to gather in The Jubilee in Ordsall, until eventually there was about sixty of them. They then headed for the Canal Bar in Whitworth Street, another Loc-19 door. 'The management were so concerned at the appearance of these people, who all wore long coats with collars turned up, that they called the police and said there was going to be trouble,' Crown prosecutor Raymond Wigglesworth told a subsequent court case. The Salford contingent were bolstered by a few Gooch faces. Some Cheetham Hill pulled up outside in cars and spoke to the ringleaders but did not join them. The police arrived, and officers started identifying faces in the crowd, so the mob trooped out and made to the nearby Hacienda where, despite a £15 entrance fee, they marched in without paying. After a drink, they set off again, walking almost a mile to their target, the Home club. The doormen were helpless to prevent them walking straight in and demanding drinks at the bar, again without paying.

Five plainclothes officers arrived shortly after midnight, took a look around the club, then retired to a vantage point on the stairs. Some uniformed officers joined them. The Salford gang geared themselves up. Some pulled on balaclavas, others baseball caps, and some zipped up their jackets to cover their faces. Then they charged across the room as if to attack the police. They stopped just short of the officers, goading them in a terrifying manner, as the dance-floor quickly cleared. Then they surged again towards the officers on the stairs. One PC testified that it was the most frightening incident he had ever been involved in. 'About twenty charged at us,' he said. 'I was transfixed, I couldn't move.' Instead of attacking the officers, however, the gang then mingled back among the 600 patrons. As more police arrived, beer bottles were thrown at them. The heavy mob from the Tactical Aid Group finally turned up and closed the club. Officers lined up by the door as the patrons poured out to arrest those they recognised.

Several ended up on the cells and later went on trial. 'It was obviously organised and the object was to exert influence,' the prosecutor later told Bolton Crown Court, where several of the men went on trial. 'A group of people tried to exert control by threatening violence. It was an organised display of force.' Eddie Taylor and Gary McDonald, both from Salford, were described in court as ringleaders and were convicted despite denying the charges. 'I have not the slightest doubt but that on that night you and a group from the Salford area went to the clubland of Manchester city centre intent on causing trouble, intimidation and violence,' the judge told them. 'I bear in mind that no-one suffered any physical injury as a result of your behaviour but it was a terrifying experience not only for members of staff but for the police officers.' He jailed them both for fifteen months. Taylor had previous convictions for public order and assault. McDonald had served time for robbery and possessing a gun. 'We've been convicted just 'cos we're from Salford,' remarked McDonald loudly.

Home would never recapture its former success. More shots were reportedly fired outside, and in June 1995 police raided the club. 'Three people were arrested and an amount of drugs and weapons were discovered during the police operation just after midnight on Saturday,' reported the *Manchester Metro News*. 'It follows an incident last month when staff were shot at from a passing car. Tablets, powder and vegetable matter – all believed to be drugs – were discovered on the dance floor of the Ducie Street venue. Police say panicking revellers emptied their pockets onto the floor rather than be found in possession of illegal substances. A Mace spray, a prohibited weapon which disables people when directed into their eyes, was also discovered along with an eight-inch chef's knife.' The police indicated that they would oppose the renewal of Home's licence. Instead its owner temporarily closed the club. 'Three or four years ago, everyone wanted to come to Manchester because of the music scene,' said one of the club's staff. 'It was really thriving. Now, because of the perception, it has changed. It is very sad.'

Clubbers were heading out of the metropolis. Other great northern cities like Liverpool, Leeds and Sheffield were beginning to woo the clientele. A low hum of background menace pervaded Manchester's nightlife. DJs were threatened with guns and sometimes relieved of their record collections. The manageress of one city centre bar was tied to a chair and told her mother would be raped. A club manager was similarly shackled and had his biceps sliced in half with hedge scissors. Taxing was rife. 'It is affecting business immensely,' said Paul Cons, one of the creators of the Manchester club scene. 'The reputation of Manchester out of town is terrible. Clubbing for a lot of people is about going to other cities. They will travel a hundred miles because of the way the doormen are, the rudeness and aggression. They treat your average customer like scum.'

* * *

The black gangs were also looking elsewhere. 'Black music' nights had the worst problems, or at least the worst image, especially those that pulled in the jungle crowd in their American look of puffy bomber jackets, baseball jackets, sweatshirts with the hoods pulled up and baggy jeans tucked into boots. This longstanding perception had been exacerbated by a mini-riot at a city venue called Checkpoint Charlie's when many of the city's young black and mixed-race gangsters attended an event featuring DJ Dave Rodigan and Papa Face. Plainclothes officers were also there. 'There appeared to be arguments developing amongst the males gathered outside the premises,' recorded a police report. 'Those present I would describe as leading members of gangs, in particular Cheetham Hill.' The Hillbillies were running the door, the club was operating without a late licence and was overcrowded. Police asked the organisers to shut down but it was 3 a.m. before people began to leave. They found dozens of police waiting in ranks outside. Jonathan Quartey, of Cheetham Hill, who had a previous conviction for assaulting a policeman, pointed his finger towards one large officer and threatened to 'blow him away'. It was the catalyst for a mini-riot. Some of the crowd were hit with truncheons and bitten by police dogs; seven were arrested and five officers were injured. The incident led to calls for a public inquiry and even saw the formation of a protest group, Action for Black Justice. Quartey later pleaded guilty to using threatening words or behaviour and was fined £500. He said he reacted after being stopped from going back inside to get his coat.

It was another coffin nail for black music in the city. Home cancelled jungle nights after just three events and most other clubs refused to host them. A Joedicy gig at the Free Trade Hall saw major problems. 'They had a nightmare down there,' said a venue manager. 'They lost control of the door and called the police who came over and stopped everyone apart from some real loons getting in. Then they had problems backstage.' UMIST staged a jungle event and had trouble all night, beginning when a young gangbanger was shot in the foot nearby. Bar staff were spat at and verbally abused and the doormen were utterly intimidated. 'At two a.m. they tried to close and were told they were carrying on for another hour,' said a promoter. 'The security team realised that dealing with drunken student rugby players was one thing, but this was completely different.' It reached the stage where no mainstream promoters would do a night that brought in young black people. Manchester's jungle studio star A Guy Called Gerald relocated to London because his kind of music wasn't receiving the support it deserved. Some black journalists complained there was an undertone of racism to the treatment of jungle and ragga but the trigger-happy gangs were a reality that could not be ignored. So the Moss Side gangs began to take their leisure excursions elsewhere: London, Birmingham, Bristol, Sheffield, Leeds.

Two of the most feared members of the Young Gooch were the half-brothers Errol and Marlon Jones, who came from a huge Moss Side family; their mother and father had twenty-two children between them. They had close friends among the so-called Black Mafia of Wolverhampton and Marlon, a rap singer, was close to securing a record contract and was due to feature in a film produced by jungle artist Goldie. His numerous bullet scars added to his credibility.

In the early hours of 4 June 1995, Marlon and some friends gatecrashed Wolverhampton's First Base club, entering through a fire escape, and a fight broke out. Doorman Tony Wilson, a former England international boxer, was hit in the face with a bottle, leaving gaping wounds that needed fifty stitches. Seconds later, Jones pulled his hood over his head, walked into the foyer of the club and levelled a silver handgun with both hands while his friends guarded the door. This was the heart-stopping apparition that confronted the doormen, including the bloodied Wilson. Jones fired, wounding a barman who was hiding in the cloakroom, badly injuring another doorman and killing his bull terrier dog.

'Who's scared now?' said Jones as he fired.

By chance, Jones was caught on a surveillance video that police had covertly planted across the road. He was acquitted of attempted murder on the directions of the judge but was convicted of wounding, unlawful wounding and possessing a firearm with intent to endanger life. Jones claimed he was the victim of mistaken identity, though he admitted being at the club. He was branded 'a menace to society' by the judge and received a lengthy jail term. His mother and supporters had to be escorted from Wolverhampton Crown Court as they hurled abuse at the jury.

Errol Jones, known as 'EJ', was every bit as capricious as his brother. On New Year's Eve 1995, he arrived in Bristol with two mates from Wolverhampton, Gary Nelson and Derek Jones. They went to a rave at the Millionaires Club, where they swigged champagne and took Ecstasy, then headed on to a blues club called Tinkles before ending up in Tasty's Café in the notorious St Paul's district. EJ was wild-eyed and abusive, according to café owner Jennifer Williams, who asked him to leave. 'I'm a black man,' he said. 'I'm from Manchester.' EJ left, but not before one of his crew had pointed two fingers at the neck of a waitress, miming a gun.

Out on Ashley Road, the trio noticed Gert Leeuwrink, a visitor to the city, sitting in a car and wearing an £800 gold link chain. They decided to take it. Jones pulled out a gun and pistol-whipped the terrified man. As he did so, three people came walking down the street, on their way home from a party. One was Jamaican-born Evon Berry, known as 'Bangy', a thirty-seven-year-old caretaker at the local Malcolm X Community Centre and father of three school-age daughters. Berry was a well-known and popular figure in St Paul's district, a gentle bear of a man who was not the sort to walk past when someone was being beaten. He tried to reason with the crazed young thug.

'Come on man, it's News Year's Day. Be calm.'

EJ gave him an evil, deranged look and lifted his gun as one of his friends sneered, 'We're going to leave a lot of dead bodies tonight.' He put the muzzle to Bangy's neck and pulled the trigger. The big man dropped with the blast. Amazingly, he pulled himself upright, and staggered towards a taxi office fifty yards away. One of Jones's gang pulled another gun and turned to Bangy's companions. Victor 'Squeaky' Dinnall raised his hands in supplication. The gangster smashed him across the face with this weapon, then shot him in the chest.

Kelly Kershaw, the fifty-four-year-old dishwasher at Tasty's Café, had just stepped out from the steaming kitchen for a breath of air when he heard the first shot. 'I opened the door and heard a bang,' he later testified. 'I thought someone was firing shots in the air and I dived on the floor. At the same time, I looked up the street. Behind a car, there was a young guy holding his hands out in front of him, pointing at another man. The other man was holding his arms up.' Kershaw crawled into nearby Sussex Place, where he heard a third bang. 'I saw a man coming up the road with a cricket bat. He was chasing someone and swinging the bat around.'

The injured Victor Dinnall ran into the café, with blood smearing his face and chest, a female companion crying and hysterical. Jones and his friends escaped. Fifty yards away, at the office of Class 1 Taxis, gentle Evon Berry died. More than 1,000 people attended his funeral in St Paul's. 'He was a man of peace who avoided trouble,' said the Reverend Richard Daly. 'He will always be remembered as a peacemaker.' Within a month, Errol Jones had been identified and arrested in Manchester.

★   ★   ★

The first warning in print of how bad things had become in Manchester clubland appeared in the autumn of 1995 in the music and style magazine *The Face*. An anonymously written story under the headline 'fear and loathing' acknowledged the explosion of bars and clubs in the city centre but noted 'a positive chill in the air'. It was followed up by the Manchester listings magazine *City Life*, which claimed in an editorial that organised gangs were now on 'nearly every nightclub door in the city centre' and that clubs had been forced to close and promoters driven out of town. The Doorsafe scheme had served only to legitimise the wrong people, who charged extortionate rates and vast retainers, hence forcing clubs to put their admission prices through the roof. 'If you can promote in Manchester, you can do it anywhere in the world,' said one Ibiza-based promoter. 'The gangs scare the life out of everyone involved in the scene.' Tony Wilson's stated in his memoir *24 Hour Party People* that the Hacienda security team was paid £375,000 in 1992. One well-known head doorman was paid at least £1,000 a week. Only mainstream music nights earned enough money to pay those sorts of security bills, so creativity was stifled and clubbers took their custom elsewhere. The twenty-four-hour party had turned into a non-stop nightmare.

Ominously, the *City Life* editorial warned that even the one area of the city free from gang infiltration was now being conquered:

> The Gay Village, previously immune to these pressures, is increasingly visited by either Salford or Cheetham Hill gangs; not only do they threaten violence if free entrance and drinks are not made available, but recently even demanded free taxis home from a local operator.
>
> In addition, the gangs are increasingly threatening live events. Several bands and international promoters now refuse to come to Manchester precisely because of the gang activity, and the ones that do have to inflate prices to accommodate the gang's demands.

The Gay Village was a nineties success story, a brave concept to transform the area around Bloom Street, Canal Street and Sackville Street – a sleazy patch of prostitutes and rent boys around Britain's ugliest coach station – into a bright, thriving quarter. Soon it was home to around twenty-five bars and clubs, supplemented by gay restaurants, hairdressers and cab companies. The Madchester scene kicked off by the Summer of Love gradually shifted from the Hacienda to the safety of clubs like Paradise Factory, attracted a trouble-free environment and late opening hours, often until 6 a.m. (partly to avoid 'queer-bashing' if the clubs kicked out at the same time as straight clubs). The Village, or 'Gaytown' as it was christened, began to attract many non-gays after the mainstream clubs finished at 3 a.m. This in turn guaranteed plentiful demand for Ecstasy and amphetamines. Spending in the area, the so-called Pink Pound, was estimated at around £26 million a year. 'Gay people don't have children,' said a doorman who worked there. 'So they don't spend their money on families, they spend it on themselves. The ones who buy drugs tend to buy a lot – and that means big money.'

The city's attempt to position itself as a twenty-four-hour entertainment capital played into the hands of the villains. What had been a gangland no-go area – 'Who wants to be seen fighting over a load of fags?' asked one gang head – was suddenly a prime target. Once the gangs got over their prejudices they realised that business was business – and there was no-one there to stand up to them. The gay clubs were unprepared. 'A group of gangsters turned up one night who our door staff couldn't refuse,' a promoter told the *Independent*. 'We turned the music off and closed. The next week they were back, more of them, and the night folded. We approached another club owner to see if we could run a gay night on his premises and he said he wasn't prepared to take the risk.'

Equinox, in Bloom Street, was perhaps the most popular club in the Village and became the locus; it had a relatively high number of 'straight' customers, which made it the easiest one to move in on. Its Manumission nights there in 1994 had attracted a big audience but at a high price. Salford took control of the door. 'It went from being a camp club to attracting every dealer, pimp and gangster in town,' a barman told the *Independent*. 'A man's ear was bitten off. There were two stabbings while I was there. One night we were threatened with a gun, the door was kicked off its hinges by gangsters, a bouncer was attacked and the promoter doused in petrol, and the police had to evacuate the club. After the gay bouncers left, and a gang took over the door, I left and went on the dole rather than work there.' Manumission was voted the best club night in the UK by *DJ Magazine* but its promoter, not surprisingly unnerved by being soaked in petrol and thrown down a flight of stairs, relocated to Ibiza, where he enjoyed immense success. 'The Village set the pace, particularly in the dance culture, and it became quite attractive to people to go there,' said Pat Karney, a city councillor heavily involved in promoting the Gay Village. 'Many of them were younger people from Salford who had influential older brothers. In particular they started going to Equinox. The police said they had taken over the door and there were dealers inside and on the door.'

In November 1995, the BBC regional documentary series *Close Up North* asserted that the Village had become the latest target for racketeers. Programme makers spent two weeks in the Village talking to people, many of them guarded in their comments. One contributor was Tony Cooper, licensee of Equinox. 'The problem we have got, which is the same as every other club in Manchester, is a rogue element,' he said. A few days after the programme was broadcast, a Salford doorman broke Cooper's cheekbone. Word spread that he had been beaten up because he had spoken on television. It wasn't true – the bouncer had reacted angrily after being sacked for taking money from customers on a free-entry night – but people believed it.

The stylish, glass-fronted Manto bar had led the Gay Village renaissance along Canal Street and had become enormously popular. It suffered the occasional scally incursion, including an attack by a gang in balaclavas who showered customers with broken bottles. More serious was an incident involving an attack on the doormen in which a gun, possibly a starting pistol, was discharged. It involved the so-called Salford 8 gang,[60] a splinter firm led by the man who had shot at police during the Ordsall riots. 'He looks very young but he will pull a gun and shoot your legs off without thinking twice,' said a doorman. Pub and club owners even discussed taking out injunctions to bar such people from their premises. 'Unless something is done, Manchester will be run by two or three gangs,' said one.[61]

* * *

At a September 1995 meeting of a group called the City Centre Club and Pub Watch Network, Inspector Shaun Currie of the licensing department reported 'an escalation of intimidation by Salford gangs taking over doors on the city.' Currie went on to mention the case of a vast new pub, the Moon Under Water, where 'tactics were employed to take over even though no door takings were involved.' The Moon, a JD Wetherspoon house on Deansgate with 8,500 square feet of floor space, had immediately come under pressure from a gang 'offering' their services as bouncers. The pub stood firm and enlisted the help of police. 'In our pubs, we don't like security, but in that pub we had to have it,' said Eddie Gershon of Wetherspoon's. 'The gang saw it as an easy touch, with the size of the pub and the money we are taking.'

Club owners persistently lobbied GMP to put officers on the doors of clubs, in the same way that football matches were policed for a fee. They got nowhere. The clubs were forced to accept the reality that often the only people who could run their doors with any authority were gangsters themselves. Who else could they employ? What non-criminal doorman could do anything against gunmen? Doorsafe, the scheme by which clubs could only employ doormen who had attended a short course and been given a green badge, did not apply to the men who *ran* the security firms; that side of the business was unregulated. In any case, even the chief inspector in charge of the Doorsafe scheme admitted, 'We don't look too closely [at backgrounds]. If we didn't allow people with previous convictions to be door staff, we wouldn't have any door staff in this city.'

Club bosses were talking in mid-1995 about a clear increase of gang-related intimidation over the previous eighteen months. 'It has escalated in the regularity of threats and people coming to the door saying that if they are not let in they will shoot you,' said one. 'A lot of it is face. They want to be seen to get in for nothing and get free drinks. You are also having a lot of kids trying it on. We know that certain individuals can control certain elements and so we have to use who they say on the door. You need to employ certain people who can talk to the nastier individuals.'

The experiences recounted by a doorman at one city centre club were typical. 'There was a well-known guy from the Gooch called Jonathan. He came to the club and I didn't know him and wouldn't let him in. He kicked off: "Do you know who you are talking to? Do you know who I am? I'll be back." You hear this all the time. Anyway, the next night a load of blacks came masked up, but just as they arrived, the police came on a routine visit. He still threatened the manager, spat in the head waiter's face and said, "You're dead." The manager resigned that night. The police had to get us out of town, escort the doormen out, because they were all tooled-up, guns and everything.

'It didn't put us off and we were back on the club the next weekend, though the adrenalin was going inside, you get like a twitch on your legs. He didn't come down and I thought it was forgotten. The following weekend, he did come back. There was a Scotsman fucking about inside the club and as we were pitching him out, Jonathan came up. We threw the Scotsman out and slammed the door in Jonathan's face without knowing. So he was banging on the door and saying, "You've fucking done it again, haven't you?" Anyway, he came in, bought a bit of champagne, then fucked off. I thought, *that's the end of him*. The following weekend he got the door slammed in his face again. He said, "I don't fucking believe this, I've never, ever been refused in a club and this is three fucking times now." He was laughing about it by now and started to get friendly with us. He said, "Nobody has ever done that to me before, you've got respect you lads." He used to buy us drinks in the end.'

The consequences for making the wrong decision could be severe. Two doormen were shot at the Brahms and Liszt club after refusing entry to a group of Moss Side men because they were wearing jeans and trainers. A black gang turned away at Paradise Factory returned and fired at the doormen, forcing them to run inside. A bouncer in the Gay Village who knocked back the wrong person was later visited by nine men who broke his nose and threw him in the canal; his fellow bouncers knew better than to intervene. A reprisal attack to someone's home was known as 'going on a mission' and it was not unusual to find various mobs of 'ballied-up' (balaclava-wearing) thugs cruising the darkened streets in the early hours looking for an address, ready to crash through the door and administer a punishment beating or worse.

Live music venues were as vulnerable as nightclubs. 'Someone tried to put a protection racket on my door,' said the manager of one. 'To say we got no help from the police was an understatement; I think they are as frightened as everyone else. But they closed all the illegal drinking dens and little clubs in Moss Side and drove those crowds into the mainstream. I locked myself in the office and spent about three hours in the afternoon waiting for the event to start, thinking, *do I go home now and never come back again?* We put crowd barriers outside so no-one could drive through the doors. As it happened, it was nice and easy. They came in and said, "It's an easy crowd, you don't need us to run the door." Others haven't been so lucky. A friend who is heavily involved in the club scene paid some of these people a small fortune to go on the door and they let in the very people he wanted them to stop.'

* * *

While the door wars rumbled on, the gang truce was under constant strain. The biggest threats came initially from shootings during taxing missions. In February 1995, nineteen-year-old Pierre 'Bishop' Webber was shot in the arm by two men demanding money as he returned from buying milk at a late-night garage, the first serious shooting on the Moss for months. Webber's first inclination was to seek revenge. 'Demons take over, bad omens around you,' he later told an interviewer. 'I chose rapping instead.' He became a founder member of the gangsta rap group Moss-Sidaz.

Another young man was shot in the arm and leg and relieved of his £3,000 car. Two fatal incidents followed. Eighteen-year-old Simon Caines was stabbed in the leg near his flat in Hulme; the knife severed a main artery and he bled to death. The attack involved the robbery of a hi-fi and a couple of rings and was carried out by a young Hulme mob with Doddington connections. In May 1995, Horace Elliott, who had several criminal convictions, called at a house in south Manchester demanding money. He was met by a reception committee with guns; they left him bleeding profusely in a heap in the hallway. Elliott lingered in hospital for six weeks before dying. Police officers said that he had connections with the Nell Lane Gang, a Gooch spin-off whose members had been re-housed on a Chorlton estate while Moss Side was re-developed.

In July 1995, one of the Cheetham Hill leaders called a national newspaper journalist to warn that the truce was breaking down. He said various 'elders' had maintained the peace by organising pay-offs for people to drop their grievances but things were slipping out of control. Further 'peace dances' had been held at the Hacienda, Sankey's Soap and Rockworld, and some senior heads had put £5,000 behind the bar at one venue to pay for everyone's drinks in an attempt to hold the ceasefire together.

* * *

Home reopened in December 1995 with new owners (a Sheffield-based leisure company) and a door team from Nottingham. 'Although the security company we are using is not Manchester-based, it is being used by a number of establishments within the area,' said a spokesman. 'It was brought in because of the problems and so far they have controlled the venues they are at. They have been passed before high-rated police officers, including the plain clothes and covert division, who are confident that not only does this firm know what it is doing, but the co-operation from both sides is one hundred per cent.' The new arrivals were greeted by a large graffiti message painted on the wall opposite the entrance, with a pair of crossed pistols and the words: 'WAR ZONE 8/12/95. LEAVE OR COMING TO GET YOU.'

The use of outside firms had been tried before, not always

with success. The Hacienda was one case in point. Another was the infamous Oasis concert at Maine Road, where security was handled by RockSteady, a large firm from Edinburgh specialising in music events. The concert was a terrifying shambles as every scally in the area turned out to prey on customers, bouncers, merchandise sellers and ticket touts alike. At Home the gangs seemed to lose interest; other clubs had become more attractive.

Holy City Zoo, a 500-capacity club in York Street owned by Allied Domecq, the parent company of brewers Tetleys, opened in the summer of 1995 and became extremely popular, especially for its Friday '2 Kinky' dance nights. Its bouncers were from a Bolton-based firm that supplied doormen to many Tetleys outlets in the city and helped to keep it trouble-free for a while, but soon the Friday nights were attracting the wrong sort of attention. In March 1996, a drunken Higher Broughton gangster ran amok in the club, urinating on the bar and assaulting customers. No-one dared stop him. The management closed the club down immediately. 'As the result of a minor incident inside the club last night, resulting in three customers being slightly injured, we have decided not to re-open until we have conducted a full review of our security arrangements,' they said in a statement issued the next day. 'It might be seen as a drastic action not to open but I would rather lose one night than risk there being any further bother,' added retail manager Mike Holt. 'If it had occurred at any other club it probably would have been brushed under the carpet but we are being very open.'

The doormen, who had lost their jobs, were especially unhappy. 'It really pissed me off,' said one. 'The gaffer at Tetleys apparently said after it that there was no way anyone from Manchester was going to run the door. The Hacienda had lost a lot of trade to Holy City Zoo and it had become the place to be but there had been bits of trouble and tension had been building up. Some of the young runners from Salford had been coming in. The management had to make the decision to close the club before something bad happened.'

The club re-opened with new video cameras and special access doors. Trouble was still expected, and all ten door staff were fitted with bullet-proof vests by the CID. One of them was an academic covertly carrying out work for a university study; he described what happened next: 'The second night the club had a visit from a very senior Salford gang leader who monopolised doors throughout the Manchester area. All the door team, except me, recognised him . . . When he arrived, one of the senior doormen hid behind the main door whilst nervously spying through the peek hole and firmly pronouncing that he was not going outside . . . The gang leader arrived with his driver and parked outside the club. His driver then told the head door person to get into the car so the gang leader could talk with him. The other bouncers waited for the news inside the club and held an emergency meeting about the situation.'[62] The club survived but would find that once a place has lost its cachet, it is almost impossible to regain it.

It was not only the most successful clubs that suffered. Utopia was a small dance venue in the basement of the Corn Exchange. 'I had sorted out the security for the club myself and made sure they weren't affiliated to any company,' said its ex-leaseholder, a clued-up young man who had occasionally worked as a doorman himself. 'I knew, or thought I knew, all about the gangs and didn't want any of them running my door.' Within a month, however, he had drawn the attention of the Salford crew. A security firm approached one of his doormen and 'made it clear that they were interested in doing the door.' He was given a couple of names they wanted him to employ, names he recognised as thugs. 'I wasn't prepared to have them on the door and went to the police and told them the club would be closed for the purpose of staff re-organisation. Then I had a phone call from a man who runs a security company in Manchester.' The man had strong connections with both Salford and Cheetham Hill. 'It was made known that if I didn't meet him he would go to my home address. I met him and sat in his car. He said he would give me one minute to decide whether or not to let him run the door. I asked him why. He said, "I want doors because doors give me power." I bought some more time and then decided to close down the club. It wasn't worth it. I had heard it said that Salford ran Manchester but I never realised how true that was until then.'

By the end of 1995, the security at many of Manchester's most popular clubs – the Hacienda, Discotheque Royale, the Academy, Sankey's Soap, Equinox, Central Park, Time, Isobar – was handled by doormen friendly with the Salford Lads. Their head doormen were often close mates with Salford, men like Damian Noonan, the hulking Hacienda door chief who habitually wore a massive gold chain around his huge neck. Noonan became almost as much of a Manchester landmark as the club itself; he once flattened Manchester United star Mark Hughes after mistaking as racist some harmless banter Hughes had directed at team-mate Paul Ince. 'The Hacienda has a good metal detector, very good cameras, and Damian, who has the respect of every psychopath in the city,' said one source. 'You want someone on the doors who the nutters respect, and he can deal with the wannabes, the young kids.' There is no doubt that such men did risk their lives on the doors; Noonan wore body armour even around his waist and groin to protect from knife attacks. The problem was who they worked for.

With similar friends on other club doors, the top Salford men could walk into most clubs in the city without paying. Few clubs would employ doormen without their say-so yet their names did not appear on any company records; in fact it was hard to pin down who was running many of the doormen. Shadowy companies with unusual names would appear and then disappear, folding before they were required to post accounts. The real bosses were far removed from the actual mechanics of running the business. It made little difference even when the Doorsafe scheme was amended under Home Office guidelines: doormen convicted of violence were to be denied their badge for five years, while drugs offences merited a three-year ban. The level of violence did appear to dip in the city at one stage but as Inspector Shaun Currie of the plainclothes division admitted, 'That may be because they have already carved up the city.'[63]

★ ★ ★

Against all the odds, the truce had held. The number of firearms incidents reported in the Moss Side area fell from 169 in 1994 to forty-one in 1995. The Pepperhill pub, bought for £10,000 by a church, was re-opened as the Saltshaker, a teetotal café, drop-in centre and youth club. A film crew moved onto the Alexandra Park estate to show how marvellous it was and a football team, Moss Amateur Reserves, was widely described as the 'peace team' for apparently having players from both the Doddington and the Gooch. While not true – most its players were identified with the west side of the estate – it did show how things had changed: four years earlier some of its players would not have been able to walk out onto a public pitch without fearing an assassin's bullet. 'It's got nothing to do with gang members,' said one player, Tiny Smith, 'and if there were gang members involved then they weren't coming with the attitude that they were gang members. It was all about football and enjoying ourselves 'cos we had nothing else to do. I preferred that they were playing football than gun-toting, drug-selling or whatever. All of us have most probably got something to do with crime 'cos there's nothing here for us anyway.'[64] They were good, winning a league and cup double in their first season despite the loss of goalkeeper Errol Jones on a murder charge.

The greatest symbolic moment came on 11 December 1995: Gooch Close ceased to exist. Remodelled and rebuilt, it was renamed Westerling Way. The altered layout did away with the maze of walkways and had bollards halfway down the road to stop drive-bys. 'The people who caused the trouble aren't here any longer,' said a new resident, 'and soon people will forget all about the Gooch.'[65]

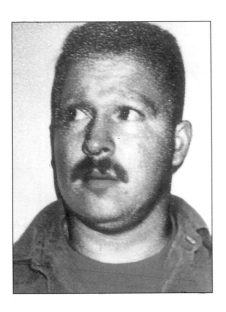

Chris Little (left) ruled the Stockport underworld with an iron hand. One man who crossed him was thrown from a motorway bridge; another was allegedly "crucified". It was inevitable that he would meet a bloody end, gunned down at the wheel of his Mercedes.

Paul Corkovic was perhaps Salford's most prolific and dangerous armed robber, whose gang were responsible for a spate of raids on supermarkets and Securicor guards. He was eventually jailed for twenty-three years.

Moss Amateur Reserves were hailed as the 'peace team' during the truce. They were also the most-shot football team in history: several players had suffered bullet wounds and had lost or would lose close relatives, including Howard Swarray (back row, sixth from left), who brother Chris would be murdered, Adrian Stapleton (front row, second from left), whose cousin Carl was killed, and Jason Bennett (front, fourth from left), whose brother Martin was shot dead.

Errol "EJ" Jones, a leading figure in the Young Gooch, was convicted of the murder of Evon Berry in Bristol during the truce and was jailed for life.

A member of the Doddington is arrested after Operation Balboa, which smashed a street drug market the gang ran on the east side of the Alexandra Park estate.

The funeral of Nicholas 'Sailor' Murphy, the first young man to be killed as the truce began to collapse in South Manchester. Soon the Doddington Gang would be torn apart by civil war.

Researchers on the Ordsall estate in Salford found that a gang was trying to replace the police as the voice of authority in the area. Anyone who co-operated with the law risked being targeted as a "grass". Ken Keating (above) even took to driving around the streets in his "Grasswatch" van to deter potential informers.

Canal Street (above) led the resurgence of the city centre enclave that became known as the Gay Village and was at the forefront of attempts to create a "twenty-four hour city". Soon, however, its pubs and clubs came under assault from organised gangs and protection racketeers.

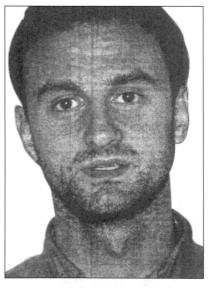

Paul Massey, once labelled "Mr Big", was jailed for ten years in 1999 for stabbing a man outside a Manchester nightclub while out being filmed for a BBC documentary.

Massey predicted that Salford would "explode" if he was jailed and so it proved: within a short space of time Stephen Lydiate (above) had been shot eight times, only to then launch a revenge plot of "Biblical proportions".

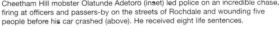

Cheetham Hill mobster Olatunde Adetoro (inset) led police on an incredible chase, firing at officers and passers-by on the streets of Rochdale and wounding five people before his car crashed (above). He received eight life sentences.

The police surprised a conclave of the Gooch Gang in this house in Moss Side and several members were later jailed. Among the hardware seized were scanners, body armour, night-vision binoculars and this Skorpion machine pistol, which fires at a rate of 800 rounds per minute.

Martin Bennett, aged 25, shot in Moss Side in 1999.

Chris Swarray, 27, shot in Birmingham in 1999.

By the late 1990s, four gangs were operating in the Moss Side and Longsight areas, locked in a series of increasingly deadly rivalries.

They also had greater access to ever-more powerful weaponry, including MAC-10 machine guns, many of them supplied by a crooked gunsmith from southern England.

The rate of killings saw a dramatic rise, including a number of innocent victims who, for whatever reason, fell foul of the gangs.

The young men pictured here were just some of those who died between 1997 and 2002.

Simon Brown, 27, shot in Cheetham Hill in 1999.

Clifton "Junior" Bryan, 29, shot in Leeds in 2000

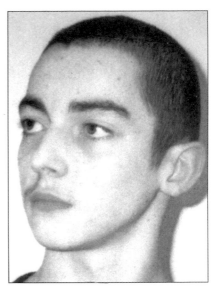

Thomas Ramsey, 16, shot in Levenshulme in 2000.

George Lynch, 36, shot in Longsight in 2001.

Aeon Shirley, 18, shot in Longsight in 2002

Tommy Pitt (top left) formed the Pitt Bull Crew in memory of his dead brother Ray and became the most feared man on the streets of south Manchester. He waged war on both his former Doddington associates and on the Longsight Crew, led by the wheelchair-bound Julian Bell (top right).

Patsy McKie with a photograph of her son Dorrie, who was shot dead in Hulme in 1999. Mrs McKie became a founder and chairman of Mothers Against Violence, campaigning to stop the gang culture and prevent further bloodshed.

CHAPTER THIRTEEN

The Mr Fairly Bigs

AT THE TIME the gang truce was being brokered, the District Auditor was putting the finishing touches to a report on Greater Manchester Police. He had found some serious flaws. He was particularly critical of the force for arresting numerous small drug suppliers but failing to target those higher up the chain. GMP drugs squad was too small to cope and its officers were reluctant to move from the city to tackle jobs in outlying towns such as Oldham. 'There has been an emphasis on quantity of arrests rather than quality of arrests, such as major traffickers,' concluded the Auditor.

The notion of an autocratic Mr Big is an enduring one with the Press and public, but the entrepreneurial nature of modern crime makes it less and less likely. The richest criminals are the major drug importers but they are not necessarily the most powerful: they might have links with international cartels but that doesn't mean they control housing estates or can call on armies of doormen. Neither Salford nor Manchester had a single criminal overlord; the men who brokered the truce were clearly highly influential but were 'first among equals' rather than dominant figures to whom everyone else deferred. 'Nobody can throw themselves over as Mister Big,' said Paul Doyle, himself an authoritative underworld figure. 'There's a lot of kids with a lot of respect, but a Mister Big, no. Any nineteen-year-old can carry a gun, so any Mister Big can be taken out. There are at least sixty or seventy people that I would carry a lot of respect for: about thirty in Salford and all the rest around Manchester.'

For many years GMP had believed that the city was run not by an autocracy but by an oligarchy, the Quality Street Gang.

Occasionally they uncovered high-end illegal activity that gave some credence to this view. On October 1994, a fifteen-month investigation concluded with the seizure of guns, drugs and cash at several homes around Greater Manchester, and waste dealer Arthur Donnelly was charged with others with conspiracy to supply drugs. Donnelly was the brother of the more well-known Jimmy the Weed; his sons Anthony and Chris had been original rave organisers and had set up a briefly successful clothes label, Gio Goi. Arthur senior, who operated out of a yard in Ancoats, had been trapped selling Turkish heroin in bulk to an undercover detective for £10,000; his partner Michael Carpenter sat in on one of the deals and threatened to use a pump-action shotgun if the buyer was a policeman. Donnelly admitted three offences of supply and was jailed for eight years. Convictions such as Donnelly's appeared to lend some weight to the QSG myth, but they were rare.

The drug trade comprises three interlocking levels, with importers at the top, middle-tier distributors in the middle, and street level or marketplace dealers at the bottom. It equates neatly to the capitalist economic system of manufacturers/importers, wholesalers and retailers, though the lines are sometimes blurred. 'There is a considerable degree of interaction between the suggested stratas of dealing, in that it is not unknown for dealers selling in market places to visit other European states and bring back supplies for their own distribution, cutting out the middlemen,' said David Brennan, the drugs squad officer who had revealed Manchester's particular gang problem to his ACPO colleagues. 'The apex of the triangle is also a little misleading in that it suggests perhaps the existence of a single Mister Big. In fact there may be a number of Mister Fairly Bigs operating in any city; and their fortunes or status may also be in a continual state of flux depending on circumstances.' The Auditor believed that the police had concentrated on street markets in places like Moss Side to the detriment of the middle-tier: the men referred to by Brennan as Mister Fairly Bigs and by the National Criminal Intelligence Service as 'core nominals'.

The Auditor did not address the very top tier, as these were mainly a concern for HM Customs and Excise, not the police. One of the most important drug barons was said by police to be a man who originated in the Rochdale area. He was involved in the jewellery and motor trades as well as protection and strong-arm work, allegedly for the QSG. He became involved in drugs in the eighties but police interest, particularly after the gruesome unsolved murder of a garage mechanic, caused him to flee to Holland 'and then to Spain, where he ran a highly successful drugs business,' according to the *Manchester Evening News*.

Police believe that one nightmarish example of his power involved Graham Boardman, the ferocious bouncer who had stood up to the Salford Firm in the pub door wars. Boardman moved into cannabis importation and agreed to buy part of a large shipment from the man. He collected the drugs but then failed to pay for them, ripping off the main man to the tune of several hundred thousand pounds. This brought dire threats of retribution, which Boardman ignored. Some months later he was lured to Spain on the promise of another lucrative drug deal and has not been seen since. It is believed that he was tortured to death over several days before his body was disposed of, probably in the Mediterranean.

In the mid-nineties, the Rochdale man relocated to the Irish Republic but soon came to the attention of the gardai and the IRA, which secretly supported anti-drug vigilantes in the Republic. Eventually Ireland's Criminal Assets Bureau, which has draconian powers to seize illegal gains, came after him and he skipped, leaving CAB to seize property and jewellery worth £100,000. His name still crops up regularly in intelligence circles. Many of his contacts remain in Rochdale, which despite its poverty is a major source of drug importation, particularly cannabis. In one case, the National Crime Squad tracked six shipments of cannabis worth £7 million coming in lorries from Spain across France and through the Channel Tunnel. Gang boss David Statham, who used a Rochdale snooker hall as his base, was jailed for nine years after admitting conspiracy to supply drugs.

Another even bigger source of supply – again with Rochdale

links – was the network presided over by the enterprising Liverpudlian Curtis Warren, said to be Britain's biggest drugs baron and labelled 'target one' by Customs and Excise. Warren rose from petty crime in Toxteth to pole position among indigenous UK importers, mainly by cutting out the middlemen and dealing directly with the sources of supply: the Turks for heroin, the Moroccans for hash, the Colombians for cocaine and the Dutch for Ecstasy. He relocated to Holland in the mid-nineties and upped his activities, aided and abetted by several men from the Greater Manchester area, in particular Stephen Mee, a burly life-long criminal with links to the Moss Side gangs. Mee already had a twenty-two-year jail sentence hanging over him, imposed in his absence – for importing Colombian cocaine and cannabis – after he was sprung from a prison bus on the M62 motorway by a black gang. Mee fled to Holland and became Warren's emissary to the Colombian cocaine barons, spending time in South America to broker a huge cocaine importation. Warren's gang was caught bringing in 400 kilos of ninety per cent pure cocaine hidden in lead ingots. Mee denied the charge but was jailed for seven years, before being deported to face the sentence he had skipped from. Yet another Rochdale man, Stephen Whitehead, was also jailed for seven years.

Warren had been a main target for an enormous police-Customs joint operation codenamed Crayfish, aimed at the main Liverpool-based drug importers. The Scousers were seen as a Customs priority in the north-west because they were so active in drugs. It meant, however, that for a long time Manchester did not receive the same Customs attention as Crayfish sucked up time and manpower. When asked in the year 2000 if there was an equivalent to Curtis Warren in Manchester, a senior Customs investigator admitted, 'We don't know because, to be honest, no-one has looked.'

* * *

One man Customs thought might fit the bill was a former Cheetham Hill robber who had gone on to amass millions of pounds in foreign bank accounts, bought property including coffee shops in Amsterdam, owned a palatial spread in Jamaica and drove a Ferrari. While south Manchester was torn apart by gang warfare, the lads north of the Mancunian Way had been getting on with business. Some had moved into door security and some specialised in taxing, levying a charge on the dealers in certain pubs and clubs, while others were still active armed robbers. Some had even gone legit.

This particular individual moved into drug importation with a close partner who had been prominent in the war with Moss Side. 'They do their own little thing in Cheetham Hill,' said a drugs squad officer. 'They have got a lot of respect and try not to use violence as a tool. They are businessmen in what they do, and that is drugs.' He forged links with other cities, notably Nottingham – where he dealt with a key figure in the main black gang, the Meadows Posse – Liverpool and London. He was also believed to work with the Turks, a group law enforcement had found it very hard to penetrate in Manchester (Turkish and Kurdish gangs control the majority of heroin supply into the UK, though Greater Manchester has a disproportionately high Asian influence). Customs marked him down as a priority target and closed in on him in an operation he was believed to be financing involving the smuggling of cannabis resin in a lorry load of onions from southern Spain. Yet though the gang was smashed and several men were jailed, the Cheetham Hill man was not convicted. At the time of writing, some Customs officers believed he had made his money and had effectively moved out of reach.

A more successful interdiction came against another international smuggling gang with Cheetham links, in an operation that showed the global scale of modern drug supply and the methods used to launder the vast sums generated. United States Customs in Atlanta developed a key undercover operative working as a money broker in Colombia, who was directly linking into the major cartels. One of his clients was a Colombian woman in her fifties called Gloria Valez, who used his services to launder payments from drug clients in the States into Colombia. She made it known that she wanted similar facilities in other countries, including the UK, so US Customs approached their UK counterparts, who set up their own 'sting' with an undercover officer called 'Ray'. His mobile phone number was passed on to the Colombians.

Ray was eventually called by Donovan Hardy, who ran a mobile phone shop in north Manchester. Hardy was buying Colombian cocaine and needed a 'safe' method of paying for it. Because Ray had been introduced by the Colombians, he had bags of credibility. Hardy met him several times and handed over £300,0000 in cash for transmission to America. This was to be laundered and sent back to Colombia in a notorious process known as the black market peso exchange, which saw an estimated $5 billion laundered every year. Hardy had access to a number of bank accounts in the Cayman Islands and he and another conspirator, Delroy Bailey, flew to the Caribbean and set up a company called Sovereign Shipbuilders. It appeared never to buy or build a single ship but large amounts of money went through its accounts and around £500,000 was transferred either to Colombia or Panama. Cocaine was then shipped from South America to Holland for the gang to collect.

A couple of couriers were picked up bringing cocaine into the country and received lengthy jail terms, but the conspiracy continued and in February and March 1998 several of the Manchester traffickers were observed making regular trips to Amsterdam and Rotterdam. A consignment of ninety kilos arrived in Holland in early April 1998 and was picked up in three bulging holdalls from a Dutch go-between and secreted in a small Rotterdam hotel, to be broken down into smaller quantities for onward transfer to the UK. Dutch Police, acting on behalf of UK Customs, raided the hotel and found the cocaine hidden in a ceiling space above a shower in one of the rooms. Cocaine worth £10 million was recovered and five men were arrested and charged.

Hardy was the only one arrested who had a legitimate income. Though his phone shop officially traded at a loss, he owned a black Porsche, a Honda Fireblade motorcycle and was in the throes of buying a £75,000 RIB fast speedboat from a boatbuilders' on the south coast: 'We couldn't have kept up with that,' admits a Customs officer. Two other gang members, both unemployed, drove a Mercedes sports and a Saab convertible respectively. Hardy was jailed for twenty-five years, two other men for twenty years and Donovan Bailey for fourteen years. Gloria Valez, the Colombian woman, has never been arrested because of extradition problems with Colombia.

Though sentences climbed during the nineties as the courts attempted to hit the smugglers hard, the money to be made was so enormous that others were always tempted. A Wythenshawe-based gang who smuggled Ecstasy from Amsterdam in cars with a hidden compartment in the petrol tank were said to have shipped in drugs worth £5 million in a few months. The ringleader was jailed for twenty years. Cannabis was slightly less lucrative but carried lower jail terms and so less risk. A Salford builder named Mark Warren, who made £430,000 from cannabis trafficking, was jailed for just six years at Stoke. He had been stopped in his BMW when returning from a smuggling trip to Spain and was convicted of possessing drugs with intent to supply. His defence claimed he was merely a courier but the judge declared that Warren had been dealing in drugs on 'a professional and massive scale.' Subsequent investigations had revealed that Warren, of Ash Street, had used money from drugs to finance the purchase of numerous houses, and had been involved in trafficking for at least six years. A confiscation order of over £200,000 was imposed on him.

There would always be others; it was no longer difficult to become a drug smuggler. 'I think the scene now is very flexible, it changes very quickly and it's market-orientated as opposed to being territorial,' said Professor Dick Hobbs, a respected criminologist at Durham University who has studied organised crime. 'You and I could empty out our pockets now, see what we've got, fly over to Amsterdam and be international drug dealers. It's as simple as that. You don't need a background, you don't need some apprenticeship, you don't need to be part of a criminal firm. Anyone really can be at it and involved in this. It's a very democratic, open economy.' A detective inspector puts it more pithily: 'Today's shithead from a council estate could be tomorrow's importer. The ladder can be climbed very quickly.'

* * *

Drugs were, of course, only one staple of the Manchester gangs. 'If you are looking for the most skilled armed robbers in the UK, the school of excellence is Salford,' said one detective. At any one time the city had up to half a dozen active robbery gangs. Perhaps the most prolific was run by one of the original Salford Lads. Paava 'Paul' Corkovic, of Croatian descent, was released from a long stretch in prison in October 1994 and apparently decided he wanted to make a million pounds, the best way he knew how. He put together a crew from young members of the firm, most of them ten years his junior, like Lee 'Tabo' Taberer, Tony Erdman and 'Ando' Anderson. 'A lot of guys who come out after a long stretch start knocking around with younger lads,' said a Salford gangster. 'It's because, in their heads, they are still the same age as they were when they went in.' The gang rented a unit on the Irlam industrial estate to use as a base and equipped themselves with sawn-off shotguns, baseball bats, sledgehammers, machetes – and a formidable Kalashnikov AK47 assault rifle. Within a month Corkovic was leading them on an unrestrained robbery spree.

They first struck at a cash-and-carry, then at a Morrisons supermarket. Next, four of the gang hit the Stanley Albion Casino in Pendleton, the heart of their territory, in a daylight raid. They threatened a Securicor guard as he went inside to collect cash, bundled him to the cash office and smashed its security screen, fired a shot into the ceiling to terrify the forty customers and snatched £100,000 in cash bags and boxes before leaving in a stolen car. This was abandoned half a mile away and they sprinted across a busy main road to a second getaway car. One of the gang was seen holding a cash box out of the window with red security smoke pouring from it. Even the police credited the organisation of the group. 'A tremendous amount of planning went into this crime,' said one officer. 'They are obviously a professional team.' Securicor put a £5,000 price on their heads.

A raid the following month at a Sainsbury's superstore, again right on their doorstep, didn't go quite so smoothly. They ambushed another Securicor vehicle coming to collect takings late on a Saturday afternoon, one of the busiest periods, brandishing guns and a sledgehammer. Two of the guards ran into a warehouse and hid in a canteen, while the gang took a female member of staff at gunpoint and demanded she take them to the cashier's office. They could not get through its locked steel doors, even forcing 200 shoppers to lie down as they tried in vain to open them. As frightened shoppers began to run from the store, they fled in a stolen Rover, one of them loosing off his shotgun as a warning, but their car crashed into another vehicle at a mini-roundabout and they were forced to run. A passing traffic officer gave chase and saw one of them caught by his trousers while trying to climb some fencing. The officer bravely grabbed and handcuffed Lee Anderson.

Despite the close escape, Corkovic refused to let up. Even other criminals considered him cavalier and many gave him a wide berth. Other raids followed at banks, stores and a B&Q hypermarket. Their attack at a Safeways in Swinton, in which their car was rammed by a guard, was the sixth raid on Securicor in five months. What Corkovic didn't know was that both he and his Irlam lock-up were under intense surveillance, and the police were just waiting for a chance to get the gang together in one place before they moved in.

In April 1995, flak-jacketed officers acting on the special authorisation of the Chief Constable fired CS gas and a stun grenade during a dramatic raid on the lock-up. Three men and a woman were arrested at gunpoint. Inside the lock-up were loaded guns, gloves, masks, handcuffs and a Land Rover equipped with a battering ram. Corkovic managed to escape in a car but was picked up at a later date. At his first trial the jury could not reach a verdict. A second followed, at which a crucial piece of evidence unavailable at the first trial was introduced: a photograph found taken at Corkovic's house showing him and another of the gang counting wads of notes. Corkovic had argued that the picture had been taken before the robberies started and the money was his, but a smart detective enhanced the photo to show a wedding band on Corkovic's finger – and he had been married after the robberies began.

Corkovic, aged thirty-three, was convicted and jailed for twenty-three years. 'You used meticulous planning and timing to steal hundreds of thousands of pounds which has not been recovered,' the judge told him. 'Firearms were discharged on a number of occasions and one man was forced to kneel down with the barrel of a loaded shotgun pressed to his neck, followed by a demand of, "Give us cash or we will kill him." Your weapon was terror inflicted on guards, bank staff and the public.' Jason McFeely was jailed for twenty-three years and Lee Taberer, Antony Erdman, James Neale and Lee Anderson for fifteen.

Another robbery gang equally as frightening as Corkovic's was led by David Adetoro, one of the family of Cheetham Hill brothers who had been close to White Tony Johnson. Adetoro had been jailed for eight years in the early nineties and was allowed out on parole as he neared the end of his sentence. With his brother Ade and a tight-knit cell of former schoolmates, he launched a ferocious robbery campaign, planning and executing fourteen 'jobs' in two years. Expert car thief Gary Pollitt stole the high-powered vehicles they needed, while the hold-up men included Gary Shearer, who had served time for manslaughter at the Leeds carnival several years earlier. The gang always carried loaded guns and seemed to like firing them, including at police. A safe-house in south Manchester was used to hide their heavy-duty weaponry and ammo.

Their rampage began in June 1995, while David Adetoro was still inside, with a raid on a bank in Stockport. One particularly dramatic assault on a Morrisons supermarket in December 1996 was caught on film: the gang dragged a store security man around the aisles while firing shots to terrify cowering shoppers. In their final robbery, they went for a wages delivery in Bredbury, Stockport. Fifty-eight-year-old Derek Monks, a worker on an adjacent industrial estate, heard a shot and saw a security guard being attacked, so he drove his sixteen-ton cement mixer into the getaway car. One of the gang fired through his cab window and

Monks was hit in the neck. He survived but had to have part of his jaw removed. A week later the police, who had been bugging one of their houses, arrested the five men. In June 1998, David Adetoro was jailed for twenty-six years and his brother Ade for fifteen. Little of the money they stole was recovered.

Corkovic and the Adetoros were capricious and trigger-happy. A more considered outfit was the combined Salford-Liverpool team known as the Battering Ram Gang, who welded a twelve-foot-long, retractable steel girder with a spike on one end to the back of a flatbed truck. This they would drive through walls or into the sides of security vans, opening them up like tin cans. Their best score was a whopping £770,000 from an Armaguard depot in Mode Wheel Road, Salford; this was followed up with a £435,000 robbery in Kent. Police eventually located their lock-up in Salford and kept watch. The gang members were finally caught but only after an abortive raid in Dorset during which they hi-jacked a police car at gunpoint prior to escaping. Seven of the gang were jailed for a total of ninety-five years.

The Battering Ram Gang pulled off some highly lucrative raids and at one time had every vault in Britain on high alert, but the biggest job of all happened right under the noses of the Salford Lads. In July 1995, a highly professional armed gang hijacked a security van at the Midland Bank district service centre in Ordsall and made off with £6.6 million in cash and cheques, in what was believed to be Europe's biggest-ever cash robbery up to that time. The local young crime gangs could only look on with envy; the raid was believed to have been masterminded by London villains who recruited help from Manchester friends with QSG connections. None of the organisers has been brought to justice, despite an enormous reward and a police operation costing millions of pounds and throwing up leads in Spain, Holland, Russia, Poland and Israel. Police believed some of the money may simply have been buried, to be dug up when it was safe to spend.

* * *

Another reason for the lack of a single Mr Big was the highly diffuse nature of organised crime. By the early 1990s it encompassed a vast range of lucrative activities, many of which had not been available twenty or thirty years earlier. Bootlegging, for example, was the fastest-growing criminal activity, and by the mid to late nineties there was not a housing estate in Britain where someone was not selling bootlegged cigarettes and booze bought in France or Belgium. Many people cashed in, not just hardened villains. Men like Barry Roycoft brought bin bags full of cigarettes from France and Belgium and sold them in pubs around Salford and Manchester, sometimes with the connivance of licensees. Roycroft was soon taking holidays to the Caribbean and America and running three family cars, including a Jaguar XJS, even though he received only £120 a week in sickness benefits. It was estimated that he had avoided over £500,000 in duty when he was jailed for two years – and his case was a drop in the ocean.

Computer theft was another crime of its time. One Salford gang based in the Charlestown area carried out more than 200 raids in less than a year, ransacking schools, offices, Salford University and the businesses at Salford Quays, where one premises was 'screwed' fifteen times. The burglars went for high-value computers, often to order, and were quickly paid off in cash after each raid by their main handler. They effectively ruled the street where they were based, so neighbours would not interfere, and their getaway vehicles were often driven ablaze into the River Irwell. The perpetual burglaries became so bad that two out of three business managers interviewed in one survey said they would like to pull out of the city.[66]

Vehicle crime in Manchester was beyond epidemic levels; by the early nineties the city was the car theft capital of Britain – and Britain had the highest rate of car theft in the world. Organised gangs stole vehicles to order or dismantled them for spare parts sold at garages and scrapyards. Four-wheel drives were exported to the Gulf States and Pakistan, where they were especially popular. Counterfeit goods were another Manchester speciality, with rip-offs of popular clothes labels, perfumes, watches. Money was laundered in myriad ways: through house purchases, bars, car pitches, gyms, sunbed studios, insolvency practitioners. The number of disclosures of irregular or suspicious cash transactions rose nationally from 600 in 1987 to 15,000 in 1994 as funny money flooded through the banking system. A 1995 report by Cambridge Econometrics, an economic forecasting group to which European research institutes contributed, said the very future of the city and the growth of its small businesses was being hindered by organised crime and the black economy. Drugs, robbery, bootleg fags and beer, fraud, stolen cars, computers, snide clothes and perfume, car-theft, computer-theft, porn: there was nothing the criminal fraternity would not turn its hand to, and the size of the city and the extent of its black economy made it impossible for any one person or group to control. Gangland is a swirling, shifting morass, with partnerships forged and broken and individuals rising and falling with equal despatch.

The influential Paul Massey, who had been labelled a 'Mr Big' during a Salford Council session, questioned why anybody would want the tag.

I don't want to be me. They want to be me, right, and be Mr Whoever, but I don't want to be that Mr Whoever. I don't want to be known as anybody; I'm no better than the next man . . . Why they want to be me, I don't know, because I'll tell you summat, if any of them was me, if I did get shot or I did go to prison for a long time, and they did end up sitting in my chair, keeping it warm, they couldn't handle the pressure. They couldn't handle the phone ringing every morning, knock on the door every morning, seven days a week, the missus putting up with it . . . just to be in my chair, the pressure of controlling everything, is not worth being sat in. I'd rather be somewhere else.

I wish I could just say to them, 'Well, you sit here and I'll go and get down the road and get on with what I'm doing.' But you can't, you don't, because there's nobody around at the moment to do that. Because the people that are around, they're game with guns and game for a battle, don't get me wrong, but that isn't the person you want sat in the seat. You need someone with a lot of respect, a lot of influence and knows how to control violence.

There were places, however, where the story was different. In the smaller towns around Manchester, a person could, with the right associates, control at least the most lucrative rackets. Many of the outlying towns in the sprawling Greater Manchester conurbation had their own 'heads', men like Billy Webb, who held a virtual monopoly of heroin supply in Bolton,[67] or the Pownall brothers, Wigan's main drug dealers. Yet perhaps only one displayed the desire to 'run' his town, to take as much of the pie as he could, to put himself up as a Mister Big.

CHAPTER FOURTEEN

Chris Little

CHRIS LITTLE LOOMED over Stockport like a storm cloud. Few men in recent history have so successfully cowed local people or displayed such arrogance. Little burned down public buildings to show his power, organised marches to antagonise the police, intimidated magistrates, journalists and crime witnesses, and publicly brutalised those who crossed him. It was inevitable that he would meet a bloody end, gunned down at the wheel of his £50,000 Mercedes.

Stockport does not seem a natural home to violent gangsterism. The official website of Stockport Metropolitan Borough Council eulogises the city as 'aspirational, accessible, diverse and friendly' and much of its population of around 300,000 dwells in leafy middle-class commuter belts, giving it the feel of a giant suburb rather than a disparate metropolis. Yet this large, bland conurbation also encompasses some tough estates. It does not have the Manchester or Salford tradition of ferocious street gangs but has always had its hard men.

Little was perhaps the most ambitious. Born in July 1963, he apparently began his criminal career when he organised the sale of drugs at his secondary school. His natural pugnacity drew him to boxing, first as teenage amateur at the Levenshulme club in Manchester, then as a professional under veteran manager Jack Trickett. His pro record was unimpressive – two wins and five defeats – although he did take Sheffield's Johnny Nelson the six-round distance to lose on points; Nelson went on to become a British and European cruiserweight champion and won several fringe 'world' titles. Little's final contest was a one-round stoppage loss in December 1988. 'He had plenty of heart, plenty of will to win,' said Trickett, 'but never the ability to learn the skill.' Little fought like a streetfighter; he marched forward throwing leather but took plenty in return. Too limited to bring success in the ring, his power earned him a growing reputation on the streets of Stockport. He grew into a six-foot two-inch bulldozer of brute power and energy. To the police he was a 'big gob' who shouted all the time and was highly-strung. 'He was always agitated and irritable,' said a former detective. 'If he was sitting down, he couldn't keep still.'[68]

Little turned his energies to organising pub and club doormen in and around Stockport and soon had around fifty men working for him. He was also prepared to venture into Manchester itself when the occasion demanded. In 1991, his younger brother Nicholas was roughed up and thrown out at an incident in Liberty's nightclub in Sale in 1991 for chucking drinks off a balcony. Little pulled eleven of his henchmen together and they set off in a car and a van to seek revenge. They burst into Liberty's wielding coshes and clubs, and hit one of the doormen on the head with a garden-edging spade 'waved about like a sabre in a cavalry charge,' according to a Crown prosecutor. Two other doormen were attacked inside the club. The gang made off but were seen leaving by a police patrol, who radioed for reinforcements. A roadblock was set up and they were stopped as they made their way back into Stockport and twelve men were subsequently accused of violent disorder. Little, then twenty-seven, of Marsland Terrace, was held on remand and was later jailed for eighteen months. 'The violence was such that Liberty's head doorman, a giant of a man, ran away in fear,' Manchester Crown Court heard. His henchmen received a variety of lesser jail terms or suspended sentences.

Inside, he built up prison muscles and brooded. Little left prison in the spring of 1993, returning to his modest house in Marsland Terrace, with its home-made gym at the back and a cage for his bull terrier and mastiffs. To celebrate – and to show the police his power had not waned – he staged a homecoming 'parade' on a Sunday morning in the Stockport suburb of Offerton. Two hundred friends, family and followers gathered and, fearing trouble, a large contingent of police turned out. A chief inspector approached Little and asked for the crowd to disperse.

'Just shake my hand and the lads will go quietly,' said Little.

'No chance,' replied the officer.

At that moment, a superintendent who was new to the area walked over, pointed at Little and told him to clear off. To his horror, Little grabbed his hand and shook it – then turned and gave the thumbs-up to his pals. 'The superintendent was horrified,' a fellow officer told the *Stockport Express Advertiser*. 'But you really couldn't tell that was going to happen. He didn't stand a chance.'

Little had a sadistic streak; those who crossed him could expect a beating or an attack by his fighting dogs; one man was forced to wear shorts to show off the scars left by their teeth. Paul Healey was thrown from Brinnington bridge onto the M63 when Little and his gang mistook him for another man. He was in a coma for ten weeks following a nine-and-a-half-hour operation to rebuild his face with metal plates and repair his smashed skull and broken bones. Little apologised for shattering his twenty-six-year-old victim's life by buying him a pint of lager. Another was thrown from the fifth floor of a block of flats. Gossip had it that he even 'crucified' one man, hammering nails into his hands and firing a crossbow bolt through his thigh. It may have been myth but it added to the ferocious public image.

His most infamous punishment beating was recorded for posterity. Little had heard that Chris Jones, a self-proclaimed local joker, had insulted him while drinking at a snooker club, and sent two heavies to bring Jones to his house in Marsland Terrace. They went into the backyard and Little asked Jones to choose between fighting his bull terriers or taking part in a boxing match. Jones chose boxing. 'Wrong choice,' said Little. Jones was given heavy sparring gloves while Little put on smaller boxing gloves. His minions filmed what followed. With his first punch, Little knocked the smaller man across the garden. His bull terrier and mastiffs went berserk in their cages as more blows thudded into Jones's body.

'Do you respect me,' demanded Little.

'Hang on,' replied Jones, even now unable to resist a joke, 'let me think about it.'

Little erupted, smashing Jones's head repeatedly into a metal fence and then punching him solidly in the kidneys as he cowered. Finally Little's men took Jones to hospital, where he discharged himself after treatment. Little gave him £10 the next day for 'a drink'. The video was taken around pubs to show people what would happen if they crossed the crime boss.

Little also derided the local police. Once he walked into a nightclub, punched his fists through the cigarette machine, turned to the watching crowd of people and screamed, 'I'm looking for a copper to beat the shit out of.' On another occasion, he went to see one of his acolytes at Stockport Magistrates Court and sat in the gallery in front of two detectives. Looking over his shoulder, he stared at the officers and he said loudly, 'What the fuck are you looking at?' The magistrates did nothing. He would phone Stockport police station, jeering at officers and challenging them to 'prove it' when they asked him about his crimes. So when an officer bluntly informed Little that they ran the city, not him, he saw it as an open challenge.

In April 1994, Little took a holiday on the Canary Islands. It was the perfect cover. In his absence, several of his lieutenants gathered a group of young on school playing fields in Offerton to issue their instructions. Darren Durr, aged twenty-three, specified the targets. Daniel McHugh, twenty-eight, and teenager Michael Murphy warned what would happen if they didn't co-operate; 'Little will go off his head,' said McHugh. With the briefing over, a flat was then used to assemble a collection of firebombs, orchestrated by Durr and McHugh. Their aim was a synchronised series of arson attacks in several areas of the city: thirteen targets had been selected. Little had also left instructions for riots to be started in Offerton, Reddish and Brinnington. He was going to show the police who was boss. On an April night in 1994, the gang set to work. In the space of an hour, eight schools, three shops, and cars in two streets were petrol-bombed. The air filled with the sound of sirens as fire engines and police vehicles roared in from all over the area. The planned riots failed to happen but the cost of damage was still estimated at £750,000.

Little put £15,000 into the Brookfield pub and used proxies to apply for a licence, but the licensing magistrates rejected the application. Little had a copy of the Magistrates' Handbook stolen from the Stockport courthouse hoping to use blackmail to get his way and some of the magistrates whose names and addresses were in the book received threatening phone calls. 'I wasn't desperately worried,' recalled one senior female magistrate. 'It was just typical of that type of mentality. I'm dealing with people [like that] in the dock. They're mostly pathetic, bless them.' Little brazenly told a senior police officer that the book would be handed over if no objection was raised to the licence, but he was caught in a police trap and charged with attempting to pervert the course of justice. Although police did object, a licence was granted, though later the pub was gutted by fire.

He also attempted to lean on the local weekly newspaper, the *Stockport Express*, which had refused to print a story about his 'charitable' donation to Brinnington Boxing Club. Little called the journalist concerned and made threats. Then he put one of his goons on the phone. 'I'll break your fucking legs for you,' said the voice. It was typical of his bullying style. 'I've been threatened in the job before but, because of his reputation, it was unnerving,' said the reporter, who was married with a son. 'Later I felt angry. Who does he think he is? He's ruining lives.' Police had by now compiled a considerable intelligence file on Little, but had great difficulty in finding anyone who would make a complaint against him.

* * *

Little was making other enemies. Despite the attack on the Liberty's bouncers, he knew enough to stay on his own patch. 'Chris wasn't interested in anything outside Stockport,' said one of his closest henchmen. 'There were a few Cheetham Hill moved in when Chris was in prison so when he came out he fucked them off. He pulled three hundred and fifty lads out.'

When a Wythenshawe gangster tried to move in on his territory, Little went after him with a gun. He regarded Stockport as his own.

He was vexed, then, when a Manchester company started taking over doors in Stockport, and attacked one of the firm's bosses at a boxing tournament. It was a big mistake. Little was out of his league and reprisals followed. His car was petrol-bombed and his house set on fire. It culminated in a mission to ambush him at a pub. 'They had made the decision to teach him a lesson, at the very least,' said a police officer who was called out to stop it. 'Twelve of them got tooled up and got in three cars. They didn't have guns but they had some nasty weapons. An informant to the Regional Crime Squad got to hear about it early that evening. He rings up the RCS and says Little is going to die. Everyone descends on Reddish Lane. The convoy is stopped and all the weapons are found. They were charged with conspiracy to commit violent disorder and GBH. At court they all turn up in sunglasses and gold. Little fears it will get out of hand and gives evidence on their behalf. In the end some of them get done for possession of offensive weapons and get a fine, but nothing more. The judge was scathing of Little.'

Little knew when to avoid a fight. Instead he continued to target people weaker than himself. He sent one of his strong-arm men and a 'negotiator' to extort £20,000 from a couple in Edgeley; Little had heard they had recently loaned a friend £5,000 and sensed they had come into money. The woman was assaulted, a cut-throat razor was produced and the terrified couple allegedly saw a gun in a briefcase one of the men was carrying. Little continually bullied lesser criminals in the city, taxing and humiliating them and building a groundswell of resentment. He threatened to break the legs of an old woman who 'spoke out of turn' when he pushed in at the bar of a pub. He also had a death wish. He told his mother Patricia, 'Mum, I am a gangster. I will be shot dead, and that's what I want.' Perhaps wanting to make sure he was not forgotten, he was planning another 'parade' of his troops for August 1994.

On Friday, 22 July 1994, Little was driving with a friend in his

£50,000, open-topped Mercedes coupé to buy some wine. He was thirty-one, in his physical prime, an imposing presence with a penetrating gaze, his short hair and clipped moustache giving him an angry look, his neck and shoulders bulging with muscle. He pulled up at traffic lights at a junction near the Jolly Sailor pub in Marple, Cheshire. A white Ford Granada with false plates pulled up alongside. In it were several men. The barrel of a shotgun extended from the window of the Granada, and two shots boomed out. Both hit Little in the head. His foot slipped off the brake and his car, an automatic, accelerated into two other cars and a bollard before crashing into the wall of the Bowling Green pub 100 yards away. Four people in a van hit by the car were injured, one suffering a broken leg. 'Even in death he could dish it out,' commented one journalist. Little's £2,000 Tag Heuer watch fell from his wrist. His reign was over.

The white Granada, stolen a month earlier and fitted with false plates, was later found burned out. As word spread, flowers appeared on the doorstep of Little's house. One neighbour even claimed Little had been reading the Bible with him shortly before driving off to his death. 'My children adored him and he loved them to bits,' said the neighbour. 'He was a superb neighbour, a big, tough, lovable fellow. He was a fitness fanatic and always working out in his gym.[69] Before he left he was reading the Bible.' The police were far more cynical. 'It was inevitable he would come to a sticky end,' said a former detective. 'He was showing all his cards and he never had that many. He was dealing with half a pack.'

* * *

Forty officers were put on the murder case and a reconstruction of Little's last journey was staged in an attempt to jog the memory of witnesses. Police believed he had been followed from his house, the assassins waiting until he stopped at the lights before they struck. Careful planning had clearly gone into his killing and the murder car had been stolen from a Stockport garage a month earlier. By the end of August, two men in their early twenties had been arrested and charged with conspiring to murder Little. They were joined within a fortnight by several others, including a twenty-two-year-old-man who was accused of pulling the trigger. Some of the accused were known car thieves, involved in stealing and 'ringing' vehicles. Their gang would look for high-value cars advertised for sale as far afield as Staffordshire and North Wales, and would visit showrooms in disguise, getting the keys for a test drive and then speeding off. 'There's no point lying: we do cars,' one of them told a newspaper interviewer. 'We chop them, swap them, change them and ring them. But we've never hurt anyone. We take them from showrooms, not Joe Public.'[70]

Three men in their twenties finally went on trial at Manchester Crown Court in January 1996, charged with Little's murder. One of the problems the prosecution had, however, was in ascribing a motive. The defendants denied knowing Little well though their paths had crossed in a Stockport club, Peaches, where he would often drink. The prosecution speculated that perhaps Little had wanted to extend his influence and, in doing so, had stepped on the toes of other criminals. 'Men like this make enemies and Christopher Little no doubt made enemies,' Peter Birkett QC, prosecuting, told the jury. 'No doubt there were many people who might have wished he was dead.'

Detective Constable Paul Moores described Little as 'a legend in his own lunchtime' and said that 'every time there was trouble, Little's name was mentioned.' He gave evidence about the intelligence file on the gangster, revealing that Little regularly collected £200 protection money from a popular snooker club in the city. There was intelligence that drug couriers were acting on Little's behalf; one was arrested with £50,000-worth of amphetamine. Moores described the stories of the crucifixion, the hurling of a man off a bridge, the video of Chris Jones's beating.

The defendants produced alibi evidence to back up their not guilty pleas. There was also an 'O.J. Simpson moment' when the alleged triggerman was questioned about a pair of badly charred, medium-sized gloves found in the torched car. He said they could not be his because of his very big hands – and demonstrated the point by pulling on a pair of extra-large driving gloves in the witness box. The other two defendants declined to give evidence. The jury deliberated for fourteen hours before clearing the trio of plotting to murder Little and of associated charges. They were cheered so loudly by supporters in the public gallery that the judge threatened to clear the public gallery. 'The jury's decision is final and it is a decision we accept,' said Det Chief Supt David James, head of Greater Manchester CID. 'However, the case was thoroughly presented and prepared. At this stage we are not looking for anybody else in relation to the death of Christopher Little.'[71]

The police had greater success against Little's firebug gang, who were put on trial in April 1995. 'The arsons were all part of a planned, organised attack which was prepared for at a meeting on school paying fields ... where instructions and orders were given by the leaders,' said Anthony Gee Q.C., prosecuting. 'They were carried out with a degree of co-ordination which bordered on military precision and behind the attacks appears to have been the desire to do as much damage as possible in the shortest time.' A total of sixteen defendants aged from eighteen to thirty-six were eventually found guilty of conspiracy to commit arson.

*   *   *

The hole left by Little's death was quickly filled, though not without further violence. Outside firms took over his doors, while the drugs trade was soon parcelled up. One gang even took a man on a punishment tour around several pubs, severely beating him in each one to set an example. 'It was similar to the flogging-round-the-fleet scene in *Mutiny on the Bounty*,' said Chief Superintendent Bill Hughes, the area police commander. 'The criminals had the audacity, the lawlessness and the arrogance to think there was a private area over which the law had no effect.'[72] The victim survived his ordeal but was too cowed to testify. To halt the gangsters, Stockport police set up a dedicated drug unit and expanded their intelligence network. An undercover unit was even set up in rural Buxton because of fears that those taking over the trade from Little were expanding into *Heartbeat* country. 'When [Little] was murdered last year, other factions moved in to fill the vacuum,' said a superintendent. 'The whole range of illegal drugs is now being seen in the High Peak.'

One of the men Little had apparently crossed swords with was Peter Fury, an ex-boxer of Irish traveller stock. One story had it that Fury challenged Little to a bareknuckle fight and Little declined, saying he would prefer gloves in a ring. Police intelligence indicated that Fury had taken over Little's mantle as Stockport's main drugs dealer. He bought a Porsche 911 with the personalised registration PPF 1 for £63,000 cash, though, true to his traveller background, still lived in a mobile home. With his accomplice, haulier 'Big' Frank Smith, he used a unit at Helmshore in semi-rural east Lancashire to store, prepare and distribute large amounts of amphetamine imported from Belgium. The drug was sixty-seven per cent pure and shaped into bricks. Smith was observed handing a rucksack full of drugs to Fury in an out-of-the-way lay-by. It contained ten kilos of speed worth about £1.5 million. Another two kilos were in Smith's Land Rover.

Fury was described in court as a man with 'considerable intelligence' who had been involved in complex business dealings using up to twelve different names and who had transactions or bank accounts in America, Jersey, the Isle of Man, Spain, Belgium and Ireland. Fury, twenty-seven, who had a car sales pitch, claimed he made his money from vehicle dealing, boxing and bareknuckle fighting. He was jailed for ten years. Smith, forty-nine, was jailed for ten years and his son, also called Frank, for six years. All three were convicted of conspiracy to possess drugs with intent to supply in July 1995.

From a completely different social background came Tony Darnell, a solicitor with a well-established criminal law practice in Middle Hillgate, Stockport. A former clerk to Stockport magistrates, he became probably the city's best-known criminal lawyer, a father of two who lived in Glossop, earned £50,000 a year and regularly paid his £1,500-a-month mortgage in cash. Darnell had a rash streak, however. In the early eighties he was fined £100 for headbutting his girlfriend's ex-boyfriend in a wine bar, earning him the nickname 'Yosser' after the character Yosser Hughes in the TV drama *Boys From The Blackstuff*. A decade later, Stockport police developed strong suspicions that he was involved in serious drug dealing.

They set up a clever sting operation to trap him. In April 1996, an undercover female officer from the Regional Crime Squad was placed 'under arrest' at Stockport police station, posing as 'Maggie', a drugs dealer from Northern Ireland who had been found with 1,000 Ecstasy tablets. Darnell was the duty solicitor and was assigned to see the woman in the station. Maggie intimated her involvement in drugs and, with relatively little prompting, Darnell agreed to supply her with Ecstasy. He took from her the key to a safe deposit box and called her contact in Belfast to let him know developments. Later that night, Darnell returned the key to Maggie after she had been released on bail. He took her to a Manchester hotel, warning her to beware of listening devices.

Two weeks later, Maggie and another officer posing as her Belfast contact met Darnell in a Manchester hotel. A hidden tape recorder captured their conversation. The solicitor offered them 5,000 Ecstasy tablets at £3.50 each and amphetamine at £3,000 a kilo. He professed to great caution: 'You don't know me from Adam. You can't trust me. We have got to be cautious. I don't know who you are. You could be anyone for all I know.' At the same time, however, he boasted of his contacts and some of the cases he had worked on. He wanted an on-going relationship with this new Belfast connection and advised them how to deposit money in a solicitor's client account so they would not need to fly back over to Manchester for each deal. Darnell then bragged that he specialised in representing clients trapped by police surveillance, insisting on anonymity when they used phones. 'I don't want to know your names,' he said. 'Nothing can ever get back to me. If ever I speak on the phone I will be called "Rumpole", as in *Rumpole of the Bailey*.'

Darnell agreed to supply an initial 5,000 tabs of E and some samples of a high-purity amphetamine tablet known as 'speedball' at £2.50 each, to be sold on for between £6 and £8. Over the next few weeks, he had a series of cloak-and-dagger liaisons with the two undercover cops, making them follow convoluted instructions to throw any police off the scent. Darnell was given £17,500 and the drugs were handed over to Maggie and 'John' in the car park of a pub in Longsight by Darnell's courier, a Stockport man in his mid-forties called Brian Farrell. A few days later, another deal was arranged, and in June it was followed by a third. A doorman, Paul Jackson, acted as Farrell's minder while he transported the gear. The lawyer pocketed a total of £52,000.

Darnell and Farrell were arrested on June 27. Jackson was picked up on his return from holiday in Florida, the police having found a stun gun and shotgun cartridges at his home. When told of the undercover operation during interview, Darnell replied that if it was on tape 'I have done it and it's a criminal offence.'Yet he initially fought the charges, his barrister claiming that the police set out to trap Darnell because he had been a thorn in their side through his successful defence work. However, at the last minute he changed his plea at Chester Crown Court and admitted two offences of conspiring to supply drugs. Darnell's barrister said he hadn't dealt in any drugs before this episode but was ensnared after falling into substantial debt with the Inland Revenue and with credit cards. Described as a 'calculating, determined and greedy criminal', Darnell was jailed for eleven years – one more than Peter Fury – and was professionally and personally ruined. Some of his assets were seized under the Drugs Trafficking Act and the court was told his home was up for sale. The Solicitors Disciplinary Tribunal struck him off. Farrell the courier was jailed for eight years and Jackson the minder for six and a half.

'We were aware that Darnell had, in the past, poured scorn on the sort of tactics we used to catch him and that of course that made it more satisfying,' said DCI Mike Keogh, commander of the dedicated drugs unit. 'He was a man with a career and a standard of life most people would dream of. His strength was that he knew the law inside out – but he wasn't streetwise. His greed and arrogance brought about his downfall.'

* * *

By the arrival of the new Millennium, Stockport's mobs were as active and as vicious as any in the country. Several brutal murders – in particular the torture and killing of a young dealer called David Barnshaw, who was covered in petrol and set alight – bore grisly testimony to the depths people would sink in the murky drug world.[73] Occasionally gangs clashed head-on, with fatal results.

Paul Reilly was a 'strong and hard man'[74] who controlled drug dealers in the Lancashire Hill area, just north of the M60 motorway. Hostilities erupted between him and a drugs gang from Adswood to the south of the city, after a fight at a nightclub. Reilly, thirty-one, decided to take over their territory as an act of revenge, attacking their property and telling them they would only be allowed back to the area if they stopped dealing and paid him £30,000. The Adswood crew was run by Andrew Synott, who was nicknamed 'Red', his brother Michael, known as 'Menace', and their half-brother Paul Arden. 'The Reilly gang took steps to exact physical vengeance on the Synotts and their associates and also to take control of their drug business,' prosecutor Alan Conrad later told Minshull Street Crown Court in Manchester. 'The Reilly gang went several times to Adswood in pursuit of the Synotts. Andrew Synott's house was attacked, windows broken and his Mondeo Estate car set on fire. So frightened was Andrew Synott of Paul Reilly that he would not even go back to his house to see if his wife was alright.' Reilly and his gang smashed up Synott properties and created spoof 'wanted' posters about Andrew Synott and Paul Arden and distributed them around their territory. They even stuck up one of the posters at the Wembley pub, the Synotts' gang base. During one incident Reilly and his men barged into the pub and ordered the licensee not to serve the Synotts. As Reilly increased the pressure, the Synott brothers went into hiding, checking into hotels with their respective partners. Humiliated and fearful, they also resolved to hit back – with outside help.

The court was told that initially they went to see a man to get a gun, but the proposed deal fell through when the alleged supplier, worried that the weapon might be used for murder, flew off to Tenerife. Later the Synott brothers recruited Kassam Essa from Cheetham Hill, who put together what one officer later described as 'a professional killing team'. The Synott gang then set about creating alibis so they could be seen in busy public places at the time of the shooting. Reilly had been out for the day but had returned home in his Escort van and had gone inside to watch TV. Soon afterwards a witness saw three men get out of a car with their faces masked. They burst into the house through the front door, stormed into the living room and opened fire at Reilly as he sat at a table. He threw a chair at his killers and tried to hide behind the table but was hit in the pelvis and chest. He was certified dead an hour later. Reilly's girlfriend and her eleven-year-old son saw some of what happened. Her other son, aged thirteen, was upstairs at the time. 'It was plain that the assassination was carefully planned and carried out with ruthless efficiency. They shot him dead in cold blood,' said Mr Conrad.

Andrew Synott, of Tintwistle, Derbyshire, Michael Synott, of Bridgehall, Stockport, Arden, of no fixed abode, and Colin Blackburn and Kassam Essa, both from Cheetham, all denied conspiracy to murder but were convicted and jailed for life.

CHAPTER FIFTEEN

Collapse of the Truce

THE DODDINGTON FLOURISHED under the truce. The least sophisticated of the four main gangs, they operated at the coalface of the drug world, using the security of the armistice to establish a simple street market specialising in heroin and coke on their Alexandra Park turf.

The cocaine was cooked into rocks of crack in a semi-detached house in a quiet Chorlton close by a man from Toxteth, Liverpool, the source of most of the cocaine in the north of England. He supplied the rocks to the Doddington via Winston Brownlow, a leading gangster who oversaw a sales pitch his gang had established in Grierson Walk, a walkway, and Portstone Close, a cul-de-sac, on the estate's east side. The crack was sealed in snap bags, usually at the home of a woman who was forced to co-operate, and parcelled out to the runners. Each dealer sold individually but would direct buyers to another member of the group if he was out of supplies. Every day saw three drops of 100 wraps of heroin and each wrap, sealed in a snap bag, sold for £10. A wrap of crack, or 'stone', sold for £18–20. The dealers worked every day and at the lower end were paid £250 a week for their work. Some wore bulletproof vests and full-face balaclavas; most carried cellphones. They hid the wraps in their mouths or down their boxer shorts, in flowers beds, under tree roots in the gardens of disused houses, or behind dislodged bricks.

Mothers and young children had to walk through the gang to reach the nearby St Mary's Primary school, a nursery and a playground. 'The dealers operated on two sides of the school quite openly and in view of children, staff and parents,' said headmaster David Keen. 'The older children have grown up with it. They deserve a chance of a good education like any other school. It's never been very pleasant to have children playing within close view of the dealers, who were still there at hometime.'

Up to thirty dealers worked the market, several of them schoolchildren themselves. One was twelve, selling under the supervision of his dad, a Doddington leader. Another was Paul Day, who though small for his fourteen years had a shocking reputation for violence. Day was in juvenile court one morning to receive a conditional discharge for possessing cannabis, then went straight to the estate and was selling more drugs before lunchtime. Some sat astride mountain bikes, others worked on foot. Their customers came from all over Manchester and regarded it as a 'quality service'; the Doddington had finally learned not to bully their buyers and would even offer drugs on tick to familiar faces.

The organiser of the market, the 'leader of the pack' as a judge would later describe him, was Pepperhill veteran Ian McLeod. He was the oldest of the group, and bore the scars of the gang wars: he had been shot in the stomach and bore a steel plate in his skull from an assassination bid. He was assisted by the three Pitt brothers, Kenneth, Ray and Thomas. Kenneth, the oldest of seven children, had been in trouble since his mid-teens and had recently emerged from a four-year sentence after being found with £1,000-worth of coke. Ray was known as 'Pitbull' and had a reputation as an enforcer, notable even among the Moss Side gangs. 'I was the first to nick Ray Pitt, when he was twelve,' said a former police officer. 'He had the attitude of a twenty-five-year-old and he spat on the back of one officer. But when we got him to the police station, he started crying. He was only a kid.' Tommy, the youngest, had received a conditional discharge for robbery at the age of twelve. He progressed through theft, burglary and dishonesty to possession of heroin, and in 1993 was sent to a young offenders institution for carrying a loaded gun and affray. When he came out, he was almost immediately re-arrested for possessing heroin with intent to supply but went on the run from a bail hostel to join his brothers at the drugs market.

Others involved included a promising young footballer, a failed student from Somalia who went around in body armour with a replica pistol, a former soldier in the Tank Regiment, a teenager who had spent time in the care of social services, had never worked and had no qualifications, and an occasional painter and decorator with a string of convictions. Many were experienced dealers with convictions ranging from weapons offences to kidnap and assault. Though crude, the Doddington drugs market raked in more than £20,000 a week, or over £1 million a year.

★ ★ ★

The Hillbillies had established their own market in a walkway in their Waterloo estate heartland and were selling around 200 wraps of crack and smack a day, for a turnover of more than £10,000 a week. They were a tighter-knit group than the Doddington, most coming from a half-mile radius. Some of the younger Hillbillies also launched a campaign of extortion against local businesses, which became plagued by robberies and protection rackets. 'Unless something is done, businesses are just going to up and leave this area,' said one company boss. 'I know many are already talking about it. [It] is affecting the whole business community. I know of Jewish properties that have been victims and I also have heard stories of Asian shopkeepers who have been robbed or their property attacked.' Attacks were often followed by threats of further violence if the victims went to the police.

The final straw for the Asian community came when an Asian-owned taxi firm was targeted. 'It started off with minor damage, breaking windows, slashing car tyres,' said one of the Asians. 'Then they came to the taxi bay, threatened a switchboard operator with a gun and demanded his gold rings. We were much more bothered about that than the damage to the cars. He was on his own and it was very frightening. They seemed aged between seventeen and twenty-one, mostly West Indian.

'We had words with some of their leaders, the older fellows, and they promised to intervene. They said they would have words and everything would quieten down. Whether they really meant it or were just pretending, I don't know. Anyway, the youths turned up a few days later and threatened us again. They wanted a thousand pounds protection money. We thought, we'll let them come but we'd rather die than pay them. Forty or fifty Asian people, mainly relatives and friends, were asked for help. They were waiting when three of the Cheetham Hill turned up in a Golf GTi. They were very arrogant. They said we shouldn't have gathered all those people and said, "Don't think this is the end of it." That is when the fighting started. One of our people was hit on the head with an iron bar and needed stitches but they came off worse. One of them got a broken arm and their car was smashed up. The police came and arrested two people.

'After that, we had another talk with their leaders and they assured us nothing more would happen, but a day later one of our drivers' cars was slashed with a knife and another one had a traffic cone thrown through his windscreen as he was driving. Then some of them appeared near one of the cab businesses, and when some Asian people confronted them, they said they wanted five thousand five hundred pounds to pay for the damage to the car and for the one who was beaten up. But the community stood together. We have faith in each other. Most of the Cheetham Hill gang are drug pushers. They ruin our youngsters as well as attacking our women and snatching their bags.' Meetings were hastily arranged between Asian leaders and senior police officers and the problem appeared to fizzle out, though it did lead the police to take a closer look at the Hill.

Other incidents were putting the gang armistice under severe pressure. 'Throughout the truce there have been a number of little incidents which the sensible guys had sorted out,' said one of the main heads, a convicted criminal with a reputation for violence, eleven months after the start of the ceasefire. 'Car damage, taxing, things which could have led to flare-ups, were dealt with. It might cost two thousand pounds to square but face was saved and the aggravation stopped. Recently though, lots of guys have lost interest in putting themselves out to keep the peace. The trouble is that in a gang situation it only takes one idiot to start a war. The dangerous element comes from the younger guys who've got nothing. All they do all day is try to hustle money and the only way they can do that is to use a little force. That's their power.'

So long as it held, the truce was a boon to the drug traders, who could operate in a far less tense environment. Greater Manchester Police seized more heroin than anywhere outside London in 1994, in a year when national seizures rose by twenty-five per cent. By late 1995, drug agencies were reporting that it was easier to buy heroin than cannabis in Manchester. A user could have a £10 bag of relatively high quality heroin delivered at any time of day or night just by making a phone call; smack was even being used in the 'chill-out' areas of dance clubs where previously cannabis had been prevalent. At the same time, crack cocaine was finally encroaching on the powdered cocaine market, an ominous sign. 'It is difficult to find anyone who has had a healthy relationship with crack cocaine,' Mark Gilman of the agency Lifeline told the annual In The City music conference. 'Most people try it once and say, "That way madness lies," or have carried on and ended up in trouble.' Ecstasy saw a fifty per cent national increase in seizures in 1994, an enormous rise.

Drugs squad officers were also finding that street markets were springing up all over the city. One on the Cardroom estate in inner-city Ancoats was shut down after a lengthy watch-and-buy operation by police. Another was discovered in Stalybridge, Tameside, on the east side of Manchester, where a drugs ring was selling mainly from houses. Tameside had to double the size of its drugs squad to combat dealers throughout the division; one gang specialised in stealing social security benefit books and using them to raise money for drug deals. In Ashton-under-Lyne, a female syndicate was run by twenty-four-year-old Amanda Elliott, who bought heroin in bulk from a Moss Side supplier and recruited a team of young women to sell at designated sites, including the cenotaph in the town's Memorial Gardens, though the site of the market shifted regularly and addicts were directed by mobile phone. Elliott was eventually jailed for six years. In Trafford, to the west of Manchester, the borough council won government funding specifically to tackle its crack cocaine problem. Even Glossop in Derbyshire saw a surge in its drugs trade, especially in Ecstasy.

Senior GMP officers took a decision to change tack. They believed that the drawn-out process of covert observation to amass evidence gave residents 'the impression that nothing was being done'. Even when successful, the result of one-off operations was often a job creation scheme for new dealers to replace those taken out, and this in turn often led to turf war. With limited resources at their disposal, the police decided that their best approach was to 'disrupt and harass the marketplace' by making themselves a nuisance to the dealers on a day-by-day basis. Within days of the new policy being explained to councillors at a meeting of the city's social strategy committee, officers moved on the Cheetham Hill drug mart on the Waterloo estate, raiding twenty homes and seizing £15,000-worth of crack and £8,000 of heroin. 'I have dedicated a team of officers to tackle the drugs problems in this area and this is the first of what I believe will be many successes,' said Supt Alan Green, the sub-divisional commander at Collyhurst. Fourteen pushers would eventually be jailed, though there was some criticism from the local community of the leniency of the sentences.

* * *

It was inevitable that the trigger-happy Doddington crew would be first to shatter the peace. One Saturday in July 1995, Robin Parkes staggered up to two Moss Side police officers, bleeding from bullet wounds. Parkes was no angel, having served time for possessing a stolen gun. Now someone had shot him in the abdomen and hi-jacked his black Golf GTi. He was taken to hospital for emergency surgery. As an angry group of friends and relatives gathered, it emerged that he had been shot by a friend in a row over a mobile phone. A notorious Doddie called Kevin Lewis was later charged. An incident that in another time or place might have resulted in nothing worse than a bloody nose had almost cost a life.

A few weeks later, on an August afternoon, Nicholas 'Sailor'

Murphy was riding on a motorbike to a christening on the Alex Park estate with a friend on pillion when someone shot at them with a handgun. At twenty-six, Sailor was a veteran of the gang world. He had survived a kidnap attempt three years earlier and a shooting that had left him with a steel plate in his skull. He had moxie, and not long after the motorbike incident was seen in a pushing-and-shoving row with two men he believed had fired the shots. Another man left the scene and returned with a gun.

This time Sailor had pushed his luck too far. The gunmen let off a hail of bullets and he was hit three times; one bullet bounced off his steel headplate but the other two hit home. Another man was wounded in the thigh and a third in the knee, both almost certainly accidentally – they were believed to have been the two men involved in the earlier row with him. Murphy was found lying on a pavement close to his brother Tony's house in Quinney Crescent, with spent cartridges nearby. He had been due to become a father in a month's time.

Murphy came from a large family and his nine siblings were distraught. His brother Carl, who was a year younger than him, made a point of visiting the scene of his death every day. On the night of September 5, he was at the spot laying a bunch of roses, against the advice of his father, who feared danger after dark. A shot rang out from the shadow of a nearby building and Carl was hit in the shoulder. He ran for his life towards Princess Parkway, thinking he could hear further shots cracking behind him. Carl was treated in hospital under armed guard. Police speculated that, as he had regularly visited the spot since his brother's death, the gunman may have become familiar with his movements. 'How could anybody do this to Carl when he was paying his respects to his dead brother?' said his father Ashley. 'I can't take any more of this. I want all this trouble to stop. I have already lost one son.'

Sailor was given a big send-off. His streetname was spelt out in red and yellow flowers, his coffin carried on an ornate glass carriage drawn by two black-plumed horses. A police outrider led the cortege through Old Trafford, and he was interred at Stretford Cemetery. 'He had his faults but he was honestly always there for us if we needed any help,' said his older sister Pamela. 'What is making me angry is that he did not die with dignity. There was no-one there for him.' His distraught family denied he was a drug dealer and described him as a loving son. 'My brother was a compassionate, unselfish young man, and had not been convicted of any drug offences,' said his sister Grace.[75]

The shooting of Robin Parkes and murder of Nicky Murphy suddenly poisoned the atmosphere on the west side of the estate, and grudges or arguments that had been suppressed now choked the air. A young Doddie called Kwame Gasper owed one of the leaders money for drugs. He was chased in his car and threatened with a gun. Gasper, however, was friends with Ray Pitt and perhaps believed this would protect him from serious harm. At 9 p.m. on 4 September 1995, Gasper was walking to Pitt's house in Levenshulme when fellow gang member Owen Roche came up behind him. Roche was a close friend of the man Gasper owed for drugs, and before his victim knew what was happening, Roche shot Gasper in the back of the leg. He spun round to see Roche again squeezing the trigger but the gun jammed and Gasper frantically limped to a nearby house for help. He ended up in hospital but initially declined to make a complaint.

Predictably, Roche was shot himself a short while afterwards at his house in Radley Walk, the place where Julian 'Turbo' Stewart had died and 100 yards from where Sailor was shot. A gunman chased Roche into his house and fired bullets through the window and doorway, hitting him in the leg in front of his mother. He was taken to the same hospital as his shooting victim Gasper. As armed police went on regular patrol on the east side of the estate to stop two factions of the Doddington from massacring each other, a planned Channel Four documentary that was to show how peace had come to Moss Side was promptly shelved. 'This violence is being carried out by a tiny number of people but they are nevertheless creating havoc,' said a senior policeman.

Gasper said nothing until four months after the shooting, when he fingered Roche to the cops. Roche was jailed for nine years. The court heard that Gasper was a 'sidekick' to the much-feared Ray Pitt, but by then Pitt himself was dead.

* * *

With the Doddington in disarray, a fluke led police to the heart of their cocaine manufacturing system. That October, officers went to investigate two men acting suspiciously on a Moss Side industrial estate at 3 a.m. The men escaped over a perimeter fence, but a search of the immediate area uncovered £100,000-worth of crack cocaine – the biggest-ever seizure in Greater Manchester – and two loaded guns: an Ingram Mac-10 machine pistol, capable of releasing thirty bullets in less than two seconds, and a Browning self-loading pistol. It was arguable which find had the more alarming implications: the Mac-10 or the crack. Crack is normally produced in small amounts but this was in sticks that the police likened to Blackpool rock. Someone was clearly trying to saturate the market and increase the number of addicts.

Officers entered the Doddington's drug factory in Chorlton, which they had been watching for weeks. They arrested Winston Brownlow and Verdaine Griffin, both aged twenty-four, and found drug-making equipment and cocaine and crack with a street value of £103,000. The police were also building a case against the Doddington trading site on the Alex estate. Despite the alertness of the young dealers, officers had managed to hide in an unoccupied house on Portstone Close, overlooking the tiny dealing area. The front windows were covered in a fine mesh and a camera was put in the bedroom covering the dealing area below. Others officers secretly watched through peepholes drilled in another boarded-up window on the landing. Over two months, in conditions of great tension and danger, observations and video evidence were collected on the deals outside using pinhole microwave cameras that could be operated from up to a mile away. 'Those viewing the marketplace were right in the thick of it and could have been discovered at any time,' said DCI Mike Williams of Greenheys police station. 'They were very vulnerable and it takes a lot of courage to do that. They were there from early morning to late evening, living and working in dire conditions, with all that stress.'

From a close-knit team of about a dozen officers, undercovers were sent in to buy drugs. It was edgy work: they were entering an intimidating atmosphere, with young men on a hair-trigger, many wearing body armour and balaclavas. Several of them were challenged over the next few weeks.

'Are you a copper,' one was asked outright.

'No,' replied the officer, who was hardly likely to admit it.

'Are you sure?' said the dealer. Again the answer was no. Satisfied, the dealer sold him a wrap of heroin.

In one six-day period, 219 sales were recorded. Cars would pull into the cul-de-sac and dealers would almost race to get there first. Junkies on foot were picked up after being filmed making buys. The key targets were soon selected and given codenames. Ian McLeod was 'November', Kenneth Pitt was 'X-ray' and his brother Thomas was 'Bravo'. On one occasion, Tommy Pitt was arrested in Grierson Walk by a police constable who was not connected to the surveillance team. After a chase and a struggle, Pitt was taken to the police station, where two small bags fell out of his boxer shorts. He promptly put them in his mouth and tried to swallow them. After a further struggle, officers retrieved crack cocaine.

Even as police were preparing their case, events overtook them. The gang had taken to preying on its own; there were un-confirmed rumours that one dealer had been taxed for £100,000 by more hardcore members and another for £30,000. Ray Pitt, preoccupied with 'war business' against some of his former friends, was rarely around on the streets but did put in an appearance at the Hacienda, where he apparently had a ruck with a former friend over crack cocaine. One story has it that Pitt owed a substantial amount of money, probably from a drugs deal, and refused to pay it. It led to a subsequent gunfight, although no-one was hit. According to testimony later given in court, Pitt then had a fight with fellow Doddie Che Cole.

Five days after Christmas, Pitt, aged twenty, was sitting decked with gold chains and rings in the passenger seat of a grey Ford Cosworth in the car park of the West Indian Sports and Social Club in Westwood Street with seventeen-year-old Marios Baama, one of his gang's young dealers. It was three o'clock in the morning. A Jamaican band had been performing and scores of young Moss Siders were enjoying themselves. People were milling around in the car park. Pitt was by now probably the most feared gangster on the streets of south central Manchester. He had a long record of robbery and violence and lived by the code: in 1993 he had been jailed for fourteen days for refusing to give evidence against a rival who had shot him. He had fired the bullet that precipitated the truce. Anyone who was going to try something with Pitbull had better make sure they finished the job.

A small, slim man sidled over to the car. He wore a dark, baggy, hooded tracksuit and a baseball hat with the logo 'No Fear' on the front, and carried a black handgun. He fired into the car, mortally wounding Pitt and hitting Baama in the legs. Pitt died almost immediately; Baama was badly hurt. There was a rush of panic as people scattered. Others spilled out of the club to see what was happening. A passing ambulance returning from another job was flagged down. One of the crowd ambled up to the ambulancemen and inspected Pitt's injury. 'He's from the Doddington,' he said. 'I'm Gooch and I know we're enemies, but he doesn't deserve this.'

The two men were taken out of the car. Pitt had a massive head wound. The two-man ambulance crew had a struggle getting Pitt's body out and some of the increasingly angry crowd attacked them but were calmed by others. One of the ambulancemen was punched. 'It is difficult to comprehend what could possess people to behave in such a manner,' said ambulance control manager Stephen Brown. 'Both members of the crew behaved with great professionalism and courage in extremely difficult and worrying circumstances.' In the commotion, someone drove off in the heavily bloodstained Cosworth; it was later found parked in a nearby close. Pitt was eventually taken to hospital by ambulance but was dead. Baama was ferried to the MRI in a car. A large crowd gathered in the hospital's reception area.

'MERCY MEN MOBBED AT KILLING' blazed the headline in the *Manchester Evening News*. It identified the murder as 'the first directly drugs-related murder in Moss Side since Julian

"Turbo" Stewart, another "Doddington", was shot in the head in Radley Walk almost exactly two years ago.' It also said Pitt had been involved in a power struggle for turf vacated by another gangster now in prison. 'There was talk that something was going to happen,' said Father Phil Sumner, the well-informed local clergyman who was always quick to pick up street vibes. 'When a truce is agreed, it is often by a particular group of people who have influence at that time. They have themselves gone through prison sentences and worked in the prisons on raising black consciousness and it was probably through that that they made the decision to go for a truce. Others in the community are not always involved in the same processes and don't always link to the decisions about truces. It is remarkable that this community, including those involved in drug dealing, has made some effort to keep away from that sort of violence. There are a group of young men who did go through prisons who are quite influential. They made decisions to be more responsible, realising what they were doing. But not everybody has subscribed to that.'

What no-one knew was that the police had been gathering evidence against the gang even while civil war was tearing it apart. They had been secretly filming the drugs market and sending in undercover officers to make buys. They were taken completely by surprise by the Pitt killing and the sudden split in the gang but their up-to-date intelligence meant they could quicky identify the two factions. On one side appeared to be a group including Owen Roche, Darrell Laycock and Che Cole. On the other were Pitt's family and closest friends.

Two days later, Laycock was in Bedwell Close in the early hours with a young woman, Adele Abdela. He knew his life was in danger and was wearing a flak jacket. Yet he was foolish, or brazen, enough to be back in the open on his old stamping grounds. Three men approached him, armed to the teeth with a machine pistol, a pump-action shotgun and a handgun. They opened fire in an explosion of cordite and metal. Twenty-seven bullets were discharged, nineteen from the machine pistol. Many thudded in Laycock's body armour and arms. He fell to the ground near a wall on which the word 'peace' had been painted in bright colours. Miss Abdela was hit in the hand. A man with dreadlocks pulled up in a car, bundled them in and drove them to hospital, where a number of Laycock's friends soon arrived. In pain and in shock, Laycock asked them if he was going to die. Armed police guarded him before he was taken into an operating theatre. Amazingly, after surgery and the removal of several bullets, he survived.

The use of automatic weaponry paradoxically saved Laycock's life. 'The reason Laycock survived is that unless you are a trained marksman you cannot control a weapon of this nature,' said a police firearms expert. 'If you open fire from more than ten or fifteen feet, the thing will spray everywhere because of the tremendous reverberation generated. What is particularly alarming is that innocent people are put in immediate danger.'

The divisional superintendent, Lilian King, looked drawn as she held a Press conference about the Doddington civil war. It was an especially unwanted development given the vast amounts of money then being spent on rebuilding parts of Moss Side and Hulme and parallel attempts to change the area's image. 'People are killing for money and status,' said King. 'They are putting those two things above life. The dealers know that children are less likely to be stopped and searched. Sadly, once these young-sters are involved with that culture it is hard to get them out of it . . . It is a perpetual and very lucrative industry. When we take out the top guys, as we have done successfully in the past, they are replaced within weeks.' Despite this, she was desperate to play down the Moss Side myth. 'In the last week there were three shootings in Manchester, of which one was here. One of the victims died. But which shooting was reported in the paper? Was the attack on Mr Laycock reported because he was black? I have to ask that because as soon as a young, Afro-Caribbean male is murdered, maimed or uses a firearm here, it becomes news because Moss Side is news.'

Superintendent King appeared to be saying that twenty-seven bullets fired in a residential street at a man implicated in a gang war was not news. While her desperation was understandable, it was misguided. Gabrielle Cox, secretary of the Moss Side and

Hulme Community Forum, was more realistic. 'There is a sinking feeling when these shootings happen,' she said. 'Why do young men do these things despite the risk of violent injury or even death?' Part of the answer was unemployment. Around forty-four per cent of Moss Side's ethnic minority men under the age of twenty-five were unemployed, according to one survey. 'These young men do not believe they belong to the wider community,' said Cox. 'They have built their own community, with its own mores and values. If they have never had a job, if their brothers have never had a job, if they see their mothers working all hours in some crap job, it's not surprising they turn to other values.' A worker at the Saltshaker, the friendly drop-in centre that was once the notorious Pepperhill pub, concurred: 'These kids are not that different from kids anywhere else. They are torn between trying to do good things and bad things. It's just that there is more scope for bad things here.'[76]

★   ★   ★

In January 1996, eighty Manchester police officers gathered for a 4 a.m. briefing, and ninety minutes later were crashing into homes in south Manchester. By 10 a.m., ten of their fourteen Doddington targets were in custody. The culmination of Operation Balboa, the raids were an attempt both to eradicate the gang's street market and to stop its civil war.

Balboa was one of a number of GMP anti-drugs operations coming to fruition under the 'harass the marketplace' policy. Operation Scorpio in Collyhurst was aimed at street heroin dealers on the new Allen Street estate. A number of those arrested claimed in mitigation that they had been forced by violence to sell drugs by unnamed 'top dealers'. It was an indication of the way street markets were moving away from Moss Side into other areas. Another group of cannabis dealers were filmed making 300 deals in three weeks outside a pub in Harpurhey; they hid their drugs under a nearby paving slab. In Denton, Tameside drugs squad seized crack, heroin, cocaine, speed and Ecstasy with a street value of more than £300,000 in Operation

Revolution, the latest in a series of raids against the main players in the east Manchester underworld. They had equal success against a drugs mob known as 'the Tee' that sold heroin by phone; records showed that, over a four-month period, 2,386 calls were made to the gang's main number from a telephone box outside Dukinfield Town Hall. The head of the gang, which had a pyramid structure, was twenty-five-year-old James Cole, from Ashton-under-Lyne, who spent his profits on foreign holidays, jewellery, a motorbike and a nine-carat gold bar. Users would call the 'dealing phone', the orders would be passed on and handovers were carried out by street-level members of the gang. Cole was sentenced to eight years and other gang members to shorter terms.

Targeting the drugs was the most effective method of putting away gang members, as convictions for serious violence were still almost impossible to obtain. Several men had been arrested and faced serious charges over the Doddington civil war but to little avail. A young man charged with the murder of Nicholas Murphy was discharged when two vital witnesses, one of them Murphy's girlfriend, failed to attend court even though they had been in the witness protection scheme and had been housed in a secure flat fifty miles from Manchester. Charges against Owen Roche over the killing of Ray Pitt were dropped by the prosecution at magistrates court – 'I was innocent and I would never do such a thing to anyone, let alone a friend,' said Roche outside the court – but he was jailed for nine years for wounding Kwame Gasper. A witness in yet another murder case, that of teenager Simon Caines (see page 190), was sent into hiding by intimidation and his failure to give evidence resulted in the collapse of the trial. 'I don't like having a son who is a fugitive but I would rather he be alive and a fugitive than dead in a gutter,' said the witness's father. David Montrose was eventually tracked down by police and jailed for two months for refusing to give evidence. He said a knife had been drawn across his mouth, cutting both sides of it, as a warning not to talk. It showed the difficulties of getting anyone to testify in this bewildering world of bullets and blood.

Another Manchester judge jailed two 'frightened' men for a

month for refusing to give evidence in another case after they got a telephone threat in a manslaughter trial. 'I understand there are professional intimidators at work,' said Rhys Davies QC, Manchester's top judge. 'Time and time again, unhappily, proceedings in cases of the greatest severity have had to be abandoned. It is becoming a plague.' He referred to 'a scourge of witness interference and witness pressure which has led to the whole system of justice being undermined in certain categories of cases.' But leading solicitor Jeff Wilner, who sat on the criminal justice liaison committee with Judge Davies, was critical of the policy of dealing harshly with those too scared to testify. 'It is not right to jail people who have been intimidated to such an extent that they are genuinely fearful,' he said. 'Judges need to explore other alternatives . . . once detailed research has been done into the reasons why they feel unable to give evidence.'[77]

This difference of opinion reflected how the explosion of serous crime was putting the relationship between various branches of the legal system under tremendous pressure. A further example came when Salford police chief John Potts, previously accused by city councillors of being deaf to warnings about organised crime, used the Superintendents' Association national conference in September 1996 to launch a ferocious public attack against judges who 'will never know the full picture if their street knowledge is based on sitting in the back of a gleaming black limousine.' He went on, 'When prisoners are convicted of operating protection rackets and receive five years' imprisonment, it gains headlines. If the same story mentioned the actual period will be nearer two years and because they have previously been remanded in custody they will probably be released in under twelve months, it would cause outrage to many and terror to those who have been brave enough to assist the police. Why don't judges announce how long a convicted criminal will be behind bars and what their day of release will be. Who are these people who keep us from the truth with this enormous sham?' Potts's outburst drew a strong response from the Recorder of Manchester, Judge Rhys Davies, who sent a letter of complaint to Chief Constable David Wilmot calling for Mr Potts to be disciplined (and pointed out that he drove to Manchester in his own saloon car, not a limo).

In August 1996, Ian McLeod, thirty-two, and his Doddington army were jailed for running the drugs market on the Alexandra Park estate. McLeod's previous convictions included possession of a gun, kidnap and robbery, and he had been shot at least twice. McLeod, who claimed to be a car trader, was jailed for ten years for conspiracy to supply class A drugs. 'You were, in my judgment, the leader of the pack,' said the judge. 'What makes your crime all the more dreadful is the employment of boys as pushers.' Kenneth Pitt, twenty-three, was jailed for six years, though his sentence was later halved on appeal, and Thomas Pitt, nineteen, was given five years. Thomas had admitted in a pre-sentence report that if he went back on the street he would 'only start dealing again' and the judge told him, 'Your brother's death seems to be no deterrent to you.' Others received sentences ranging from three to six years. All except McLeod and one other had admitted the offences.

Two of the defendants were young enough to be in the care of the local authority. Paul Day had been fourteen at the time of the offences. He had been one of the more active dealers, acting under the instructions of someone else. He said he was forced into it; he thought he would be 'killed like Ray Pitt' if he didn't deal. Day had previous convictions at juvenile court including possession of Ecstasy with intent to supply, possession of heroin and possession of cannabis. Even the prosecutor admitted he 'has had a troubled young life' and had wanted to impress his peer group, but argued that the gang might be deliberately using such young lads as runners because they would be treated leniently by the courts, and that 'had to be wrong'. Day was detained for three years under the Children and Young Persons Act. Another boy who had been twelve at the time of the offences was detained for two and a half years. 'It is an attempt by ourselves to rid Moss Side of this image it has of being the drugs capital of the country,' said DCI Mike Williams. 'We are taking a lot of major players out of the game and there is a lot of positive attitude in the area now. We haven't had anywhere near the same level of drug-related violence since this operation.'

At a separate hearing at Manchester Crown Court, Verdaine Griffin, from Toxteth, was jailed for twelve years after admitting being concerned in the making of crack cocaine, and Brownlow was jailed for seven years after admitting plotting to supply crack and possessing it. The prosecution accepted Brownlow was a customer of Griffin and was not concerned in the production of the drug. Both were 'intelligent, able young men,' said the judge. They were also 'two of the major players in the north-west drugs business . . . involved in the manufacture and supply of large quantities of crack cocaine throughout the region,' according to DCI Kevin Haig.

Balboa was the most successful operation against a single gang since Operation China five years earlier, yet the drug sales continued, remorselessly. Some members of the anti-Pitt faction who escaped the round-up began selling from blocks of council flats in Northern Moor, in the Wythenshawe area. They terrified families and quickly set up a new market. Operation Airduster began in July 1996 when residents in flats on Garthorp Road complained they were living in fear. A number were forced to leave after intimidation, including one man who was ordered out after being burgled. Others asked to be re-housed. Most of the dealing had been in heroin. The estate's four blocks of three-storey flats were turned into a dealing zone reminiscent of the film *New Jack City*. By October 1996, only one tenant remained. The council decided to waste no more money on improvements but to raze the post-war flats and sell the land.

In November 1996, Che Cole went on trial charged with murdering Ray Pitt in what the prosecution said was a violent internal feud in the Doddington Gang. Three eye-witnesses, giving evidence from behind screens, named Cole, then twenty-six, as the gunman. Two of the witnesses were identified by false names. They said Cole had been wearing a baseball hat with a No Fear logo and had fired a black handgun. One of them, identified by the pseudonym 'Simon Walker', said he, Cole and Pitt were all members of the Doddington. There had been an argument between Pitt and another gang member that led to a gunfight, although no-one was hit. 'Then Pitt and Cole had a disagreement over something,' he testified. Walker said he was in the car park of the club when he heard a gunshot. 'I looked over and everyone was panicking. Then I noticed Che at Raymond's car letting off two more shots.' Everyone scattered. Walker admitted he did not tell police what he saw until he was arrested several days later for supplying heroin, but denied he was giving evidence only to earn lenience in his own case. 'I am doing this because Raymond was a friend,' he said. 'It just can't go on, what happened.' Another witness said he saw a fight between Cole and Pitt just days before the murder.

In his evidence, Cole, of Kensington Street, Moss Side, said emphatically, 'I did not shoot Raymond Pitt. I was not the gunman.' He said he was drinking inside the club with two friends when there was a commotion and they heard someone had been shot. It was only the next day he learned the victim was Pitt. The jury believed his story, and Cole was acquitted. He grinned and thanked the jurors.

★   ★   ★

The county's armed crime unit had made some major weapons seizures since its inception but had begun to notice a disturbing development. A young man being chased through Moss Side dropped something that looked on first sight like a rectangular block of lead with a muzzle sticking out. It was a Mac-10 machine pistol. Originally manufactured by the Ingram company in the USA, the Mac-10 was designed for American troops operating at close-quarters in the Vietnam jungles. It holds a thirty-round magazine of nine-millimetre ammunition and fires at the rate of 1,100 rounds a minute; in other words, it can empty an entire clip in less than two seconds. It is crude but shockingly deadly. 'It is for special forces or police use, in as much as it's not an accurate weapon,' said a constable in GMP's armed crime unit. 'It's not a weapon you would use single-shot. It's a weapon you would stick round a door and empty into a room in order to clear that room of any would-be problems. There's absolutely no legitimate civilian application.' Labelled 'Big Macs' by the media, the guns were known among the criminal fraternity as 'raincoats', presumably because of the way they showered bullets.

The armed crime unit quickly realised the terrible implications of finding a Mac-10. What they did not then know was that a single source was running a supply line to send the weapons throughout the British and Irish underworlds. Anthony Mitchell was a licensed firearms dealer with a passion for macho pursuits. He lived in a terraced house in Brighton with his common-law wife, loved motorbikes and competition shooting, and served as a special constable with Sussex police. There was something odd about him though. In 1993 he was stopped coming through Gatwick airport and was found to have more than his permitted allocation of ammunition. He was forced to resign as a special. He and his mates also posed as police officers to enter police and military shooting contests in Europe and North America. They wore black boiler suits and named their team Black Shod. They were good, and sometimes they won.

'They did it for the thrill of being able to beat a police or army team,' said Detective Constable Cliff Purvis of the National Crime Squad. 'I think Mitchell was one of these frustrated SAS boys. He used to go baton training, abseiling from helicopters, even man-tracking.' Mitchell's darkest secret, however, was hidden in his workshop. There he worked on firearms that, by law, could only be bought, sold and kept if they were deactivated – rendered unusable. Mitchell bought more than 100 such guns from one company: they were Mac-10s. He found it easy to put them back into working order by fitting new barrels and breech blocks. He then sold them on the black market, usually through well-connected London criminal John Ackerman. The going rate for a working Mac-10 with silencer and ammunition was over £1,000.

Mitchell's guns made their way to at least four major cities: Dublin, Glasgow, London and Manchester. The first known murder committed with one of them was a Jamaican hit with ten bullets outside a pub in Brixton, south London. The connection in Manchester seemed to be through Salford, where whoever was receiving them was then selling them on to the south Manchester gangs. One day officers chased some suspects in Longsight, south

Manchester. 'They found one hiding under a vehicle in the road,' said Keith Jardine, head of Manchester's armed crime unit. 'When they extracted him he was carrying one of these machine pistols, fully loaded.' Soon after, another one was pointed at a Moss Side police constable by a nineteen-year-old; he was jailed for ten years. At least eleven machine pistols reactivated and sold by Mitchell made their way to Manchester between 1992 and 1997. Many of Mitchell's had a unique breech-block which he had designed and which worked better than the original. He also liked to leave his own trademark. 'Mitchell was something of a surrealist,' said Purvis. 'He wrapped his guns in hessian and marked the package with a kind of Cyrillic writing. It actually meant nothing. It was his version of the rose that the Scarlet Pimpernel used to leave.'[78]

And as those guns seeped to the gangs of south Manchester, signs on the Alexandra Park estate were making people uneasy. Graffiti began to appear on school and health centre walls: 'West Side Killer Zone' and 'YGC', short for Young Gooch Close. The remodelling of the estate was supposed to have got rid of the drug dealers and gangbangers but residents were beginning to ask if the £30 million spent had been wasted.

A spectacularly ill-timed report in the *Guardian* declared that the Manchester gun wars were effectively over. 'As 1996 draws to a close,' it claimed, 'a bunch of hooded teenagers, none of them more than 16, is all that is left of the drugs and guns scene . . .' Those same hooded teenagers and their 'spray-and-pray' guns were about to unleash a wave of carnage unprecedented in modern Britain.

CHAPTER SIXTEEN

The Longsight War

HE WAS SEVENTEEN years old, unemployed, wore a long gold chain and drove a sports car. His cellphone held the numbers of his string of girlfriends, one of them the 'baby mother' of his daughter. He had police cautions for possessing drugs and ammunition but nothing too heavy. On the street they called him 'Bigga'.

It was 9.30 p.m., the light almost gone on an October night, and Orville Bell was in his red Honda CRX in Linnet Close, a cul-de-sac at the southern end of a housing estate in Longsight. Beside him sat fifteen-year-old Emma Mullin, his latest girl. They were talking when two teenagers, their faces masked by bandanas, cycled up behind. One, on a Claud Butler mountain bike, tapped on the driver's window – with a gun. Bigga wound it down slightly. The youth poked the nose of his gun through the gap – then fired twice. A bullet went through Bigga's jaw and lodged in his throat. Whether through conscious effort or unconscious reaction, Bigga threw the car into reverse and it lurched back for several yards, dragging the shooter's Claud Butler under its rear bumper.

Bigga got his door open, staggered for a few yards across the road, and collapsed on the pavement. One of his attackers reached down and yanked the gold chain from around his neck as blood began to form a pool around Bigga's head. Emma ran for help to a nearby pub and someone phoned Bigga's mother, Victoria Laing. She was there within minutes. Emma was trying to keep her son warm with a coat. 'I found my boy lying in a pool of blood and calling for his little daughter, Kasha,' Mrs Laing told the *Manchester Evening News*. 'He said repeatedly, "Mum, I've been shot." I told him he'd be all right. I held him tight and waited for the ambulance.'

A life-support machine kept Orville Bell alive for several days at Manchester Royal Infirmary, until he died on 29 October 1996. 'He was just a teenager who loved music, girls, his car and go-karting,' said his mother. 'I don't know why anyone should hate him enough to want to kill him. I had heard there was an argument but I don't know if that's true. I know there has been some taxing going on by some lads from Moss Side. Perhaps they wanted his gold chain. But if they did, he wouldn't have let them have it.' Within a fortnight of Bigga's death, a youth of eighteen known as Tin-Tin was being questioned.

The police floated a theory that Bell's death was part of a battle over drug turf in an area south of the city centre and east of Manchester University, encompassing several modern estates in Longsight, West Gorton, Ardwick Green, Brunswick and Levenshulme. Trouble had been brewing in this area for several years; it had become known as the street robbery centre of Manchester, and police had been forced to draft extra officers to deal with muggings, theft and burglaries. The young lads responsible for this crime wave were now growing older and moving into drugs, augmented by some Moss Side players who had been moved off the Alex Park estate during its renovation. Residents of one housing area, the Anson estate, had been complaining for months that it had become plagued by drug dealing and bored, lawless teenage gangs. One heroin pusher sold at a bus stop on the busy Stockport Road; his clients would wait there, ignoring all buses, until he turned up. On one occasion, police saw eighteen addicts at the stop when he arrived with their gear.

There were several reasons why the drugs market gravitated towards Longsight, including the closure and renovation of Gooch Close, the arrests of the Doddington gang and the regular mistreatment of junkies by the Moss Side pushers. 'They realised they had killed the goose that lays the golden egg,' said a former gang member. 'They wanted the action back, so they got down to Longsight. For the Longsight boys, who had quietly been doing their own thing, it was a case of arm and defend yourself, or die.'

The growing drugs trade meant that many of the Longsight youths could afford guns and they were not slow to arm.

The Longsight lads were marked by their extreme youth; many were no older than their mid-teens. One of them, arrested behind the New Victoria pub with eight snap bags of brown heroin, a mobile phone, cash and a knife, was fourteen and had not been to school for over a year. He was caught again a month later, again with drugs and cash, and again got bail, only to rob a local store wearing a ski mask, pointing an imitation gun at the shopkeeper and making him empty the till. Another youth, Hagos Youngsam, was detained for eight years after admitting four offences of possessing heroin and cocaine with intent to supply, two counts of possessing an imitation firearm, robbery, attempted robbery, assault, possessing cannabis and attempting to escape from custody; he was sixteen when most of the offences were committed. He had marched one young man to a cash machine, pistol-whipped him to the ground and kicked him until he revealed his PIN number. While held in custody at Longsight police station, officers had to call the fire brigade as he became wedged when trying to escape from his cell through a ventilator shaft. Youngsam dealt from his home in Langport Avenue. He lived there with his brothers and sisters. He hadn't been to school for a year after getting expelled.

Youngsam and others like him came from the same Longsight estate where Bigga had been shot, a cheerless patch of low-rise dwellings isolated between the major A6 Stockport Road on one side and a railway mainline and stockyard on the other. Relatives and friends of Bigga from that estate now formed the nucleus of an emerging gang that became known as the Longsight Crew. Many of them were so young that they could not hold a driving licence, drink in a pub or watch an X-rated movie. Their nerve centre was Langport Avenue, yet another planning mistake hidden in the belly of the estate, where the gang would gather to scheme.

Bigga's assassin turned out to be yet another teenager. Eighteen-year-old Leon 'Tin-Tin' Kenton, from Chorlton, was found to have a jacket stained with blood that matched the dead youth's, and a witness saw him with Bigga's gold chain. No motive for the murder was put forward when he went on trial in June 1997, though police believe he may have mistaken Orville Bell for another man who was the real target. Kenton claimed he was playing computer games and smoking cannabis at the time of the shooting, and said someone must have borrowed his jacket, but the jury didn't believe him and he was jailed for life. 'This was a murder which had all the trappings of a form of execution,' commented the judge. Kenton showed no emotion as he was taken down.

The Longsight Crew regarded Bigga's death as a Gooch hit. It was the Gooch's first serious violation of the truce, perhaps because they did not see the Longsight lads as being a party to it, and so were fair game. Young as they were, however, the Longsight lads were not prepared to lie down to the bigger and more powerful Gooch – and they had the means to fight back. Central to the gang was the figure of Julian Bell, Orville's older brother. Julian had broken his back on a stolen motorbike at the age of twelve, an accident that left him confined to a wheelchair. He had received £500,000 in compensation, and now used it to arm and lead the Longsight Crew in an all-out assault on the Gooch, funding the purchase of a range of weapons including Mac-10s and Uzis. At the start of the decade, the dealers had upgraded from standing in a shopping precinct alone to riding mountain bikes, using mobile phones and forming gangs. Now they had fast cars, steel-plated body armour, sub-machine pistols and the impregnable bravado of youth. Longsight went to war.

★   ★   ★

Their first attack was a drive-by deep in enemy territory at Westerling Way, the new name for Gooch Close. On 6 January 1997, a Longsight hit team sprayed shots from a car, hitting two teenagers, one of them only fifteen, in the legs. On January 20, another squad headed onto the Alex estate and spotted two young men hanging out on Gooch turf. A gunman unleashed thirty bullets from a machine pistol held out of a car window. Mark

Watt was hit in the leg and needed surgery to remove a bullet, while Chris Moodie escaped with a graze.

The Gooch hit back. Two men on bicycles fired nine bullets at the Bells' house in Langport Avenue, and there was another shooting nearby. The police acted quickly. On February 4, they raided homes in Longsight and Moss Side, arrested six men, seized a large quantity of drugs and found a fully loaded .357 Magnum of the type made famous by Clint Eastwood in the *Dirty Harry* movies. Three weeks later, officers from the armed crime unit raided a Longsight Crew stash house and uncovered a Mac-10, an Israeli-made Uzi machine pistol, three loaded hand-guns and 300 rounds of live ammunition. They had 'prevented a bloodbath,' reported the *Manchester Evening News*. Their difficulty was in proving that the guns belonged to any of the gang members.

In March, the Young Gooch again headed into the secluded Langport Avenue late at night. This time their plan went badly wrong. One of their number was Zeus King, a nineteen-year-old whose late father Marcel and his pop group Sweet Sensation had topped the charts in 1974 with 'Sad Sweet Dreamer'. The Gooch lads spotted two of their Longsight enemies and one of them opened up with a rapid-fire gun, spraying several cars but accidentally hitting Zeus. The teenager died instantly.[79]

It was not long before the Doddington, too, were dragged into the killing spree. Someone went looking for twenty-seven-year-old Kevin Lewis, a major Doddington player since the earliest days of the Alex Park War who had survived at least two shootings. In 1996 he had been charged with attempting to kill a friend as his gang slid into civil war, but a paucity of witnesses meant the case was never brought to trial. Some heavy people had asked Lewis to cool it, warning that his behaviour could cost him his life, but he didn't listen. 'Kevin Lewis said he wouldn't have people telling him what to do,' said Damian Noonan, the massive Hacienda head doorman, who knew him well. 'He was a top lad. You didn't fuck with Kevin Lewis.'

Lewis was out with friends one night and early in the evening noticed a small gang of masked youths. According to a friend,

Steven Morrison, they made Lewis 'a bit uneasy and we all decided to go home.' Lewis parked his BMW in one of the old Moss Side terraced streets outside a club called the Shamrock. The gang reappeared. 'I saw one of the riders mount the pavement and, when he reached Kevin's side, raise his right arm and point something at his head,' Morrison later told an inquest. 'There were about ten to twelve shots and then the gang rode off.' Lewis took a single bullet to the head from the rapid-fire weapon and was killed. A woman walking 150 yards away was hit in the thigh by a stray bullet.

Thirty-six officers worked on the inquiry and conducted more than 100 interviews, but Lewis's killer has not been brought to justice. Some of his friends did end up in court, however: Keith Perkins and Hugh West spent a day at Lewis's home paying their respects, then got drunk and smashed up the Big Western pub with pool cues, demolishing glasses, bar pumps and optics. A fruit machine was turned over and a brandy bottle thrown through the giant TV screen. Perkins claimed someone had made a derogatory remark about Lewis, and one of the pair was heard to shout, 'Gooch men are coming in here and we're Doddington.' Both were jailed for what the judge called 'a disgraceful exhibition of unbridled and ungoverned violence.'

Two dead in a month, and the next body was not long in coming. Henry Ajilo, a twenty-nine-year-old with several girl-friends and a wardrobe of designer clothes, was a wheeler-dealer motor trader from Gorton who skirted the edge of the law. He disappeared that April; the first clue to his whereabouts was the discovery of a blood-soaked car. It transpired that a Jason 'Dog' O'Driscoll, said at trial to be a man with 'a fearsome reputation', had shot Ajilo twice in the back of the head, put his body in the boot of a car and dumped it under bushes down an isolated farm track seven miles south of the city centre. The next day Dog stripped his victim's flat of valuables, including his expensive hi-fi equipment, but two days later he was stopped in the heavily blood-stained Rover after a chase. He was wearing a tee-shirt Ajilo had bought on the day of his death and had his victim's cloned mobile phone; half a litre of blood was still sloshing in the spare wheel well in the boot. Ajilo's decomposing body was not found until seven weeks after the murder when a farmer went to investigate an unpleasant smell coming from his land. Dog claimed in a statement that Ajilo was his friend and had been killed by Moss Side gang members who believed he was a Hillbilly. He was not believed and was jailed for life.

All the police could do was keep up the pressure. In their biggest action yet, 120 officers raided twenty-four homes in a bid to break the Longsight-Moss Side. Some of those arrested were questioned about the shootings of Lewis and Zeus King, but there was little hard evidence against any of them. It was announced that Longsight was to get an extra forty-three constables to combat the problems there but frontline officers were sceptical. At the sharp end was GMP's armed crime unit, set up specifically because of the south Manchester gun wars and based in a secret location on the east side of the force area. It relied heavily on intelligence on the new names and faces to unravel the motives for their feuds. 'Our work is far more intelligence-based than it was several years ago,' said one detective. 'The armed crime unit and divisional CID have pulled off some highly successful operations but the bottom line is that drugs are a lucrative market. There will always be young bucks coming through to claim their share of the spoils. It's like a production line. It's a macho thing as well to have a tasty weapon and then be prepared to use it. They have some frightening armoury. The trouble is that they don't know how to properly use something as potent as a Mac-10 and invariably spray bullets way off target, which puts innocent people in the firing line.'

The break up of Anthony Mitchell's Mac-10 ring by the National Crime Squad that summer was a notable success, while Manchester officers raided homes on the Racecourse estate in Sale which, like Nell Lane in south Manchester, had become satellite territory for the black gangs. They also smashed several more drug markets, busting a gang described as 'the most dominant heroin dealers' in Rusholme and Fallowfield. The gang, who also sold crack cocaine, operated in streets near Manchester City's Maine Road football ground and made up to £1,000 a day each. Their leader was said to have received 150 calls a day on his mobile from just two public phone boxes in the area. Another crack cocaine pitch outside a fast-food takeaway in Claremont Road was dismantled and two Jamaican yardies, both illegal immigrants, were among those arrested. Police even speculated publicly that they had removed the last of the street markets from Moss Side but Labour councillor Richard Leese, who had Graham Stringer as leader of Manchester City Council, was unconvinced. 'Every agency we work with here tells us the drugs war is being lost,' he said. 'Levels of crime associated with the drug trade are increasing and enforcement measures to combat the illegal use and supply of drugs are failing.'[80]

* * *

'We only kill our own' was a gangland myth prevailing from the Kray era of the 1960s. If it had ever been true, times had changed; by the mid-nineties the gangs were leaving a trail of innocent victims. In March 1997, shopkeeper Ian Marshall was shot dead at his off licence on the Racecourse estate after trying to defend himself with a machete when armed robbers burst into the store. A young rapper nicknamed G-Rok was one of two men later convicted of his killing, though he continues to claim a miscarriage of justice. In July 1997, Errol 'EJ' Jones of the Young Gooch was jailed for life with his two Wolverhampton friends, Derek Jones and Gary Nelson, for the pittiless street killing of caretaker Evon Berry in Bristol. A judge in Bristol described it as 'one of the most dreadful crimes in the city's recent history.' All three had denied any part in the killing.

A month after EJ was sentenced, two more innocent lives were lost. Jason Schultz, who was known to associate with the Gooch, was at the wheel of a hired Ferrari Spyder when he overtook two cars at seventy miles per hour on the wrong side of the road in Whalley Range. He lost control of the car and hit two sweethearts, social sciences graduate Stuart Ward and his French girlfriend Nathalie Monier, who was studying for her PhD at Manchester Metropolitan University. Both were killed. Schultz, who was a banned driver, and passenger Paul Donaldson both fled the scene. Schultz was later jailed for four years for causing death by reckless driving, plus a year for perverting the course of justice.

The next innocent victim was Davinia Smith, out celebrating her sixteenth birthday in January 1998. She had been for a Chinese meal with her mother and had gone on to a club with two young friends. Later, Davinia and her pals took a taxi with some youths they had met to an all-night blues in Laindon Road, a few hundred yards from where Orville Bell had met his death. The girls had a look at the party but decided they did not want to stay and were climbing back into the cab when someone opened up with a Mac-10. The gunman was possibly aiming at the gable end of the house but had difficulty controlling his weapon as more than twenty bullets crackled out in a single second. The cab was sprayed with hot metal, its windows shattering. Davinia was hit in the head, a bullet piercing her brain. The taxi driver had the presence of mind to speed off and drove straight to the Royal Infirmary, where Davinia underwent emergency surgery to remove part of her brain. Davinia, described by neighbours in Ardwick Green as a 'very decent, law-abiding and God-fearing' girl, was not the target; the shooter may have been after the youths who had been with her just minutes before. He was believed to be one of the Longsight Crew, which had acquired a new armoury after the police weapons seizures of the year before.

With Longsight rearmed and the Gooch-Doddington truce shattered, the next few years would take the gang warfare in Manchester to a level unimagined even in the worst scenarios of the armed crime unit. The shooting of Davinia Smith seemed to mark the start of a merciless spate of tit-for-tat attacks that made past events look tame. An extraordinary series of gunfights began with a full-blown shootout between Longsight and the Gooch on grassland at Bold Street, on the Alex Park estate. Soon after, the Gooch bushwhacked two youths taking a taxi from a pub in Longsight territory to the same estate; a car overtook the taxi and forced it to stop, then a man jumped out and fired three bullets, hitting a sixteen-year-old in the abdomen. He managed to stagger to a house in Doddington Close for help. Next, Che Cole was wounded in a drive-by. Cole, cleared of killing Ray Pitt in the Doddington civil war, had already been shot three times in the leg the previous autumn; when police asked to look at the bullet holes in his trousers, he claimed he had been wearing Bermuda shorts, uncommon garb in Manchester in late October. Within a few more days, two more teenagers were wounded in the legs in Claremont Road and two young men were shot at by a gang on mountain bikes in a cul-de-sac in Beswick, east Manchester, indicating a further expansion of gang turf; some young men linked to the Longsight Crew were selling drugs behind a bookmakers in Beswick precinct. Elements of this group would, a few years later, form the nucleus of yet another gang, the Young Longsight Soldiers.

Armed police took to the streets of Longsight and Moss Side, patrolling with their guns on show. GMP had already boosted the number of armed officers to cope with a doubling of armed operations over the previous three years and had increased the number of ARVs (armed response vehicles) on permanent standby. Unsurprisingly, however, there were complaints about low morale in C division, which included Moss Side, Longsight and Wythenshawe. The division was deemed to be about 115 officers below strength. 'Having been a street warrior for a number of years on the C, I had to write a few home truths,' one unnamed officer wrote in a force magazine. 'No-one I speak to has any morale.' Constables starting in the area found themselves poorly informed. 'You don't get briefed on anything, you just pick it up as you go along,' said one officer based at Longsight. 'No-one tells you. It is like a moving conveyor belt and you are jumping on it. There is no gang unit; the nearest thing they have is the armed crime unit.'

★　★　★

'I was in the house when it happened. Someone came to the door and said Julian had been hurt. I went outside and there was a large crowd gathering. I went closer and then saw my son on the ground bleeding. He had been shot by a bullet in the head. He was also bleeding from a leg. He opened his eyes and looked at me as I spoke, but he could not reply. It was terrible and I shall never forget it. His friends tried to save him and tried to stop the bleeding but he was too badly injured.'

Sylvia Wagaba was a committed Christian who worshipped at the Global Revival Church, where the congregation regularly prayed for an end to gang violence in Manchester. In March 1998, her eighteen-year-old son Julian was ambushed as he rode his bicycle by two hooded men outside her home in Levenshulme. They shot him, ran to a car and were driven away. Mr Wagaba cradled him on the ground as neighbours brought blankets to keep him warm. 'It is every mother's nightmare to watch their child dying and feeling powerless to do anything,' said Mrs Wagaba. Her son had apparently argued with someone over a cheap car stereo. Two men charged with his murder later went free when a main witness refused to testify, having been told that he and his girlfriend would be 'smoked' if he went ahead.

Soon after, Che Cole's charmed life continued when he survived a third assassination attempt in six months. Cole, twenty-seven, was in a taxi when a car pulled up and someone fired a dozen shots. His bulletproof vest saved him, though one bullet went under the jacket and hit him in the abdomen. It was not unusual for young men to suffer repeated gunshot wounds; being shot once was a strong predictor of being shot again and such scars were no longer a novelty. Tundy 'Trigger' Smith, eighteen, survived a ferocious attack in Quinney Crescent when a first shot shattered the back of his skull and exited through his eye socket and a second and third broke his ribs and narrowly missed his lungs. 'God Jesus Christ, they've mashed me up,' he kept repeating, as he lay covered in blood. Smith, a talented drum 'n' bass artist, survived and, with a glass eye, later became part of the Moss-Sidaz hip hop group with his friends Pierre 'Bishop' Webber and Mark 'LA' Roberts. They could boast of being Britain's most-shot vocal trio: Webber carried bullet scars on his shoulder and belly and Roberts on his thigh.

The armed patrols seemed to have no deterrent effect on the

fresh-faced school-leavers who lived by the law of the gun. They did not seem to fear arrest and displayed a numbing lack of empathy with their victims, as though it was all some terrible virtual reality game. The *Observer* dubbed their gunfights 'playground shootings'. They were adopting their own slang, subculture and quirks of behaviour. For example, groups of young bike riders would often adopt a diamond formation when travelling with a gun.

The Gooch made several raids on the Longsight Crew's home estate that April. A gunman fired a number of shots outside the Cottingham Road home of Julian Bell, Orville's brother, wounding bystander Craig Bayliss in the arm. Bell himself was shot in a car outside his house; the bullet went through his hand and embedded itself in the leg of a teenage friend in the next seat. A few days later, David Shirley, fourteen, and Chris Thomas, seventeen, were shot with automatic weapons on the same Longsight estate. Bones in Shirley's ankle, groin and elbow were smashed. Five people had been shot and wounded in the vicinity in seven days, yet the new police sub-divisional commander for the area, Superintendent Tony Porter, told a public meeting that the gun war sparked by Orville Bell's murder seemed to be slowing down. It was one of those optimistic public pronouncements that always seemed to preface a further ratcheting of the carnage.

* * *

Thursday, May 21, and a teenager made a lunchtime visit to two gang members in HMP Manchester (formerly Strangeways) on attempted murder charges. The teenager himself was a murder inquiry suspect but had not been charged. As he left the prison, he was confronted by several of the Longsight Crew, carrying knives and screwdrivers. He ran for his life back into the visitor centre outside the main prison. The centre was invaded by the Longsight youths but their target managed to get behind a security screen before prison officers were alerted.

The next day, the same teenager was taken with fellow Moss Side gang members to the new police station in Longsight, where they were put on an identification parade in connection with a previous serious incident. The Longsight Crew discovered they were there and laid another ambush. As the Moss Side mob left the station, the leader of the Longsight crew appeared in a car and hurled abuse. There was a stand-off as police prepared to take the Moss Siders to Tactical Aid Unit vans. Then two masked gunmen appeared from nearby Richmond Grove West – and opened fire. Officers and gang members dived for cover as one bullet shattered a window at the station. 'Luckily they opened fire from a fair distance,' a detective told the *Manchester Evening News*. 'If they had been closer, it could have been a different story.'

The attempts to assassinate rivals at a prison and a police station were firsts even for the Manchester gangs. 'It was reckless in the extreme but typical of the disregard for human life these people have,' said the detective. 'Anyone could have been killed.' So shocking had the shootings become, and so long had the litany of mayhem grown, that mere woundings now barely merited a mention in the media. School-age teenagers shot with automatic weapons began to rate just a paragraph or two in local newspapers or a few seconds on regional news reports. Only the unusual or outlandish made for a lead story, such as the accidental death of Orville Bell's cousin Jermaine, a sixteen-year-old basket-ball player who shot himself with a converted air pistol while messing around with some friends. The air pistols, which looked like genuine guns, could be modified to fire live ammunition yet were legal to sell.

Another story that briefly broke through the media apathy involved the visit of a boy in his mid-teens to try on a heavy-duty bulletproof vest at an army surplus store in Tib Street, in the city centre. Told that is was £500, he said he would return. He came back soon after, put on the vest and walked towards the exit. When the father and son who ran the shop shouted at him to stop, he said, 'I've got a gun,' then he opened up with a .22 pistol. Frank Lanagan, fifty-four, was shot in the throat and his son Stephen, twenty-five, was hit in the leg and lower abdomen, rupturing his bowel. Both men survived but were badly hurt. The gunman, who was only about five-foot seven, pedalled off on a bicycle.

Even murders had become unremarkable. When teenage music student Leon McKenley was blasted twice in the chest and once in the back at the front door of his home in Old Trafford in January 1999, neither the local nor national press paid much attention. Councillors and community groups in wards like Moss Side and Ordsall, and even police officers, had routinely complained about 'misleading' headlines during the gang wars and about places being unfairly tarred, but now something even worse had happened. Gang-related crime in Manchester had become so common, so deep-rooted, that the media had lost interest. It had became a non-story. Only the truly bizarre or horrific would make the national media take any interest at all.

⋆ ⋆ ⋆

Just before 1 p.m. on Friday, 23 April 1999, an off-duty police officer noticed three suspicious-looking men on a slip road of the M6 near Lancaster. Tunde Adetoro, aged thirty, and fellow Mancunians Andrew Dennis and Francis Dixon, both in their early twenties, were dressed in the classic armed robbery kit of boiler suits, balaclavas and firearms. The officer followed Adetoro and Dennis in their red Rover, while Dixon was apprehended separately. The two men sped off down the M6 heading back towards Manchester and soon a motorway patrol took up the pursuit. Eventually Adetoro and Dennis pulled over to the hard shoulder and PC David Bentley got out of his car to approach them. Adetoro pulled on a balaclava, produced a handgun and braced himself to fire. The officer dived for cover as one bullet shattered his car door window and other shots ricocheted off the ground and hit his leg. 'I was lucky in that I just ducked and felt the bullet part my hair,' he later said. 'If I hadn't ducked, it would have hit me straight in the chest.'

Adetoro was a very dangerous character, a Cheetham Hill wildman who had counted White Tony Johnson among his close friends and whose brothers were serving long jail terms for armed robbery. He was prepared to kill to avoid capture. The men took off again, down the M61, which they left near Bolton's Reebok football stadium. Adetoro fired two more shots at the police car as the GMP helicopter, India 99, was scrambled. The officers stuck to their pursuit as the pair then drove towards Horwich. The men abandoned their car and hijacked a Ford Fiesta from a woman sat at traffic lights; a hooded man pulled her from the car, threatening to shoot her if she didn't get out. Adetoro also aimed his Kalashnikov at a lorry driver who tried to stop the Fiesta, but missed. The men then headed back towards Bolton and this time hijacked a BMW, taking twenty-seven-year-old Amanda Ryan hostage while firing at the windscreen of a police Range Rover that had taken up the chase. They skirted Bolton town centre and revved off through Bury towards Rochdale. Their hostage, cowering in the back of the car, heard Adetoro suggest to Dennis that they should shoot somebody, apparently with a view to slowing down their pursuers.

Their first victim, a fifty-one-year-old cable installer working on the main Bury to Rochdale Road, was shot in the leg. The second, a forty-six-year-old Asian doctor, was shot at through the window of his car in the Bamford district of Rochdale as he drove to work, breaking his arm. Martin McKay Smith, a solicitor, was shot in the leg as he passed the BMW on his motorcycle, and a fourth victim, Jim Gallagher, aged seventy-five, was hit in a leg when the gunman fired on a bus queue opposite a shopping centre. 'I heard the screeching of cars and police sirens and then I heard a shot,' a witness told reporters. 'I saw three lads in a car speeding off and Jim was down on the floor at the bus stop. I don't think they were aiming at him, they seemed to be aiming at the police who were chasing them. It was absolutely crazy.'[82] Two bullets narrowly missed another pensioner also at a bus stop while others almost hit police officers.

The fifth person shot was father-of-three David Hassall, who was cycling home from work near the Rochdale football ground when a bullet tore into his right side and went out of his back. 'I saw three police cars come past very fast,' witness Jason Brierley told the *Manchester Evening News*. 'The next thing, someone was lying on the ground. He had been on a mountain bike and at first I thought it was a road accident, but then I saw he had been shot in the hip. There were crowds of people trying to help him. He was shaking a lot but was very calm and didn't shout at all.' The denouement came when Dennis lost control of the BMW, veered off the road and crashed into a lamppost in a Rochdale street. Five people had been shot, apparently with the sole intention of forcing the police to stop and tend them.

Armed police patrolled the courtroom when Adetoro, Dennis and Dixon went on trial for what was described as one of the most remarkable episodes in recent criminal history. All three of them denied a lengthy list of charges. The prosecution asserted that Adetoro had repeatedly fired a Kalashnikov AK47 and a Smith and Wesson pistol at civilians and police cars during a fifty-mile chase in his desperation to escape. Adetoro denied charges of attempted murder, kidnapping, possessing firearms and conspiracy to rob and claimed he was the one being fired at, by police or by other drugs dealers. He admitted in court that he worked for three 'Mr Bigs' in the Cheetham Hill area but denied being a key player. 'I am on the borderline of the Cheetham Hill gang,' he said. 'I am nowhere near the top of it. I do the running about.' It was alleged in court that Adetoro may have been in Lancashire to collect guns from an Irish gang and that he supplied weapons to the Gooch. He admitted that two guns he had with him during the mayhem had previously been used in other shootings, but denied he was an underworld armourer, claiming he had hated firearms since his friend Tony Johnson was shot. Yet he admitted he constantly wore body armour. 'It's either wear body armour or carry a gun,' he told the court. 'People have been shot in my family and I hate guns.'

Dennis claimed in a police interview that he did not realise it was police that were chasing him, claimed to be unable to remember having shot any of the civilians and professed himself full of remorse. 'He stated that he wore body armour because he had been living in fear, having had some dealings in drugs, which meant that people were after him,' said the prosecutor. Adetoro was convicted of twenty-one charges and was given eight life sentences. Dixon was jailed for life for carrying firearms with intent to commit robbery and Dennis was jailed for fifteen years for the same offence. Three constables who pursued their car for more than twenty minutes despite being fired at received the Police Bravery Award.

* * *

Death was now a constant reality for anyone associated with the gangs. Despite the lurid headlines of a decade earlier, gang-related killings had been rare in the late eighties and early nineties; certainly nowhere near the levels routinely reached in cities in the United States. The breakdown of the truce, however, and the growing availability and affordability of lethal weaponry – a Magnum handgun for as little as £200 – loosed the shackles. Suddenly all bets were off and no-one was safe.

Anthony Stevens, the former Pepperhill man, was now a successful legitimate businessman, with his own media company and nightclub interests, but kept in touch with his old friends. He had also become a confidant for some of the Gooch lads. Two in particular, Martin Bennett and Chris Swarray, had strong family and friendship ties with their gang but told him they both wanted out. 'Martin and Chris confided in me that they were absolutely terrified for their lives. Martin Bennett in particular just seemed to know that his time was coming. He asked me how he could get out of it.'

Bennett, whose streetname was 'Remy' for his fondness for Remy Martin brandy, described a recent occasion when he had pulled up at a Moss Side restaurant for lunch and saw a couple of old enemies coming out. They spotted him and stiffened. 'They are walking very slowly to their car and he's coming out of his car very slowly, looking at them,' said Stevens. 'He's walking over towards the restaurant door looking at them, they are slowly getting into their car looking at him. They start their engine and, whilst they are still looking at him, he's walking to the door of the restaurant still looking at them. They have driven off very slowly, still looking at him. He's gone in and ordered his food and the woman says it is going to be about five minutes and all of a sudden he has lost his appetite.' Bennett was seriously considering turning his back on his old gang contacts. He just hadn't yet had the heart to do it.

On July 31, a group of young men were involved in what police called 'a minor fracas' outside a Moss Side newsagents. One of them was Martin Bennett, aged twenty-five. Shortly afterwards, at 6.30 p.m., he was shot in the chest while walking down Great Western Street. He was bundled into a car and taken to hospital but could not be saved. He left two young children. One theory is that Bennett had argued with some young lads and one produced a gun, which Bennett took off him, only to be shot by another. The youths concerned were loosely affiliated to the Doddington, and at the hospital there were stormy scenes as those close to Bennett swore vengeance. Tragically, word had already reached the Doddington leaders that they were being wrongly blamed. They decided to get their retaliation in first, and shot up the house of a Gooch man's relatives; indeed, there were six further reported incidents of gunfire before dawn. That was it: full-scale war was declared. While flowers were placed at the spot Bennett was shot, youths in bandanas patrolled the streets. Officers in armed response vehicles stop-checked cars to hinder drive-by hit squads and plainclothes spotters discreetly watched for signs of trouble.

★　★　★

Four days after Martin Bennett's death, twenty-year-old Dorrie McKie was shot dead in Leaf Street, Hulme. He was not a gang member but had lost friends to the gun, including Leon McKenley. McKie was ambushed by a gang on mountain bikes and was shot three times as he and a friend ran from their car; he was found lying on grass with a fatal chest wound. Extra police patrols had been out in Moss Side because of fears of a gang backlash over the murder of Martin Bennett, but the killing occurred half a mile from where the patrols were concentrated. Officers did not immediately link the two murders, and two separate incident rooms were established. Again, the Doddington were blamed.[83]

Then, on August 15:

> The black Volkswagen Jetta tore down the road at high speed just after midnight. Inside were two panic-stricken men. Following closely behind was a grey BMW whose front-seat passenger was spraying the car with an automatic weapon.
>
> The VW approached a T-junction a mile from Manchester city centre and swerved to the left in Kincardine Street, a fatal move. Here it slammed into the back of a car before ricocheting into a lamppost and coming to a juddering halt.
>
> The chasing car casually pulled up alongside and a man stepped out. He walked up to the passenger of the VW, Antony Cook, 24, and shot him seven times in the head and chest, killing him instantly.
>
> He then turned his attention to the 20-year-old driver and shot him three times in the stomach. The injured man managed to escape by appealing for help to a couple who had been in the vehicle he had hit. He staggered to them, begging: 'Help me, I've been shot.' He is still under police protection in hospital. Police said the attack was a 'premeditated, cold-blooded murder.'

That, in purple prose, was how the normally sober *Independent* described the assassination of Antony Cook. Journalists were privately briefed that Cook was a 'rising star' of the Doddington; certainly he was a hothead, running around with a 'gat' and causing trouble, and may have been killed by the Gooch in a row over a woman. As bunches of flowers and rain-smudged messages later appeared around the base of the lamppost, amid remaining pieces of glass from the car, one of the Gooch apparently phoned the Doddington leader on his mobile to gloat.

'We killed your boy.'

'Who do you mean?' he asked. When told about the shooting of Cook, he reportedly replied, 'You just saved us a bullet. We were after him ourselves.'

The police now had a triple murder inquiry – Bennett, McKie and Cook – but astonishingly said that none of the deaths of the previous sixteen days was gang-related. Others were having none of it. Father Phil Sumner, whose parish at Saint Wilfred's RC Church covered most of Moss Side, officiated at the funerals of all three of the most recent victims. 'It is nonsense for the police to say it's not gang-related,' he said. 'They may not necessarily be linked but there have been a considerable number of shootings and people know it's gang-related.' Fr Sumner tried his best at Martin Bennett's funeral to persuade the gang members to reinstate their ceasefire. 'I'm aware there will be people in church who can re-instigate a truce and I would appeal for them to do so,' he told the congregation at a church in Old Trafford. 'I ask people where the killings get them? What happens to the families and the children of the victims? The credible message on the street is that Martin and Antony's deaths are gang-related but not necessarily tit-for-tat shootings. What I do know also is that the community has the power to stop this process here and now, to say enough is enough before it spirals down again further.'

If GMP were trying to avoid bad publicity for the city, it was futile. The Britain's Bronx tag was back. Parallels were inevitably drawn with the bad days of the early nineties and no amount of official whitewash could cover it up. 'These are indeed grim times,' opined the *Daily Telegraph*. 'After more than six years of comparative calm and many millions in investment, Moss Side is again standing close to the abyss. But the first step is for the police openly to accept the depth and seriousness of the problem. Underplaying it in the hope that it might go away has not worked so far and there is no evidence that it will do so in the future.'

* * *

Chris Swarray was the other young man who had confided his fears of being shot to Anthony Stevens. He seemed to know that something bad was coming. In September 1999, Swarray, aged twenty-seven, was sitting with two companions from Manchester in a parked Golf GTi in the Ladywood area of Birmingham when another car containing several men pulled up alongside and a gunman opened fire. Swarray was killed by two bullets, in what police described as an assassination. 'I remember speaking to someone who was very close to Chris who said Chris knew that he had trouble in Birmingham, and he would have to go in a different car,' said Anthony Stevens. 'He even said to somebody that he had just got a feeling that his time was going to come very soon, but there was nothing he could do and he was going to try and enjoy himself the best he could until it happened. People thought he was big, bad Chris Swarray but he was scared for his life. If you have got people like Chris Swarray and Martin Bennett frightened for their lives, just imagine what the rest of them are feeling.' Home Office Minister Paul Boateng condemned the killing and GMP offered a £30,000 reward to catch the killers. At the time of writing, it had not been claimed.

Two searing feuds, the Gooch-Longsight and the Gooch-Doddington, were being conducted in tandem, and in the hostile atmosphere it was inevitable that non-combatants would suffer. In October 1999, courier Judah Tafari Dewar, aged thirty-five, was shot dead in Blethcley Close, Longsight. Dewar, the father of nine children, was an ex-Sale Grammar School pupil who had no connection with gangs or drugs and may have been targeted because he was in the wrong place at the wrong time in the wrong car, a BMW coupé. He had been visiting a friend and had returned to his vehicle when he was shot in the chest. He was found slumped on the ground beside the car with the door still open and died within seconds. Police believe his killer was a fifteen-year-old boy called Thomas Ramsey, who was part of an as yet unrecognised gang forming from a faction of the Doddington. Ramsey was charged but walked free when the case was thrown out for insufficient evidence. Convictions were secured in only eight per cent of shootings in Manchester.

Three more men died over the Christmas and New Year period. Simon Brown, twenty-seven, killed with a close-range shotgun blast to the head outside a Boxing Day party at the Manchester Black Community Trust building in Cheetham Hill. Brown had been fighting a campaign of violence and intimidation against his family by members of the Gooch. He was ambushed by a group of men as he left the party with cousins and friends at 5.30 a.m. On 5 January 2000, the body of Roger Ormsby, thirty-four, was found in his burning BMW in Whalley Range. He had been shot three times in the back of the head; the fire probably started when his foot slipped onto the accelerator, leaving the engine revving for up to half an hour. Ormsby had an expensive lifestyle and owned a garage and several properties but police refused to speculate on his source of income. Again the Gooch were suspected. 'Roger would stop his car and greet me in the street whenever he saw me,' said Fr Phil Sumner. 'He was a likeable character to those who knew him. Obviously, there may have been people who met him in different circumstances.' He left a long-standing partner and three children.

Nine days later, two young men on a motorbike cut down seventeen-year-old Gabriel Egharevba in Longsight. Neighbours found him bleeding heavily on a grass verge shortly before 10 p.m. 'His mate ran back and kept shaking his friend,' said one. 'When we arrived we could see he had been shot in the left temple. He wasn't breathing and there was blood everywhere.' The small crowd tried unsuccessfully to flag down traffic on Hyde Road before paramedics and police arrived, but Gabriel died where he lay. He was known to have been shot by a teenage member of the Longsight Crew, though lack of evidence meant no-one would be prosecuted for the crime. It was the ninth fatal shooting in eight months.

* * *

That January saw heavyweight boxing icon Mike Tyson visit Manchester to fight Julius Francis. Tyson, whose lifestyle had a particular appeal to the gangbangers, made a point of urging the Moss Side gangs to make peace. Within days, however, members of both the Doddington and the Longsight Crew had been hospitalised in shootouts with the Gooch, the police had received intelligence that a Doddie had obtained three Uzi machine pistols and been ordered by his boss to carry out taxings, and three

Young Gooch were spotted in the Great Western pub with a Mac-10. One of the Doddington's heaviest hitters had to be stopped by his mother from going outside to confront ten men in balaclavas outside his house, while two Gooch were stopped in a Honda Integra in the early hours of the morning, both wearing body armour with steel plates front and back.

These were signs that something big was brewing. On April 20, according to police records: 'At 13.50hrs, an anonymous female contacted police stating: "Lee Amos is keeping someone hostage at 66 Ruskin Avenue." ' Amos, known as 'Cabbo', was a Gooch member wanted for questioning in connection with serious crimes and the house, a two-storey, mid-terrace, was a known Gooch address. Covert observation specialists were despatched to watch the house while a large police firearms team was assembled. They fidgeted until a 'firearms investigative authority' was obtained, giving them permission to storm the building. The officers were all conscious of Tunde Adetoro's shooting spree and of the fact that loaded weapons, including a Mac-10, had been pointed at policemen in Moss Side on several occasions in recent months. It could only be a matter of time before one of them took a bullet.

Five hours after the initial tip-off later, heavily armed officers crashed through the front door of the house. There was no hostage; what they found instead were seven members of the Gooch apparently having a 'war council'. With them were six women. In the living room was a fully loaded Colt 45 with the safety catch off and in the back bedroom was a Skorpion machine pistol – which can fire at a rate of 800 rounds per minute – and a loaded revolver. Also found were five suits of body armour, two Alinco scanners tuned to the frequency of the local police division and a pair of night-vision binoculars. Amos and Meshack Gordon were wearing body armour, while Gordon and Colin 'Piggy' Joyce were wearing jeans that had been adapted to conceal guns in the pockets. 'GANG LEADERS SEIZED AT MAFIA-STYLE SUMMIT,' declared the next day's *Daily Record*. 'MURDER SUSPECTS HELD AT "DRUG GANG SUMMIT",' reported *The Times*. This was a dramatic way of saying some of the gang had been meeting to rearm and to plan their on-going conflicts. Their weapons were believed to have been recently purchased from a Birmingham gang. 'We have been after these people for a long time,' said a police source. 'This is a significant breakthrough in our inquiries.'

It was the biggest blow the Gooch had suffered since Operation China years before, and offered hope that more killings might be averted.

CHAPTER SEVENTEEN

Crackdown

PAUL MASSEY'S INFLUENCE on the feuding gangs of Manchester came not from his size or muscle – unlike, say, a Chris Little – but from his mettle.

> It's in your heart, isn't it? It's got to be in your heart because you look around, all your tough fighters, they're crazy. Like Lucky Luciano [founder of the US mafia] and all them, all your gangsters all over, they're not big, are they? They're all little guys, but with big hearts. And you know you've got a big heart. Like my brother, he's six-foot odd, a big hard guy, and to look at him and look at me you'd think he was the one who could handle himself. A lot of people when they cross me . . . they underestimate me.

He was able to command great loyalty through favours done but also through force of personality. Massey had an intensity that others lacked. No-one, not the police, the prison authorities, or rivals, could make him back down if he believed he was justified; he would go all the way on a matter of principle. It made him an anti-hero.

> What it is, I can be trusted. You have got to have trust. I am honest with people and straight. I don't lead people down roads that I wouldn't go down. Basically, I wouldn't use anybody. It is not my style. If I do anything with anybody, we have a discussion and we stick to it. Then you will be recognised as a person to follow.

Massey liked to see himself as a person to whom others turned for help and advice. In October 1996, he even appeared in a bizarre Channel Four documentary about feuding families that included the story of Ken Keating and his son Sean, both from the Ordsall estate. Sean claimed that a £10,000 contract had been taken out on his life by his own father because he was regarded as being a 'grass'. Ken said, 'If I'd have known what Sean was going to do I'd have smothered the little bastard. As far as I am concerned, if people want to be gangsters and mix with the criminal fraternity then they know the consequences if they turn police informer.' Sean, for his part, felt that 'the sooner Ken and all my family dies, the better for me.' Massey appeared as an unspecified intermediary, regretting that father and son had fallen out. The documentary team were impressed by the esteem in which he was held, and sensed Massey was a good story in his own right. They kept in touch, with a view to making him the subject of his own documentary.

Not even Massey could stop the renewal of hostilities in south Manchester, a terrible rollercoaster that now had unstoppable momentum, but his influence had extended beyond the city. Through friends and contacts, he was also instrumental in arranging a truce between two warring factions in Sunderland. On one side was Ernie Bewick, a rugged but reputable man who ran many of the doors in the industrial north-east city; on the other was a family called Waters, with whom Bewick had fallen out. The Waters faction asked Massey, through a mutual friend, to go up and ensure peace. On his intervention, Bewick agreed to leave them alone. Unfortunately Tony Waters broke the agreement and attacked Bewick. In the ensuing fight, Waters suffered fatal injuries.

Massey had similar contacts all over the country, men like Paul Ferris, Glasgow's most famous gangster. According to Ferris, the two met through Scottish drug smuggler Rab Carruthers. 'Rab had been well-established in Manchester since the early 1970s. Through Rab I met a group known as the Salford Gang, in particular Paul Massey. These guys were the tightest, most self-supporting characters you could meet and their reputation was second to none in our world. I took to the group immediately and they've stood by me ever since.'

On home turf, Massey and several of his friends were expanding into the site security industry. When a Salford firm called JS Security, owned by a couple of older men from the area, folded over VAT debts, Massey apparently lent one of the owners £20,000 to start up again. A limited company was registered called PMS. The initials stood for Professionally Manned Security, but everyone assumed it stood for Paul Massey Security. Massey was employed as a consultant.

It came at an unsettled time in the security business in Salford; there had been a spate of mysterious attacks on other security firms, apparently intended to drive them out of the area. Massey insists they were nothing to do with him.

> When PMS started off, right, when other companies, other sites and other properties was getting attacked and burnt and guys getting beaten up and all that, they was blaming PMS. But that never happened . . . and for people like myself who back PMS up, they aren't going to ask me to get involved attacking other sites with other businesses for them to get work . . . We're not out there to get security by violent means.

Someone clearly was, however. In April 1995, two security guards were on duty in a brick gatehouse at the entrance to a business park in Ordsall when petrol bombs were hurled at their lodge. One landed on the roof and another hit a car. It was the first of four similar attacks on sites guarded by the same company. Guards were stoned, abused and some had a burning mattress thrown at them. Others were threatened while out with their families at Salford market. At Easter 1996, someone made a hole in the roof of a sales office on a Salford building site, poured inflammable liquid in, then fired it. Twenty-four hours later, a primary school guarded by the same company, Marpol, was set on fire. The school was paying £1,800 a week for security after yobs had broken forty windows and stoned the headmistress; she had been taunted as a 'grass' for giving evidence to police about youths breaking into a teacher's car. The case attracted national attention because the headmistress Judith Elderkin, of Marlborough Road primary school, stood up and talked about it at the National Union of teachers annual conference. Rumours began to emerge of other schools paying protection money but no-one would go on the record.

Massey said PMS won contracts not by intimidation but because it did a good job. After all, he was associated with it, and few would mess with Massey and his friends in Salford.

*   *   *

One of Massey's principles was that heroin would not be sold in his area. 'Massey has this almost philanthropic attitude about not allowing hard drugs in Salford,' said a journalist who has worked in the city for many years. 'It is known that you just don't go to Salford for heroin and crack. One story circulated that an acquaintance of Massey's became addicted to heroin while in prison. When he came out, Massey kept him in a house for a week until he went cold turkey and came off it.' Some police officers have claimed that this public stance was no more than a sham but it seems to have been true. 'Brown' was perceived as something that black gangs sold, and other Salford men such as Paul 'One-Punch' Doyle were equally opposed to it. 'The guys I knock about with, they won't sell brown,' said Doyle. 'If anyone gets arrested for that, they deserve to. It's just a vermin drug. The nickname of it is smack and it smacks people out of their heads. You see kids on it and they're not capable of anything, they're just monged out.'

The problem was in enforcing such a ban. No-one could regulate the young bucks of Salford for long, and new faces not beholden to anyone were making their mark. One was Vinnie Clay, a six-foot-four terror who scared everyone. He once walked into a pub, put a gun on the bar, loaded it and fired into the roof – for no particular reason. Clay and his mates were suspected of being behind a string of violent incidents, including one in which a policeman was hit over the head with a rake. On another occasion, an officer turned up to deal with a dispute in a chip shop on Langworthy Road. He parked his patrol car and went inside. Clay appeared with a chainsaw and sliced off the car roof. 'I liked Vinnie, he was a character,' said Paul Doyle.

Clay was one of many, and they were uncontrollable. Some of them fell out with Massey over heroin and, perhaps sensing a weakness after some of his friends were arrested for a series of armed robberies, they made a spectacular attempt to kill him, as Massey described.

We had the machine gun fired at us outside my friend's house one day, a Mac-10. Missed, anyway. But y'know, them guys who fired that machine gun, right, they just thought they was going to walk up, pull the trigger and [we] was all going to drop dead like in a film. They didn't even hit anyone. Because it's not how you think it is when you go out to do that. People don't just die that easy.

That was, in my eyes . . . because I'm not letting coke and heroin be sold on the streets. But if them bullets would have fucking hit and done the damage, they wouldn't have been around to sell the coke and the fucking heroin anyway after it. So what's the point of doing that? It's just pointless. They must have thought, *oh, he's got a couple of friends, we'll kill him, the rest will fucking fall in line because we shot the main one.* It doesn't happen. That's in films. This is reality. These people are my friends, they ain't going to go to bed and just leave that guy who's laying there dead.

When it happened, I had a lot of friends, I'm talking, I couldn't put the number of people that come to me and said, 'I'll go and whack them out.' And I went, 'No.' And they just couldn't get their head around it. But they don't understand the background of it and that, you know, friends of ours are friends of [the gunmen], and some of their friends and brothers are friends of ours. It was a bit of a complicated thing really and they was only young kids. So, y'know, we just left it. Really, we give them a squeeze – let them off.

'Giving them a squeeze' was an ambiguous phrase; certainly some of those involved were in mortal fear. Two brothers fled their Salford homes to hide in a caravan park in North Wales, where one of them blew their cover by getting drunk and discharging a machine gun during an argument with some people on the site. When arrested at a railway station with the gun, a silencer and ammunition in a duffle bag, he said he had bought it because he was in fear of his life from organised criminals in Salford. He was jailed for eight years. A young man in Strangeways on a wounding charge was also believed by police to be under a death sentence and was not allowed out for the funeral of his baby daughter in case he was attacked there. Handwritten notes began to appear on lampposts in the Ordsall area, declaring, 'Don't mess with smack or you'll get a crack.' The threat appeared to subside; it seemed that Massey had won again.

He had also scored another victory over the police, walking free from charges of involvement in a full-scale riot at a boxing match in Birmingham. Just a few weeks after the first truce meeting, the popular Salford boxer Steve 'Viking' Foster had challenged Robert McCracken for the latter's British title at the National Exhibition Centre. McCracken himself had a large and boisterous following among Birmingham City's football hooligan gang, the Zulus. So when a coachload of Foster's fans arrived and began chanting abuse, McCracken's followers responded by standing on seats and goading them from the other side of the hall. Scuffling started in a bar during the undercard and soon spilled into the main hall. Dozens of plastic seats were thrown and eventually the two sides clashed on the main floor of the arena, to chants of 'Salford, Salford'. They exchanged punches and used chair legs as iron bars during several minutes of intense fighting while the terrified security team retreated to the back of the hall. The rioting, said to be the worst ever during a British boxing bout, was shown live on national television and when Conservative Party chairman Jeremy Hanley ill-advisedly described it as 'just exuberance' in an interview, the gaffe was partly responsible for him losing his job. Massey was one of several Salford men charged after a police appeal to help identify faces taken off TV footage and security cameras but the case against him was eventually dropped because the identification was inconclusive.

Perhaps his resentment towards the police was partly responsible for his cavalier behaviour when, on Boxing Day 1997, he was stopped on suspicion of drink-driving in his Rolls-Royce. 'This is what I like about having money – I'll get you sorted out,' he said to three police officers. When arrested and put in a van, he pointed at them aggressively and said, 'I will get you all shot. Remember the riots? I told you then, wait till the fog comes down, some bobby will get it. It will be your fault.' His tirade continued on the journey to the station as he banged on the side of the van and hurled abuse: 'I will have you shot. You will have to watch your backs. I don't need to do it now, I will wear a balaclava on a dark night.' The intoximeter showed Massey was twice the legal limit. He was charged with threats to kill and released on bail.

It did not stop him participating in another TV documentary. Amber Valley Productions, a Derby-based independent production company, had been given a reported £100,000 commission to record a programme for *Modern Times*, the quirky, slice-of-life documentary series on BBC Two. The programme would portray the lives and views of certain 'Salford lads', with Massey to the fore. He recorded several interviews and was filmed on a trip to Amsterdam and a family holiday in Scotland. He told the film-makers his hero was William Wallace of *Braveheart* fame: 'Because when he had a fight, he had a proper fight, that kid. You have got to admire him for the courage. People have stood by him and fought with him as well. He fought for a good cause.' Massey was a canny interviewee, careful not to incriminate himself or others and often hinting at things rather than saying them outright. One particular outburst, however, seemed calculated to cause the maximum concern among Salford's local government officials and the police. 'I've got a bit of a surprise coming for Salford council soon,' he said.

So what we've decided to do, on the next election we're going to put our representatives forward, you know, as an independent state, which is going to be Salford. We're going to get a respectable person who's going to stand forward to be elected, because we've give Salford Council chance after chance after chance. They've been there forty years, there's only one way to move them – get a candidate, put him forward. We know a hell of a lot of people in Salford. I think the last councillor who got any votes, he got four hundred. There's a crisis in Salford at the moment because nobody votes. Now, if we put a candidate forward, I reckon a lot of people will decide . . . Salford will be a better place. We've sat down, I've discussed it with quite a few important people who I know, not villains, I'm talking educated people who go to university, college, deal in politics … and they all say it's a brilliant idea.

* * *

The boom in Manchester's leisure economy continued through the latter part of the nineties, an entertainment, shopping and architectural renaissance barely restrained even by the most significant event of 1996: the detonation of Britain's largest-ever peacetime bomb by the IRA. The massive blast wrecked a large part of the city centre but was almost immediately seized on as an opportunity for further re-building by planners, developers and entrepreneurs. Above all, the number of licensed premises continued to surge ahead as the thrust for a 'twenty-four-hour' metropolis continued.

For one club, the most important of them all, it was too late. The Hacienda had been living on borrowed time for years, and in 1996 the police carried out another long undercover investigation there into ecstasy dealing. They then called in the owners and told them that while they would not apply to close the venue, the dealing had to stop. Under an Act passed in the dying days of John Major's Conservative administration, local councils had the power to revoke club licences immediately if they believed there was drug-taking or dealing 'on or near' the premises. No convictions were required: it fell to the clubs to prove they were innocent. A year later, however, the police took a tougher line and applied simultaneously to revoke the licences of the Hacienda, Generation X and Central Park.

Perhaps the club could have been saved had it not been for an extraordinary incident in July 1997, when a minibus carrying seven licensing magistrates, a court official and two senior police officers arrived for a Friday night spot-check. They found a Dantean commotion of bloodied youths, the aftermath of a Salford attack on some young men from the St Helens area who had walked unsuspectingly into the 'wrong' area of the club. Before their eyes, an eighteen-year-old from Haydock was hit across the head with a car jack and then run down, apparently on purpose, by a car outside the club's front entrance. He suffered a fractured skull and was 'critical' for two days.

There was no coming back this time. Two days later, the Hacienda announced it was closing for financial reasons. Fac 51, as the Hacienda was also known, had debts of debts of £500,000 and, anyway, the game was up. The police had been 'regrettably' planning to oppose its licence; they said that despite continued warnings about the way the club was being run, its problems had persisted. Talks were reportedly held with a Mayfair-based leisure company in a last-ditch attempt to keep the venue alive, albeit as a more upmarket club. The company was seen as respectable though the police wanted assurances that the security would be run by a recognised out-of-town firm; Manchester door agencies were no longer trusted. The talks came to nothing. After fifteen years, the party was over.

★　★　★

The city's most powerful politician had had enough. Richard Leese had taken over as leader of the Labour-dominated Manchester City Council just four weeks after the IRA bomb. He had seen the city centre transformed by spectacular development and bold architecture. Manchester was changing, and for the better. Memories of its forlorn application to host the Olympic Games had been dispelled by euphoria at a successful

Commonwealth Games bid. Leese had also presided over an entertainment boom that saw the number of licensed premises in the city centre rise from 250 in 1996 to more than 400 in 1998. Brown-field development, warehouse conversion, loft-living and modernist canalside café-bars heralded a sea change in the city centre. 'Even *urban* has come to mean something different,' said developer Tom Bloxham, who played a substantial role in the transformation of the city. 'It used to be urban decay, urban deprivation, urban blight. Now urban means modern and progressive.'[84]

Yet crime and loutish behaviour were a constant drag on the city's image. The triangular war in south Manchester had plumbed depths of horror unimaginable a decade earlier. Property crime by junkies to fund their habits had cast Manchester as Britain's crime capital. On top of that was the constant encroachment of violent disorder into the very city centre Leese and others were so keen to champion. Over a period of twelve months, four innocent young men were killed while out at night, including two on the same Saturday night: Simon Speakman was punched and kicked to death when he intervened to help a woman in a row with a man in a café while out celebrating his twenty-seventh birthday, while Steven Hughes, twenty-two was stabbed less than 400 yards away. The popular J.W.Johnson's bar in Deansgate put a sign at the door: 'Please check your firearms at the bar.' Having just suffered a violent robbery, they were only half joking. The club scene was in a malaise compared to the more vibrant Leeds and Liverpool; many Manchester promoters and club owners didn't feel it was worth the hassle any more. Even clubbers moving outside the city to popular nights like Peruvia in Cheshire found the gangs there too, taking over the VIP room and bullying staff into supplying cheap champagne.

Leese had none of the machine politics or the public profile of his predecessor Graham Stringer; indeed, most Mancunians would not have known who he was. A former teacher and youth worker with a degree in pure maths, he was a personable, committed politician, one of a new generation of civil entre-preneurs more interested in end results that politicking. He liked to get things done. So in March 1998, Leese composed a highly critical letter to Chief Constable David Wilmot. He said the problems of 'thugs and gangsters seem to have escalated, spreading to other areas of business activity within the city centre. And now they are seriously undermining business confidence so vital for the city's regeneration.' He complained that 'rampant lawlessness' was overtaking the city's clubs, leading to a crisis of confidence among potential investors in the city, yet the police seemed 'either unable or unwilling' to tackle the gangsters.

Somehow the letter was leaked to a reporter at the *Manchester Evening News*. When its contents appeared on the front page, a political storm broke. The inescapable conclusion was that, for Leese to make those comments, things must have been far more serious than most people realised. 'While the city had been bidding for international sporting events, inward investment and a place among the European elite, he'd always been upbeat about Manchester. But the remarks addressed to the Chief Constable seemed positively apocalyptic. The marketing mask had slipped.'[85]

Within twenty-four hours, the leader of Salford City Council weighed in. Bill Hinds said David Wilmot should be 'called to account' for 'the cancer of crime dragging us down and suffocating us.' He added, 'It is not just a handful of nightclubs which are suffering, it is the ordinary man and woman in the street. The public are scared and they are not getting the policing service they are paying for and deserve. Crime is the number one issue in Salford and we want something done. We are just not satisfied with the policing in this city. We have regular meetings with the police but things never seem to improve.' Again, the story made headlines and was a further embarrassment to the police. The officer in charge of the city centre's pubs and clubs, Ch Supt Peter Harris, did say that new measures had been drawn up after a crisis meeting the previous year. 'So far this has involved gaining more information and intelligence about those responsible. But disruptive tactics may come in – and our methods will be sophisticated.'

On April 5, bank worker Nick Centi was stabbed to death on

Whitworth Street while trying to stop a fight. It was the fifth murder in the city centre in a year and the third on Whitworth Street. None of them were specifically gang-related – just thuggery – but they reflected the tense nature of the city, the readiness to use weapons. Violent crime in Manchester had just risen forty-nine per cent year-on-year under a new recording method.

Centi's killing was followed within a couple of weeks by an old-fashioned door war. Applejacks, on Portland Street, was a popular venue, often frequented by gang members, and its door had had a chequered history, changing hands between a Salford-backed firm and Loc-19 Security. After closing for refurbishment, the club reopened with a new team, Platinum Security, from the London area. They installed state-of-the-art CCTV and liaised closely with the police, as they were expecting trouble. The Manchester men were not happy and one night a mob steamed into the club and attacked the doormen. The bosses of Loc-19 were arrested and subsequently jailed for the disorder, though they denied the charges. The prosecution claimed they had lost the Applejacks door in Portland Street to a 'more professional outfit' and had caused trouble inside and outside the club in order to get the contract back.

It seemed to be the best and most upmarket club nights that suffered the most, those that brought in the soap stars and footballers and prettiest women. 'Our core audience are successful people,' the co-promoter of the Devotion night told *City Life*. 'They wear expensive clothes and they look fantastic. Members of the underworld want to mingle with these people.' They also wanted to get in without paying, haggle aggressively over bottles of champagne, or even run the doors and levy protection money. The *Manchester Evening News* ran a spread under the headline 'CANCER IN CLUBLAND' bemoaning the damage being done to the city's night-time economy and quoting an unnamed club manager: 'There is a cancer in clubland and it's spreading throughout the city. Clubs are being closed because of the activities of perhaps 100 criminals. These people are eating their way through clubland.' The problems had become so acute that people were finally prepared to speak out, even at the risk of damaging the city's image.

For Chief Constable David Wilmot, under fire from the council, the Press, the public and even some of his own officers, it was time something was done.

★ ★ ★

Drivers heading into Manchester for a night out on the last weekend of April, 1998, must have felt as though they were rolling into Belfast or Gaza. Roadblocks stretched across the main routes into the centre. Cars were stopped and their occupants questioned by officers in Kevlar shot-proof vests while armed officers clasped Heckler and Koch guns nearby. Some were asked to step out of their vehicles and were body-searched right there under the streetlights as passers-by gawped. Known faces were filmed, quizzed and warned off. Highly visible foot patrols toured the central areas, walking into pubs and clubs, scanning the crowds.

Operation Sulu was David Wilmot's response to the public criticism of city centre policing. It was an approach unprecedented in mainland Britain except in the aftermath of terrorist attack. In the first two weekends, ninety-six cars were stopped and 170 people were questioned. 'We aim to show the villains who's in charge,' said Peter Owen, the city centre police chief. 'They've got too big for their boots. Half the people checked were target criminals. This is our town. It doesn't belong to small, arrogant groups who think they own it.' Wilmot also agreed to a PR interview with the *Manchester Evening News* in which he denied the charges of rampant lawlessness while managing to say little of interest. Wilmot was certainly no James Anderton in the attention-grabbing stakes, but he had been stung by the public criticism.

The gangsters took it badly. One carried his own hand-held camcorder around and filmed the police filming him. Another delivered a sinister warning to Pat Karney, chairman of the council's city centre committee and an energetic advocate of Manchester as a 'twenty-four-hour' leisure and entertainment centre. Karney had publicly supported the crackdown. 'I had a personal threat from a particular gang leader. He passed a message to somebody that works for me in the town hall saying that they were finding out where I lived. It's an indication of how far this cancer of fear has spread where they can put indirect threats to elected people like myself. Once that happens and if elected people get them we might as well give up and go home.'

Operation Sulu continued, eventually topping 150 arrests. The council agreed to pay almost £500,000 for eighteen city centre security cameras to monitor the city centre around the clock, the first phase of a plan to have 100 cameras overlooking the centre. 'People need to know Big Brother is watching everyone,' said Pat Karney. 'We want Manchester to be a safe place for everyone to enjoy.' A few years earlier, a Labour council would have freaked at accusations of 'Big Brother' surveillance. Now it was positively bragging about it. The change did not go unnoticed. 'It is interesting to see the shift in politicians from the early seventies, when they were very anti a strict regime, to the scene now, where Labour politicians are cracking down on law and order,' said Frank Halligan, the former divisional commander who is now retired from the force. 'That is because they are getting stick from their constituents. They are now hand-in-hand with the arch-demons of capitalism and the police.'

* * *

It was Paul Massey's finest hour. Independence Day, 1998, and a sultry July night. Massey in beige sweatshirt, blue-grey jeans and white trainers, driving a silver R-reg Audi through Salford into Manchester. His friend Michael Adamou next to him. Trailing them are several members of the film crew working for an independent production company. They had both a minicam and a DV cam. Massey wanted to show them *his* city at night, and the power he wielded once the sun went down. No police clampdown was going to stop him.

Massey stops outside the offices of PMS Security. He dials someone on his mobile phone: 'I've got your champagne. We're in Salford now. We're going to the Kentucky to get a sandwich and we'll meet you there.'

They set off and meet three men in a blue, N-reg BMW convertible with the roof down. The driver is Greg Hayes. In the front passenger seat is the shaven-headed figure of Paul Flannery and behind him is Mark Boomer. There are shouts and whoops between the two cars. Music bangs out of the stereo in the BMW. They move off together, the Audi, the Beamer and the film crew in a Peugeot 306. At Oldham Street in Manchester city centre, they pull up outside a club. 'This is Idols nightclub,' says Boomer. 'One of the boys'.'

Next they are off to Discotheque Royale, the camera so close it shows the scar on the back of Flannery's head. They call over the head doorman and shake his hand. Then they choose a bewildered, apprehensively smiling couple from the crowd and have them let into the club for free. Then they are off again, to Sankey's Soap, where they shout, 'Damian Noonan,' but the former Hacienda doorman fails to show his face.

They head for Joop at high speeds, with whooping, jeering and banter between the cars, like urban cowboys, then on to Canal Street, heart of the Gay Village. Next it's Holy City Zoo. Massey is smoking a fag. The bouncers, clearly unhappy to see them, close and lock the door. Flannery throws a Budweiser bottle at the security camera, rudely ordering people in the queue to move aside. Then he throws a glass. 'How do you smash this camera?' he asks, of no-one in particular. A police van, unseen, pulls up alongside and Flannery spots it. 'It was him . . . it was you . . . that's the man,' he quips. The cops move off, slowly.

Back to Joop, driving fast, Flannery holding a traffic cone onto the front of the windscreen. Massey is now in the back of Flannery's car and they have been joined by 'Mike', a mean-looking man with a goatee. Someone throws a glass towards Joop. This time the camera crew is stopped by cops for leaning out of the sun roof of a Peugeot 306 to film the BMW convertible. The officer gives the cameraman a ticket for not wearing his seatbelt. The crew rejoin Massey and friends outside 21 Piccadilly. A small crowd gathers around the BMW.

Now en route to a club called the Beat N Track, Massey lets loose. 'We hate the fucking police,' he shouts. 'We leave 'em six feet under.' He stands up on the rear seat of the BMW and holds his arms aloft, a champagne bottle in one hand, the buildings blurring past as he sings the 'viking song':

> *Da-derrr der. Da-derrr der.*
> *Da-der, da-der, da-der, da-der, da-der.*

It was a perfect cameo: a king of the city with his film crew in tow, chauffeur driven in an expensive car, swigging champagne and declaring his contempt for the law.

They pull up outside the Beat N Track club. Some friends come over and they shake hands, Massey still standing in the back of the car. In the club doorway, a man in a white shirt with what looks like blood on it gets up off the floor and walks in a dazed state down the road. Perhaps he has been thumped. The film crew take some shots inside the club. Then things start to go wrong . . .

A section of the film recording is taped over. There are meaningless cutaways of carpet and a cigarette lighter. It looks like the inside of a house. Suddenly, it cuts back to outside the Beat N Track again. It is 4 a.m. and there is a scene of commotion. Flannery, in his car, is arguing with an Asian male. Sirens flash. An angry crowd of black youths has gathered in the street. A young man saunters over to the film crew. 'Someone's dying, mate,' he says.

Something terrible had happened between the group pulling up at the Beat N Track and the later scenes outside, something not shown on the film. When the group arrived, they came across the parked coach of a stag party from Leeds, most of whom were inside the venue. Massey urinated against the side of the coach. Some of the Leeds group, who had gone to the coach for a break, remonstrated with him. He reacted by smashing a window with a champagne bottle, reaching through the broken glass and grabbing a bag. Another bag was snatched and the driver, increasingly alarmed, drove off, with some of the Leeds group on board. The minibus was chased by the BMW, with its soft-top down. As the two vehicles drove neck-and-neck, the occupants of the BMW made threatening gestures. Massey was seen to have a knife.

The terrified coach driver was forced reluctantly to return to Whitworth Street to collect the rest of the Leeds group. Massey and friends arrived back there too. Soon after, some men were seen in heated conversation with the large figure of Wayne Wisdom, one of the Leeds men. Wisdom launched headbutts at the two men but was himself stabbed in the groin. A British Transport Police sergeant returning home from his shift intervened and grabbed the knifeman but was manhandled and the stabber got away. Wisdom managed to stagger to the coach, blood literally spurting from his wound, before collapsing. Paramedics were so worried he would die that a policeman drove their ambulance to hospital while they tried to staunch the bleeding. Wayne Wisdom lost so much blood that for a while he was without pulse or blood pressure. Only the skill of the trauma surgeons saved him.

There followed a flurry of phone calls over the next few hours to and from the mobile phones of two of the film crew to an address in Salford and a pager later found at Massey's mother's home. Meanwhile, Paul Massey disappeared. A huge manhunt began and detectives, alerted to the presence of a film crew at the scene, began a search for the tapes they hoped might give clues to the identity of his attacker. Eventually they were granted a court order by the Old Bailey to seize the film from the BBC in London. Each film had a time code on it that showed when each frame had been filmed. It did not show what they had hoped; the film had apparently been edited within a few hours of the incident and sections of it now featured irrelevant but extended footage of carpet and a cigarette lighter.

> Shortly after 7 a.m. the editing of the original film took place at 4 Brown Street [in Salford]. In short, it was tampered with . . . the sequence of events shown on the video was interrupted, and sections of the original tape were filmed over and replaced with apparently disconnected film taken at

4 Brown Street . . . it was therefore no longer a film of events of that evening, but a film in which a series of sequences was interrupted and anything of real probative value over-filmed by inconsequential footage.[86]

While it was later accepted by the Crown that the moment of Wisdom's stabbing had not been filmed, it seemed the film had been doctored, for whatever reason.

Between July 14 and September 19, efforts were made to locate Massey through his solicitors. He failed to attend Liverpool Crown Court in August to face charges of threatening to kill police officers, informing his solicitor he would not be attending. 'He has more pressing matters on his mind,' said his solicitor. Police eventually traced him to Holland, where he was arrested on September 19. He was eventually charged with wounding, conspiring to commit violent disorder and violent disorder. In the meantime four members of the film crew – the director, producer and two cameramen – had been charged with conspiracy to pervert the course of justice.

★   ★   ★

Massey had predicted what would happen in Salford if he was locked away again. In an interview recorded by the film crew before the events of July 4, he had outlined an apocalyptic scenario:

It'd fucking explode if I took off from Salford. It's as simple as that. Because I know all them people around Salford, different units of people, don't like each other, and there's only me stood in the middle of them all keeping them apart. So you know, take me, then you'll see. Because you see what happened when they took the Krays, you know what I'm saying? They had them streets fucking cleaned. And as soon as they went, it just fucking sunk, didn't it? Like the *Titanic*. And that's what'll happen with Salford.

The first sign that he might be right came within weeks of his arrest, not in Salford but a few miles away along the East Lancs Road. First, five men blasted their way into a house in Atherton, near Leigh, with a shotgun and brutally chopped the thirty-seven-year-old occupant with a machete. Another man was attacked at a house nearby. Two weeks later, twenty-five-year-old Louis Makin was sitting in his friend's house in Leigh watching the highlights of the Charity Shield football match on television when two men in balaclavas burst in, one carrying a Samurai sword. The friend made a run for it but Makin was caught in the kitchen and hacked down like an animal. When he raised his limbs to protect himself, they were chopped almost off. It took surgeons forty-eight hours to stem the bleeding and his right arm later had to be amputated above the elbow. 'There's something organised building up in the area and it's very, very worrying,' said an ambulance officer.

Makin had been in the wrong place at the wrong time, caught up in a dispute that did not concern him. A Salford crew was making moves to take over heroin and cocaine distribution in the Leigh area by displacing the existing dominant gang. The machete seemed to be their favourite weapon. The next couple of months saw several more attacks, including one on a young man trapped in the toilets of the Salford Arms pub. Two Salford men, Bernard Cleary and the terrifying Vinnie Clay, were later charged with the attack on Louis Makin. Both were cleared but Cleary was imprisoned for six years for offering to supply heroin.

Another gang from the seething Salford underworld targeted Sheffield, where the club scene was thriving and where they were not known to the police. The Niche club, an alcohol-free dance all-nighter, was open for longer hours than any other club in the city and was a magnet for dance-drug suppliers. Three hundred people were still inside at 7.45 one morning when a young woman told door staff that three men were taunting her boyfriend. The doormen tried to eject them but four others joined in and launched a ferocious, Salford-style assault with bottles, knives and bricks. Club owner Mick Baxendale, aged forty-eight, was stabbed through the heart and died.

The Salford underworld was further destabilised by a wide-ranging and spectacularly successful police inquiry. Hundreds of officers raided sixty houses in March 1999 in the culmination of Operation Victory, a year-long probe into criminal activities ranging from drug supply to ram-raiding, handling stolen goods and weapons offences. Planning for the operation had started the year before, when Salford police chiefs convinced commanders that two hotspots – Little Hulton and Eccles – needed special attention, and trained undercover detectives infiltrated the gangs. 'SWOOP ON THE UNTOUCHABLES,' proclaimed the *Manchester Evening News*, which called it 'the biggest-ever attack on criminals in Greater Manchester.' Forty-six defendants were eventually charged, including Paul 'One-Punch' Doyle, who later admitted conspiring to supply cannabis and cocaine and was jailed for seven years. Doyle, then forty-one, was not a coke dealer but had been persistently asked by an undercover officer if he could help him obtain 'powder' and eventually passed him on to someone who could. It was enough to trap him.

Removing Doyle and his closest associates from the streets added to the unstable situation created by Massey's incarceration, and more anarchy was to come.

*   *   *

Salford is a hotbed of Manchester United support, and so dozens of people were crammed into the Ship pub in Pendleton at lunchtime on Saturday, 24 April 1999, to watch the Reds play away at Leeds live on TV. Among them was a thirty-two-year-old Stephen Lydiate, a well-known face in the area. Lydiate had been sent to youth custody when he was nineteen for robbing an off licence, and later served a longer jail sentence for kidnap. He was a violent man and had been making waves since coming out of jail with his own young firm. He was also the director of a reclaimed brick company.

Just after 1 p.m., a powerfully built black or mixed-race man entered the pub wearing a three-quarter-length, waterproof coat, combat trousers and a scarf covering his face. He was holding an automatic handgun. He walked straight towards Lydiate, stood about twelve feet from his target and fired … again and again and again. Lydiate was hit eight times in the chest, stomach, left arm, elbow and upper thigh. Ricochets or bullet fragments hit two other people as drinkers dived under tables and chairs. Others ran for their lives through the pub doors. The bullet-riddled Lydiate was taken to the intensive care unit at Hope Hospital where he was put on round-the-clock police guard.

The story behind the attempted hit was a complicated underworld saga that will probably never fully be revealed, but it seems that the men who ordered it feared that Lydiate had accepted a contract to kill *them* and got their retaliation in first. It was later alleged in court that Lydiate believed two men called Deaffern and Calderwood were behind the hit and had brought in two brothers named Jamma to carry it out. Deaffern was an international drug dealer who lived north of Manchester. Though the hit failed, it must have seemed to them that Lydiate would be out of action for a long time, if not permanently. They were wrong. Lydiate not only survived but even from his hospital bed conceived what was later described as 'a revenge plot of biblical proportions'. He vowed to track down the men he held responsible, and decided to kidnap their friends and associates and, if necessary, torture them to extract information.

Just twelve days after being blasted almost to oblivion, Stephen Lydiate discharged himself from hospital with a bullet still lodged inside him, and gathered his 'firm' around him. Over the next few days, a number of vehicles were stolen or bought for cash around Manchester. Then the plot began in earnest.

May 19: Just after 9 a.m., two men attempt to force their way into the home of self-employed builder Tony Shenton in Monton, Eccles. His girlfriend screams from an upstairs windows, and the men walk off. Two hours later, David Foster is abducted from a house in Salford, stabbed three times in the legs, and a gun is put in his mouth. 'Shall we murder him?' asks one of his assailants. Instead they take him to Hickey Farm near Tyldesley, west of

Salford. He is pistol-whipped and forced to give up the address of his brother-in-law, Jimmy Kent, then released.

May 20: Lydiate's gang book three rooms in the Campanile Hotel in Salford and establish it as their base of operations. Lydiate later collects his belongings and retreats with his wife to a hideaway caravan in Wales while the plot unfolds.

May 22: Thirty-seven-year-old Jimmy Kent is woken at his home in Lowton, near Leigh, in the middle of the night by four men in balaclavas. They shoot him once in each leg and drag him out to a white van. A short distance away, he is transferred to a car and the van is set on fire. They take him to Hickey Farm. He is hit on the head with a machete, asked where Deaffern and Calderwood are, and is told he is going to be killed. A man is brought in to commit buggery on him as a further means of exerting pressure, but the man refuses because Kent is bleeding so heavily. Salt is poured into Kent's wounds and a branch is forced into them and twisted, causing extreme pain. Shortly after noon, Kent rings a man asking for £50,000 for his safe release. The ransom demand is passed on to Kent's brother.

May 23: Kent is moved to a first-floor council flat in the Lower Kersal district of Salford and handcuffed to a cot. In the meantime, Kent's brother finally contacts the police and tells them of the ransom demand.

May 24: At a quarter past midnight, Tony Shenton, the target for an earlier abduction, is snatched from his home by five masked men. He is blasted in the leg with a 12-bore gun, then thrown into the boot of a car and taken to the same room as Jimmy Kent. There the two wounded men lie in agony. Shenton is held prisoner for fourteen hours and questioned over the whereabouts of Deaffern, Calderwood and the Jammas. Salt is poured onto his leg wound, a pillowcase put over his head and a gun shoved into his mouth. He hears a number of clicks but the gun is empty. He is told that his wife has been captured and is going to be raped.

Kent's brother is contacted and directed to an address. He carries £10,500 for the return of his brother. Officers from the National Crime Squad observe him meeting some men in a stolen Rover Coupé.

At 11.30 a.m., Michael Davidson rushes out of a Salford shop to his girlfriend and two children waiting in their BMW and tells her to drive away quickly. They are pursued by a Rover and shots are fired at them. The Rover forces the BMW to stop. Davidson gets out and bravely struggles with his attackers. He is shot in the leg. The Rover drives off.

At 5.09 p.m., police receive a call stating that a man they are looking for is in a van opposite Pendlebury Children's Hospital. They find Tony Shenton in the back of a stolen Transit. He has gunshot wounds to his leg and knee.

May 25: Jimmy Kent is given sleeping tablets in a drink. He manages, when his guard is not in the room, to exchange his glass with the guard's glass and his captor later falls into a drugged stupor, allowing Kent to escape. That night men are observed taking bloody floorboards from the flat where he had been held and loading them into a van. A news blackout imposed by police since the beginning of the attacks is lifted. At the same time, four of the conspirators decide it is time to hide out. They decamp, bizarrely, to a warden-controlled flat for elderly people, where they hide for a week.

On June 17, three men were arrested at a flat in Weaste, Salford, and guns and ammunition were discovered. Various other gang members were arrested over the next few weeks, including Lydiate himself. The old folk's accommodation was searched and a holdall hidden in a roof space was found to contain two shotguns and a self-loading pistol.

Ten men, all from the Salford area, eventually stood trial at Preston Crown Court for a variety of charges including conspiracy to kidnap, conspiracy to murder and possession of firearms. All pleaded not guilty. After a lengthy trial, Lydiate was jailed for life. Michael Boyle was given fifteen years, Jason Danson

ten years, Paul Allerton eight and Asa Dwyer eight. The other
defendants were acquitted. 'In a city where shootings have become
common, this is a case set apart by its savagery and brutality,'
said Judge Peter Openshaw, QC, as he passed sentence. 'This
success belongs not only to Greater Manchester Police but also
to the people of Salford, those who have lived with the fear
generated by men who believe themselves untouchable,' said
Chief Superintendent Chris Wells afterwards.

★ ★ ★

Paul Massey's trial was to be conducted amid extraordinary
security. Journalists were vetted and issued with special laminated
passes under the Official Secrets Act, while armed guards stood
both outside and inside the court and the courtroom door was
locked even though no specific permission had been given by the
judge to do so. Gareth Hughes, Massey's solicitor, protested to
the judge at a preliminary hearing about the measures, which he
believed would give the jury a jaundiced impression of his client.
'Mister Massey has never misbehaved in a court,' he argued.
'There has been for many years bad blood between Mister Massey
and the police. I say there is an element of window-dressing in
the presence of these armed officers.' Prosecutor Peter Wright,
however, argued that 'the defendant has set himself up as a
gangster figure.' The judge expressed unhappiness at the guns in
court but said he had to operate under guidelines laid down by
the Attorney General and his hands were tied.

The few national newspaper journalists who turned up for
the trial were distinctly sceptical about Massey's alleged status,
especially on seeing him in the dock in his sweatshirt and
jeans. 'Is that him?' snorted one. Massey did not fit their
stereotypes. They didn't get it: Massey was a Salford lad; he
didn't do suits.

The court was told that Massey and friends were out that
night being filmed for a planned documentary. Their conduct
degenerated through a 'cocktail of drink, the attention of the
film-makers, the public and a degree of self-adulation,' said Peter

Wright, prosecuting. The group were 'bent on trouble' and, following an argument, Massey and Wisdom clashed. 'He was seen to headbutt Mister Massey, who then lunged at him before pulling away. He was holding a knife. Mister Wisdom had been stabbed in the groin and was losing blood at a most alarming rate. He staggered to the bus and collapsed.' A major artery had been severed. Massey then threatened others with the knife before a passing police sergeant tried to arrest him. The officer saw him with a metal object and heard him shout, 'Get rid of this.' Mark Boomer then attacked the officer and he and Massey made off. The knife also disappeared.

Massey, then thirty-nine, denied wounding Wisdom with intent, while Boomer denied assaulting the officer to prevent the lawful detention of Massey. Both men, along with Flannery and Hayes, denied plotting to commit violent disorder. It was Massey's case that he was inside the Beat N Track at the time of the stabbing, not outside, and both Flannery and a doorman testified to this. Wisdom himself said he could not identify his attacker, in fact he 'had no idea' who it was; his eyes had 'gone out of focus' when he felt the pain caused by the wound.

Though the circumstantial evidence was strong, the Crown case was far from watertight. Charges of conspiring to commit violent disorder against Massey, Boomer, Paul Flannery and Greg Hayes were dropped because of 'evidential problems'. Massey continued to deny wounding and Boomer denied assaulting the policeman.

The day of reckoning came on 28 April 1999, the fifteenth day of the trial. The jury deliberated for just under five hours before finding both Massey and Boomer guilty. Massey, in electric-blue polo shirt and grey-blue canvas trousers, remained impassive, only a slight clasping and unclasping of his fingers suggesting any nerves. Boomer sat next to him, looking dopey.

Massey's antecedents – his criminal convictions – were read out: in trouble as juvenile; first appearance at Crown Court, sent to borstal for burglary and later for an offence involving violence and criminal damage; 1977, fined for ABH and criminal damage; dishonesty, recalled to borstal; suspended sentence for dishonesty; ABH, criminal damage and assault, jailed for six months; 1981, unlawful wounding, jailed for nine months; July 1986, offences involving the importation and distribution of counterfeit currency, five years; the same year, twelve months consecutive for dishonesty; 1990, conduct causing alarm and distress, fined; 1991, criminal damage, suspended sentence, and public order offence, sixty days in jail reduced to twenty-one on appeal and suspended.

'This offence was one of the most serious of its kind in relation to consequences and method,' Judge David Owen told him. 'You know full well it carries a potential sentence of life imprisonment. You were equipped with a knife which you used in a manner calculated to cause at the very least grievous bodily harm. You stabbed this man . . . damaging the femural artery. In consequence your victim lost so much blood he was left without pulse or blood pressure. People thought he was dead and he very nearly was. Miraculously he came back from the brink. The fact he is alive is due to the skill of those who treated him. Crime has consequences. You knew of them and fled the country.' He jailed Massey for fourteen years for the stabbing and an extra nine months for skipping bail.

An armed officer in blue uniform burst out of the courtroom to tell his colleagues: 'He's got fourteen years and nine months!' A second later came a shout of 'bastards' and Massey's friends came through the doors from the public gallery. 'You've got what you wanted, you've got what you wanted,' Eddie Taylor shouted to the police guards, who began to finger their weapons nervously. 'Leave it,' growled the massive, gold-decked figure of Damian Noonan. Some of the cops eyeballed them but none said anything and the Salford contingent disappeared down the stairs. Just one person remained in the public gallery to see Mark Boomer sentenced. He was jailed for twenty-one months. Judge Owen thanked the members of the jury, hailed the jury system 'that has stood us in good stead for hundreds of years', and departed. 'It was a show trial,' complained Massey's junior counsel, while his client waited for an armed motorcade to whisk him the short distance to Strangeways.

'MR BIG JAILED,' declared the front page of the next day's *Manchester Evening News.*

* * *

Paul Massey would subsequently appeal against his conviction and though he did not succeed, he did get a reduction in sentence, from fourteen years to ten. In October 1999, however, Massey was convicted at Liverpool Crown Court on three counts of making threats to kill police officers. He denied the charges, though admitted he had been drinking and smoking cannabis on the night in question and said if he had made the threats, they were hollow. 'You know when you are drunk you speak a load of rubbish,' he said. He was sentenced to two years' imprisonment, to run consecutively to the sentence he was already serving.

The film-makers from Amber Valley Productions were cleared of conspiracy to pervert the course of justice when, after five days of argument over the admissibility of certain witness statements, the prosecution offered no evidence against them and the jury was directed to reach a verdict of not guilty. Four men had denied erasing crucial film footage and said they had not filmed the stabbing. 'They did not believe us because they had pinned all their hopes on the fact that the stabbing was caught on film,' said producer Marcus Sulley outside court. 'The police were a little unhappy with the fact we were making this film, thinking it was going to glamorise the crime and become "The Paul Massey Show".' Their documentary was completed but has never been broadcast.

The arrests and convictions of Massey, Doyle and Lydiate were a major success for Greater Manchester Police, who saw them as top-end men who others looked up to and followed: men who ran firms. 'Local practitioners distinguish between "crime firms" and "gangs". Crime "firms" are seen in Greater Manchester to be more organised, more instrumental, and more specifically focussed on crime than street gangs. Members tend to be white, older and less visible in public places. There have evidently been conflicts in the past between South Manchester gangs and "crime firms" of this kind based in Salford. The latter have reputedly tended to traffic mainly in different drugs from the South Manchester gangs, have been more involved in providing protection for clubs in central Manchester, and have been more organised.'[87]

There was no cure-all for the problems of Manchester city centre, however. It remained a violent place; it always will. A gang ejected from Royale's on Peter Street returned with a shotgun and machete and chased doormen into the club, firing. Ben Kamanalagi, a doorman at Epic nightclub, was beaten to death in a Salford street by a young gang he had previously thrown out of the club; he tried to defend himself with a retractable cosh but was overwhelmed, beaten with bats and a wooden post and suffered twenty-three separate injuries, included a fractured skull. Even Damian Noonan was shot on the door of the Phoenix Club in Oxford Road. He went to casualty for treatment but refused to co-operate with police.

In October 1999, the police mounted their biggest-ever crackdown on 'nightlife predators'. Treble the normal number of officers swamped the city centre from 10 p.m. onwards to target known criminals. Roadblocks were once again erected to intercept motorists heading into the centre, mainly on the south side of the city, while mounted officers, dog handlers and special constables augmented a force of dozens of bobbies and plainclothes officers. Cars and people were searched for drugs and weapons and a mobile CCTV camera car called the Spy Hawk recorded faces. 'A lot of puzzled people asked what was going on,' said Inspector Pat McKelvey, 'but when we said we were just trying to protect their city, they seemed more than happy.'

CHAPTER EIGHTEEN

The Pitt Bulls

TOMMY PITT CAME out of a young offenders' institution and hit the streets of south Manchester like an electric charge. Just as each generation of gangbanger seemed wilder than the one before, from the Gladiator to White Tony to Ray 'Pittbull' Pitt, now Thomas was the baddest of them all. He had grown up steeped in gang culture, been a gunman and drug dealer while barely out of junior school, served time in youth custody and secure units, seen family and friends die. The gang life was all he knew.

Pitt found his faction of the Doddington in disarray, reeling from civil war and deadly assaults by the Gooch. Through the fearful force of his personality, his drive to avenge his dead brother, and his utter ruthlessness, he forged a new and incomparably deadly gang: Slips, Little T, Mo, Pinky, Mango, Simo, Wazza, Big Dougie, Little Porky, Chan, Zed and a dozen others. While the implosion of the Salford underworld involved big-hitters – Massey, Doyle, Lydiate – aged in their late thirties, the south Manchester hoods seemed to get consistently younger; many were naïve and pliable, and Pitt could bend them to his will. He called his followers the Pitt Bull Crew in memory of his dead brother.

Pitt had a debt to settle with those elements of the Doddington responsible for his brother's death – and used their own weapons against them.

The Pitt Bull Crew had access to quite a frightening array of weaponry, from Smith and Wesson revolvers through to Mac 10 machine pistols, some old shotguns. Some first weaponry that the Pitt Bull Crew had were a couple of shotguns and a machine gun which they actually stole from the Doddington gang from Moss Side. The founders of the Pitt Bull Crew used to be Doddington gang members until Raymond Pitt was shot dead . . . and his younger brother Tommy Pitt and his associate Paul Day formed the Pitt Bull Crew in honour, in the memory of Raymond Pitt. And one of the first things that Tommy and Paul did was, in Paul's own words, rob guns from the Doddington, and went to war with Doddington tit for tat for two weeks. So their first weapons they actually stole from another gang.

His venom turned also towards the Longsight Crew, who seemed to be expanding their drug dealing into what he considered his turf, along the Levenshulme-Longsight border. Pitt's team cruised in pairs on mountain bikes – to 'ride' became a euphemism for gang membership – ferrying heroin, cocaine and cannabis, almost always with one gun between them. His enforcers wore uniforms of dark clothing with hoods pulled over their heads, bulletproof vests and single golf gloves on their shooting hands so police would not get DNA or fingerprints from their weapons. They used the homes of girlfriends as bases and safe houses. Young recruits had to impress Pitt and gain his trust before they could join his gang; he would give gold chains as gifts if they pleased him, but death could be the price of failure. Pitt had his own favourite weapons, including a Mac-10 fitted with a silencer, that no-one else was allowed to handle.

With the rise of the PBC, the underworld of south central Manchester now had four main gangs, arrayed against and with each other in a complicated series of feuds and alliances. Simplistically put, Longsight and most of the Doddington were at war with both the Gooch and the Pitt Bulls. One survey of the gangs found that they had grown to a total of around 200 members or associates under the age of twenty-five, broken down as follows: Gooch, sixty-four; Doddington, thirty; Longsight Crew, sixty-seven; Pitt Bull Crew, twenty-six. 'Each gang comprises a core of main players, together with "ordinary members", "runners" acting on behalf of members, and "associates", who may have connections with more than one gang or provide networks of support, for instance safe houses.'[88] Their killing grounds covered a semi-circular patch around the city centre, from Old Trafford in the west around to Openshaw in the east and as far south as Levenshulme. The PBC was the youngest gang, with one in five of its members aged sixteen or younger, while the Doddington had the oldest members.

Towards the end of March 2000, some Pitt Bulls were at a blues party organised by an older Moss Side head when a gunfight broke out with the Doddington and one of the PBC was wounded. A few days later, two Longsight lads were shot in Gorton, probably by the PBC. Both discharged themselves after surgery. A seventeen-year-old friendly with Tommy Pitt's younger half-brother Michael was shot in the stomach in Chorlton-on-Medlock, possibly as a reprisal. On May 5, a carload of PBC had a shootout with a car containing two members of the Longsight Crew in Prout Street, Longsight. Gregory 'Pinky' Day, a feared lieutenant in the PBC, was one of those arrested. Battle lines had clearly been drawn.

Within ten days, the Doddington had suffered a terrible blow. A man walking his dog in the early morning in the Harehills district of Leeds found the bodies of Clifton Bryan and Denis Wilson bundled like sacks into the boot of a car. Both had been shot in the back of the head. The muscular Bryan was a Manchester bad boy who had relocated to Leeds, probably to sell drugs; the Yorkshire city saw an upsurge in gun crime and Bryan had survived at least two previous hits but had rejected police offers of protection. 'We were beginning to think he was the Sandman,' said an officer leading the hunt for the killers. 'He was a big, powerful man and his strength might have got him out of this kind of situation in the past.' Wilson, a member of the Doddington, was the elder half-brother of Kevin Lewis, who had been shot dead in Moss Side in 1997. Police eventually ascertained that the men had been killed after entering a house in Chorlton-on-Medlock; their bodies had then been driven to Leeds. Various members of the Gooch were questioned and three

Manchester men were subsequently cleared after two trials, despite one of them making a confession that he later retracted.

That summer the Longsight Crew and the Pitt Bulls clashed repeatedly while the Gooch launched a concerted assault to wipe out a clique of younger Doddington who had remained in Moss Side after some of their older heads had left the city. The Gooch were intent on destroying their traditional enemy and concentrated their fire on this stricken outpost: they threatened them, robbed them, chased them in cars, lured them into traps or ambushes and fired at them in a bid to drive them from the area. To complicate the situation further, shots were fired in yet another dispute when a man with Doddington connections tried to corral several others into a new gang with himself as leader and they refused to comply. The Moss Side carnival that year was a muted event; many young men were too scared to attend.

Tommy Pitt was constantly in the thick of it. One young man was foolish enough to confront the gang boss when Pitt started going out with his girlfriend; he even traced the pair to the Palace Hotel on Oxford Road and berated Pitt. The next day he was shot in the leg, probably by one of Pitt's lieutenants. A week later Pitt was at the centre of what a police intelligence log recorded as 'a large scale disturbance in Longsight between black and Asian males'; approximately thirty people were seen fighting in the street. In August Pitt's crew shot a young man who refused to pay them £10,000 extortion money.

Power and rage drove Pitt on. On September 3, the PBC shot Devon Bell in the Longsight base of Langport Avenue. On September 9, Pitt himself raided Longsight territory and tried to shoot Scott Morrison and Imran Temsamani as they sat in a car. His Mac-10, fitted with a silencer, jammed and he went around the corner, where he encountered two of their friends, Marcus Greenidge and Gary Riley, on bikes; Morrison and Temsamani tried to phone Greenidge to warn him but his number was engaged. He didn't stand a chance. Riley heard a loud bang and saw a flash. Realising it was gunfire, he jumped off his bike and ran for his life, dodging a hail of automatic fire. Greenidge, aged twenty-one, died instantly from a bullet to the head at close range.

He was found with a loaded Chinese Tokarev handgun still in his pocket. 'I've just whacked one of the Longsight boys,' bragged Pitt soon after.

That night, he ordered one of his young soldiers, Thomas Ramsey, to move a gun that was hidden in a flat in Longsight. Ramsey, who was heavily involved with the PBC and had been the chief suspect for a previous murder, forgot. When police later searched the flat and found the weapon with Pitt's DNA on it, the gang leader was furious, and apparently summoned Ramsey, who was just sixteen, to a meeting behind Levenshulme Baths. Ramsey arrived wearing his black balaclava and a black glove, part of the Pitt Bull uniform, and carrying a copy of the search warrant the police had left behind. He was shot twice and died within seconds. 'One shot to the head and one point blank to his shoulder,' said a Longsight officer. 'He was found by a guy with his dog. He had cannabis on him and a copy of the section-eighteen house search.' Whatever Ramsey's past, he was a sixteen-year-old boy, barely out of school.

The PBC was running amok. One rival was kneecapped on Pitt's orders. On September 13, Longsight crewman Stephen Roberts was captured, bundled into a car, beaten and frog-marched to a park, where Pitt took out a revolver and played Russian roulette, loading the gun with one round and spinning the chamber before sticking the barrel to Roberts's head and asking, 'Is it your time?' He clicked the trigger but the weapon did not discharge. Roberts was then beaten with bricks but was allowed to live.

After seven shootings in three weeks, stopping Pitt became a matter of life or death for the Longsight Crew. In mid-September one of their gunmen saw him in a car at traffic lights in the Victoria Park area. He promptly cycled up and fired into the car with a Mac-10. Pitt was hit in the leg and was taken to Manchester Royal Infirmary, where he was kept under armed guard in a secure unit within the hospital. It gave the police a chance to observe him at close quarters. 'Pitt is a small lad but he has presence,' said an officer who knew him. 'Most prisoners, you get a rapport with. They tend to be all right once they are with you;

they might want a cigarette break or whatever and so they want to stay onside with you. Even though they are lying, they will be all right. But Pitt, you just couldn't get into. If you were getting along with him, he would suddenly stop. He had to be watched constantly. It was amazing, this presence he had. He was very scary. Everyone was scared of him, even the officers guarding him.

'He is almost a schizophrenic. He could be laughing and joking with the nursing staff, watching TV, but on one occasion when he wasn't getting enough attention off the nurses and the police guarding him, he threw a Lucozade bottle at an officer's head. He was allowed as many visitors as he wanted, which seemed a bit strange, given that he was under arrest. Pitt also had about three girlfriends on the go, who all came in at different times, and the guards had to leave the room when he had visitors. But, of course, the room had a camera hidden in it, though even the police guards didn't know it.' Pitt said nothing in formal interview. He eventually was well enough to be moved into custody and was held initially in Longsight police station, where he missed the special perks he had enjoyed in hospital. 'He was pulling the stitches out of his leg so he could go back to the hospital, where he had all these rights,' said the officer.

No sooner was Pitt back in circulation than the police began arresting members of his gang, some of whom had been forging an alliance with a gang in Birmingham with a view to an arms deal. In November, they arrested Pitt at a house in Hulme. He was wearing combat trousers with traces of shotgun residue on them, and searches of various Pitt Bull strongholds resulted in the recovery of guns, ammunition, body armour, balaclavas, golf gloves, quantities of crack and heroin, drug paraphernalia and radio scanners. The PBC and Longsight had engaged in at least seventeen gun battles since Pitt's release from his previous sentence.

Detectives made a crucial breakthrough when they persuaded twenty-four-year-old Joshua 'Slips' Mensah, one of Pitt's main men, to testify against his own gang. It was an almost unprecedented breach in the code of silence. Thomas Pitt was charged with the murders of Ramsey and Greenidge and many of his most important lieutenants were also charged with serious offences. Not all of them, however; some were still at large, and in March 2001 showed they could be just as merciless without their leader. Taxi driver Mohammed Ahmed, who sometimes worked as a courier for the Longsight Crew, was ambushed while taking gang member Lee Fielding to a meeting. Two Pitt Bulls appeared on the scene and shot Ahmed four times in the head as he sat in his cab. They then bundled Fielding into a stolen car and took him to a disused railway line in Longsight, where he was blasted with a sawn-off shotgun, doused in petrol and set alight. Somehow he survived, despite horrific burns.

*   *   *

The end of the Twentieth Century found street gang culture embedded in south central Manchester. It also saw, belatedly, a more considered approach to understanding and policing the gangs. Operation Chrome was inspired by the success of an initiative called Operation Ceasefire in Boston, Massachusetts, which had produced a rapid and sustained fall in deaths and serious injuries from gunshots and knives. In Manchester, the police appointed a researcher and an assistant to work with a Home Office team collecting and analysing data about the Doddington, the Gooch, the Longsight Crew and the PBC, in the same way that a team from Harvard University had operated in Boston. The researchers did not speculate on what caused gangs to form in the first place but tried to describe their make-up and identify what specific events triggered their feuds.

However, interviews with anonymous gang members did reveal how the lure of the gangs was felt at an early age. The Chrome researchers found that seventy per cent of south Manchester gang members were under the age of twenty-five, with thirty per cent under eighteen. Youths usually became involved between the ages of twelve and fourteen.

I became aware of the gangs when I was 10 or 11. I didn't

really meet any gang members until I moved to Longsight when I was 14 . . . I knew them but didn't really meet them. My brother was in the gang. They came to our house. There were a few others I knew from school. I got to know X [a main player]. He was with my brother and asked me to work for him, selling drugs. You can make some money with them. It makes you hard.

A kid I knew was related to one of the [gang members] maybe. They hung around together. I knew they were different from other lads. They had money and drove around in cars. I did stuff for them – delivered drugs, I suppose. Some schoolmates have joined gangs. They were attracted to the cars and money. You can get girls. You see the older guys and they're living it up. It's one way of living that seems good – money and respect and if you're 'in' you're 'in'. But it's scary getting in too far.[89]

During their period of study, the deaths continued to rack up, despite the successful destruction of the Pitt Bulls. Eighteen-year-old Alan Byron was shot dead with a Mac-10 in Longsight in June 2001. Alphonso Madden, twenty-seven, died two months later on August 27, shot dead as he drove along Northmoor Rd, Longsight. Dean Eccleston was shot dead in Chorlton-on-Medlock in October 2001; one of the Gooch's most active soldiers was a suspect. A few weeks later George Lynch, a father of six, was shot dead in his car shortly after dropping off his son at a friend's house in Longsight.

By the summer of 2002, the city had seen at least four more gang-related murders, including two in a single February weekend: Chinadu Iheagwara and Stephen Amos. Iheagwara, who thirteen years earlier had been one of the Hillbilly team that butchered two security guards in a raid at Coin Controls in Oldham, died in bizarre circumstances after apparently giving his thirteen-year-old nephew a 'tap on the chin' to chastise him. This led to bad feeling with others and a peace meeting was arranged at the house of Ray Odoha – whose shooting in Moss

Side in 1994 had led to the brokering of the Manchester gang truce. Six people were present, but the meeting broke down when Iheagwara and another man began to argue. 'I'm not frightened,' said Iheagwara. 'There's nothing you can do to bother me.' In response the other man pulled out a gun and started firing. Iheagwara suffered massive head injuries from two bullets and died, while everyone except peacemaker Ray Odoha fled. He refused to identify the shooter – 'If I give a statement I'll be shot,' he told police. Later, through a solicitor, Odoha added, 'Chinadu was a very close friend of mine. I was standing nearby when it happened and tried to prevent it. I never thought he had a gun and was shocked and horrified. I am fearful of repercussions. He acted cold-bloodedly and could do the same thing to me or, more importantly, my family.' The police traced all the people believed to have been in the house at the time but they either denied being there or refused to comment.

Amos, twenty-one, was shot dead by a Longsight Crew enforcer outside Bexx bar in Ashton-under-Lyne. A good friend of Manchester United footballer Wes Brown, he was also the brother of Lee Amos, a member of the Gooch serving nine years for possessing guns with intent to endanger life. Longsight leader Julian Bell, only recently released from a jail term for threatening to kill a witness in a gangland assault trial, was later arrested in connection with Amos's death and was found in possession of £38,000 in cash. Police also tracked down the shooter – Bell's cousin and bodyguard, Richard Solomon – to Bell's smart bungalow in Lostock Hall, near Preston. A search of the house uncovered guns, ammunition, a drugs cutting agent called Mannitol and an inventory of customers. A linked raid on another property in Salford, found a heavy drugs press capable of producing kilo-sized blocks of heroin or cocaine for wholesale distribution and traces of the drugs in a microwave, blender and sieve.

Another shooting by the Longsight Crew led to a retaliatory raid by the Gooch in April 2002. The Longsight lads were waiting for them at their Langport Avenue headquarters and what was described as a 'sustained gun battle' took place in the residential close. Eighteen-year-old Aeon Shirley was struck down by four bullets, the fourteenth person to be shot dead since July 1999 in the triangle of Longsight, Hulme and Moss Side. The police responded by putting armed officers on the beat in Longsight and Moss Side. They had seen four incidents of officers being threatened with guns in a six-week period. GMP now had 120 full-time firearms officers, each kitted out with a Heckler and Koch single carbine shotgun and a pistol secured in a lockable holster. Armed response cars also carried non-lethal rubber baton guns.

The Operation Chrome team eventually produced a report with six recommendations to tackle gang-related violence: continuing highly publicised 'crackdowns' but utilising many agencies, not just the police, to ensure their long-term success; building stronger community relations to deter bad behaviour; engaging with gang members to understand their problems and try to divert them from crime; developing an inter-gang mediation service to defuse potentially lethal tensions; identifying those most likely to be shot and protecting them; and 'sensitising' various bodies to the effects their actions may have on gangs, from housing policy to street lighting to school exclusions.

Perhaps partly because of Chrome and partly because the terror had become so bad, the community in south Manchester began to mobilise. There had been occasional public meetings in the past, such as the three-day event held in February 2000 under the banner of Unity in the Community, but now the protesters were bolder and more vocal. Gangstop was a movement launched by two friends, Gary Gordon and Michael McFarquhar. Gordon had grown up in Longsight, while three members of McFarquhar's extended family had been shot. Both in their early thirties, they found themselves meeting at the funerals of men or boys much younger than themselves. 'At the last funeral, we looked around,' Gordon told the *Guardian*. 'There were hundreds of people there, and we thought, why do you only get this level of community spirit at funerals? It's time to do something about it.' They helped to organise a march through Longsight, Rusholme, Moss Side, Hulme and the city centre in the summer of 2002;

305

four hundred marchers brought traffic to a standstill and listened to emotive speeches by mothers and relatives who had lost loved ones. 'The gangs move in on areas where the community is weak,' said McFarquhar. 'People there have to take a stand.'

At the forefront of the march was a group called Mothers Against Violence, born out of the heartbreak of bereaved parents and the fears of the families of gang members. Another organisation, the Community Alliance for Renewal Inner South Manchester (CARISMA), aimed to provide young men with viable alternatives to gang culture and organised an emotional memorial service at Manchester Cathedral for the victims of gun crime. Pictures of young men murdered in Moss Side, Longsight and surrounding areas were displayed as relatives lit candles, read poems and sang songs.

Official bodies launched their own response, the Manchester Multi-Agency Gang Strategy (MMAGS), a Home Office-funded project to slash crime by gang members. Primarily involving the city council, GMP and the Probation Service, its purpose was to put into practice some of the recommendations of Operation Chrome, including employing outreach workers to go into schools, youth clubs and onto the streets to befriend gang members and discuss their lifestyles and problems, and to divert them and others onto safer, better lifeways. In an echo of Tony Blair's 'tough on crime, tough on the causes of crime', Chief Superintendent Adrian Lee, commander of south Manchester division, said MMAGS would investigate the reasons for gang membership as well as the crimes the gangs committed. 'Why do young people join gangs and what can we do to stop them?' he said. 'These gangs have been born out of lack of hope in young people and we have let a lot of them down in our society.'

* * *

Even in jail, Tommy Pitt was able to exert a svengali-like grip on those close to him. A young legal secretary who became besotted with the gangster tried to smuggle £5,000-worth of heroin to him on a visit to the high-security Whitemoor prison in

Cambridgeshire. The drugs could have been used as currency in prison and would have given Pitt a great deal of power, but she was caught by sniffer dogs and was later jailed for three years, her career in tatters.

By then, Pitt himself was serving life imprisonment. He had gone on trial at Preston Crown Court in October 2002, charged with the murders of Marcus Greenidge and Thomas Ramsey and trying to murder three other men. Eleven people alleged to be members of his gang faced conspiracy charges, while two women were accused of possessing guns, but Pitt, twenty-four, of Southsea Street, Openshaw, was the focal point. 'He gathered around him young males from the Longsight and West Gorton areas of Manchester, young men who would carry out his criminal bidding whether it was the supply of controlled drugs or the use of violence,' said prosecutor James Pickup, QC. 'He was comfortable with violence; indeed he seems to have enjoyed involvement in the inter-gang rivalry. He had his favourite guns and had exclusive use of the Mac-10. The Spanish Bronco handgun was his favourite. He was ruthless in his dealings not only with the Longsight Crew, which he hated, but also with members of his own gang. He was not one to be crossed.'

Pitt denied all charges but the evidence against him was strong. Though he was cleared of Ramsey's murder, he was jailed for life for murder, twenty years for three attempted murders and fifteen years for conspiracy after a fourteen-week trial. 'He is an infinitely cruel person in my view,' said the judge, Mr Justice Michael Sachs. 'He is obsessed with his own importance and power.' Gregory Day, Warren Coudjoe, Mark Simons, Douglas Thorne and Sandra Thorne were convicted of conspiracy to possess firearms and plotting to deal drugs, while Stefan Proverbs, Moses Boakye, and a sixteen-year-old youth admitted firearms and drugs offences. Supergrass Joshua Mensah was placed in the witness protection programme, as were two other former PBC associates. At a later trial, Abdul Butt, Paul 'Casper' Day and Mikey Gordon were jailed for life for the murder of a Longsight taxi driver. Butt, twenty-four, was described as the PBC leader after Pitt's arrest and Day as its chief hitman and torturer. 'Any decent right-minded person who walks into court would have been horrified at what they heard,' said Mr Justice Sachs. 'Your activities defy sensible belief. You showed no mercy to your victims and you will receive none from me.' It marked the effective end of the PBC.

★   ★   ★

As one fell, another rose. A new gang, the Young Longsight Soldiers had split from the Longsight Crew and struck off on their own. They forced the occupant from a house on the edge of Belle Vue/Gorton and began dealing heavily from a nearby telephone kiosk. They also had several run-ins with their former homeboys in the Longsight Crew who were unhappy that they had broken away. They had good reason: it seemed the YLSS had allied with their deadly enemies, the Gooch. It gave them access to weapons and drugs. When Gooch associate Stephen Amos was shot dead by the Longsight Crew outside the Bexx bar, several of the YLSS showed up at the hospital to show solidarity. Later that month, they shot one of the Longsight Crew in a drive-by in Gorton. 'They tend to stick around the Levenshulme area and go round all in body armour,' said a Longsight police officer. 'They keep their drugs under their armour. It is a very small gang, but all the more dangerous because they are trying to make a name for themselves.' By March 2002, police intelligence suggested that a leading member of the gang had acquired a Mac-10 and 'is threatening people in Longsight with this weapon.' Tee-shirts on sale at the Dickinson Road flea market showed a picture of a chalk outline drawn around a dead body, above the words 'Welcome To Longsight'.

The YLSS were soon well-enough established for magistrates to impose an extraordinary sanction on one of them. Sixteen-year-old Nathan Wadley was banned, under an anti-social behaviour order, from showing his gang tattoos and from wearing a balaclava or a single golf glove anywhere in the country in public. If he breached the order he faced five years in jail. Wadley was not allowed to display the L$$$ tattoo on his upper right arm in Longsight, Belle Vue or part of Victoria Park. He was also banned from displaying any symbols or insignia which showed him to be part of the Beswick Crew, the Young Longsight Soldiers, the YLSS, YL$$ or L$$$, was forbidden from going to the gang's headquarters in Shelford Avenue, Belle Vue, and was not allowed to congregate in public with groups of more than three people, including six named teenagers. Wadley was fairly typical of the young gangbangers: at thirteen he had been placed under supervision for carrying a rubber mallet and robbing a woman of her mobile phone, and at fourteen he was on a curfew for possessing heroin and crack. He persistently abused beat officers as he rode on his mountain bike. 'There is no doubt that the gang culture is a particular blight on the city of Manchester,' said city council lawyer Mark Watling at his hearing. By then, almost 500 people were estimated to be part of the south Manchester gangs.

In February 2003, the Attorney General, Lord Goldsmith QC, swished into the Court of Appeal in The Strand to make a rare personal intervention in an individual case. Britain's senior law officer argued before three judges that jail terms handed out to Manchester's Pitt Bull Crew were 'unduly lenient'. It was a highly unusual intervention; Lord Goldsmith had only once previously appeared in person to present his case. The judges agreed with him in four of the nine PBC cases put before them and increased the jail terms accordingly. Pitt himself was already serving the maximum. Lord Goldsmith also took the opportunity to point out that recorded firearms offences in Britain had increased by over a third between the years 2000 and 2001. 'For the people of Manchester, this would not have been such news,' he added.

Epilogue

SHEILA ECCLESTON AND Patsy McKie are temperamental opposites: Sheila shows her feelings more readily, an emotional, occasional volatile Liverpudlian prone to outbursts and recriminations, while Patsy is cooler, more reserved, a stately black lady who keeps her feelings in check. The storm and the calm, they have been united by grief, and their intention is to do something about it. Together they are vital members of Mothers Against Violence, a Manchester organisation to support grieving parents, connect with youths and lobby politicians about gang violence. They have helped to transform it from a small talking shop for mums to a pressure group with a national profile.

Their sons, too, were different. Dean Eccleston was tall, broad-shouldered and a handful. Dorrie McKie, known to his family as 'Junior', was ebullient too but less of a hard-knock and rarely in trouble. Both, however, fell victim to the south Manchester gangs.

PATSY McKIE: 'Dorrie's father was very quiet and my son was very quiet; a normal, happy child, though he was knocked down at six or seven – I thought I had lost him. In school, his report was: "Dorrie is a very lively young boy. He is always helping people. He will leave his work and go and help the others in the class, especially if they are younger." He loved basketball, riding his bike, listening to his music, all that rap stuff I don't understand. He was only in trouble with the police once, in his early teens. They said he was riding a motorbike with a friend in Longsight; they had seen two young lads on the bikes go into Plymouth Grove estate and they picked up Dorrie a little later. He was taken to the police station. They put him in a cell and when I got

310

there he was fast asleep. I got his stuff back and took him out. They didn't find the bike and I wrote a letter and got one back of apology.'

SHEILA ECCLESTON: 'My son was hyper even from nursery. He was born in Manchester but we left when he was six months old. He was quite a bright boy but no good at reading. A lot of them feel if they are not doing well at school, they are a dunce, and if they cause trouble at school they are not worth the trouble. Quite a lot of these lads in the gangs have felt rejection from an early age. Most of them are from one-parent families and my son was as well, and there was a lot of anger in him because he never knew his father.

'Dean was in trouble from young. We were living in Bristol at the time and we had a social worker because Dean did my head in. He was escaping out through the window at night when he was nine. I tried talking to him, battering him, nothing worked. The social worker said we could get him in a school in Bath and he loved it. He was there for two weeks and wasn't messing about, but then the social worker came to me and said, "We have to put Dean in this place in Devon." It was an approved school and he started running away from there, then stealing the staff's cars, and it persisted and then he got lost in the system.

'He got five years for a post office robbery and ended up doing six. He was always down the block, and a lot of things happened to him inside that he wouldn't tell me about. When he was sixteen in Gloucester Prison he was put on the men's wing. I think these young lads live in fear in the prison system and it hardens them. He was seventeen when he went down for the five years. He was skinny when he went in; when he came out he was full of muscle. He used to say to his mates, "You aren't getting in my car with your skinny arms. Get down the gym." I thought, *we will go to Manchester and hopefully Dean will have a new life,* but he went back to prison for seven months for not having a driving licence – he has never had a licence. He had been like that since he was nine with driving.'

While Dean was being hardened by the system, Dorrie was also moving on the edge of trouble. An acquaintance told his mother that he was hanging around with boys who robbed people. She confronted him but he denied it. Then there was the time armed youths came to her door.

PATSY McKIE: 'Three months before he was shot, there was a knock at the door and I came face to face with two young men in balaclavas, one with a gun in his hand. One put his foot in the door. They had the coats and the bikes. And this lad says, "Does Raymond Pitt live here?"

'Then Junior came down and said, "What do you want?"

'And he said, "I'm looking for Pitt. Where does he live?"

'Dorrie said, "Round the corner." He didn't, it was his girlfriend's house.

'The boy pulled a gun out of his coat, one of those shiny little guns. I wasn't scared. They did go round and try the door, because the woman who lived there told me the next day that they had heard someone trying it.'

One day a friend of Dorrie's called Leon McKenley was shot dead. He went to the funeral and kept the programme from the church service in his room. Dean, too, knew friends die; Antony Cook, a Doddington member gunned down in a car, was a mate. Almost certainly there were things that the two young men did not share with their mothers. When someone fired bullets through the window of Dorrie's house, Patsy found out only when the father of another boy told her at church. Dean was also shot at with his girlfriend in a car chase.

SHEILA ECCLESTON: 'Dean was no innocent. He was a ruler. He wouldn't give in to anybody. The lads around here [Longsight] in the gangs had respect for Dean. They wanted him in a gang, the Moss Side lads wanted him in a gang, but he was a man on his own. He tried his best, started working on the doors in the clubs. But mainly he did robberies. Dean used to do either bookies or bank jobs and used to say, "But mum, at least I have got money to spend, even if eventually I have to go back to prison. I don't want to be standing in no dole queues."'

Dorrie McKie was shot dead at about 11 p.m. on 3 August 1999 in Leaf Street, Hulme, by members of the Doddington Gang. He was twenty years old.

PATSY McKIE: 'My son was picked up by a young man in the day and was taken to basketball. Usually he would go on his bike but not this time. Then the young man asked him to go with him to collect some money. I believe it was a set-up. He went to the house to collect whatever and my son stayed in the car. Then he came out and went home with my son, then came back again a second time, and it was then that these young men were waiting on bikes. Apparently they saw them and the other fellow said, "Dorrie, this doesn't look good."

'Dorrie said, "I'm not getting out. I've done nothing against anyone."

'He said, "Dorrie, get out of the car. Get out of the car! Let's go!"

'Eventually my son got out and they started running and these lads were on bikes and that was when he got shot. I was told that the shot was meant for my son's friend. He has to live with that for the rest of his life.'

Dorrie was found lying on grass with a fatal chest wound; he had been hit three times. His friend was injured. Two Doddington gangsters were later jailed for possessing the weapons used. Dean Eccleston died at 9 p.m. on 9 October 2002 on a Longsight housing estate, while wearing a bulletproof vest and, according to his mother, carrying a gun. He was twenty-four, and is believed to have been killed by members of the Gooch Close Gang.

SHEILA ECCLESTON: 'He was set up as well. He came in here, got some things out of the cupboard and said, "See you mum, I'm going." He was with this boy, Darren Shields. They went to the lad's house near Shakespeare Walk. When they came out, as they turned the corner three youths jumped out on them. They never had masks on. The boy with my son knew who they were. These three came over and had a gun and Darren said, "Quick Dean, run."

'But my lad said, "I'm not running from no-one." If they hadn't had the gun he probably would have beaten them all. The next thing, my son has got eight bullets in him. He got two in the head and others all over his body. Darren Shields took my son's big bracelet off him and whatever else my son had. His chain was worth about four grand. He ran to his cousin's and hid it. Then he came back and a man in the corner house had come out and, as my son was dying, he was praying over my son. Then a drug addict came along and took my son's other bracelet off him. Darren Shields kicked the drug addict but he ran off with it.'

No-one has been convicted of either murder, despite huge police investigations. The two mothers reacted to their sons' deaths in different ways.

PATSY McKIE: 'I really believed that I was there for a purpose and it was much bigger than I was. Something must be wrong when young men can do that, and that was my focus: I wanted to find these young men. I wanted to know the reason why they were killing each other. I know some people talk about the drugs but to me it was more than that. It is not the drugs that take up the gun and pull the trigger, it is the person. I did walk around looking for them but didn't find them. People said, "Oh well, they meet here and they meet there," but when do they meet? I would have gone to see anybody and still would now. I wasn't afraid. I didn't mind dying and still don't. I was driven by the passion that was in me.'

SHEILA ECCLESTON: 'I was full of anger. I went round telling everybody, "You can tell this person, when I find him he has had it." I was like a raving lunatic. I took an overdose, slit my wrists. I was in a terrible state. Dean has left two children, both daughters. It is constant worry, though I know he is saying, "You don't have to worry now mum.' It is hard. All I have left are his crash helmets, his Jeep, his CD system and photos and that is it."'

PATSY McKIE: 'A young man came to me, one of my son's friends, and said he had heard there is a group of mothers getting together to discuss what had happened in the community and what they could do about it. He said to me, "I think you will be really helpful to them." My son had just been killed and I went to the first meeting and that was it. There were about fifteen women and we just talked. There was a bit of an argument about "them and us", this side and that side. The mothers were talking about this and I was naïve and didn't know about the "them and us".'

SHEILA ECCLESTON: 'That was my fear, because I knew the side that killed my son and I said to Patsy, "I don't know what I am going to do because at the end of the day that lad's mother is going to be sat by me." I'll have to listen to her talking about her wonderful son, how worried she is for him. But we should be here for them too. It's not their fault. We all want to stop the violence.'

MAV began meeting once a month and giving regular media interviews. Patsy became its chairman, while Sheila gained a diploma in counselling. The group found an office, arranged a visit to Boston and even had a half-hour meeting with Prime Minister Tony Blair in the summer of 2002.

SHEILA ECCLESTON: 'He was on telly in Parliament saying he wanted to speak to us and as he was coming up here he spoke to us and then put his arms around us. He listened and was a really nice fellow. He just listened – he is a politician and wouldn't make any promises. Even if you just save one lad it will be worthwhile. Another thing we would like to do is get round the prisons and talk to these lads about what life will be like when they get out. We want the Mothers Against Violence all over the country.'

PATSY McKIE: 'When Mahatma Gandhi marched in India for

independence, when the mothers in Argentina march for their missing sons, something happens in the course of history. Suddenly, the world sits up and listens.'

* * *

Some commentators have speculated that the United Kingdom stands on the brink of a US-style gang culture. They are wrong; it has already happened. It began some time in the early eighties, taking root in the loam of high unemployment and urban riots, fed by growing drug importation and nurtured by the ubiquity of 'dance' drugs on the rave scene and the quasi-legitimisation of crime gangs by the private security industry. To draw a criminal map of Britain in 2003, with the gangs and firms and allegiances and feuds in every region, and match it to one from 1973 would be like comparing two different countries, so great has the change been.

Yet change, despite its obvious implications, has for a long time been inadequately researched and rarely acknowledged. When a bright and ambitious Manchester detective, Peter Stelfox, wrote to every police force in the country in the mid-nineties to undertake an audit of gangs for a Home Office-funded study, he found not only that no-one had ever done such a project before, but also that many forces denied they had any gangs. Yet the signs had been clear enough for anyone who wanted to look. As early as 1994, police leaders suggested that the Home Office should consider making membership of criminal organisations illegal, in the same way that the IRA and INLA were proscribed, because of 'the difficulties experienced in instituting proceedings of conspiracy against key organised figures, who distance themselves from the criminal activities carried out by junior members, but enjoy the profits of those crimes.'[90]

If evidence were needed, the body count alone should be enough. London has the most gangs and the most killings, but then it always has; it is the spread to provincial cities that most clearly tells the story. In Birmingham, the turf war between the Johnson Crew and the Burger Bar Boys threatened to knock

Manchester off its 'Gangchester' perch. In Sheffield gangs are a present danger, partly because of the temporary relocation of Manchester's Doddington Gang there, which may have acted as some kind of catalyst for local youths. The murder of a prominent black member of the Blades Business Crew soccer gang may be an ominous signpost to the future. Leeds has seen an undeniable increase in gang-related murders, while Nottingham, with its Meadows Posse and St Ann's Crew, has seen armed police patrol the streets in another echo of Manchester. Bristol may face more feuds such as that between the Aggi and Hype crews, while Liverpool has as tangled and deadly a gang culture as its great regional rival along the East Lancs Road. Glasgow remains a law unto itself.

Manchester, however, is unique for the intensity and duration of its gang wars. According to one report:

> It is clear that gang culture has spread over the past 15 years and, left unchecked, it will spread further. It has become endemic, and through constant exposure to the superficial glamour of the gang, youths are being attracted in ever-increasing numbers. To a youth, these are gangs that offer a viable alternative to a life of economic and social margin-alisation. More than 500 individuals are known to have been involved in these gangs over the last five years, ranging from the hardcore to peripheral runners and supporters. Estimates suggest at least 200 more are involved, many of them juveniles.[91]

Figures released in July 2002 showed that Manchester had the worst record of violent crime of any city in the country – once again. Drivers were more likely to have their cars stolen in Salford than anywhere else in the UK. Manchester had eight times more robberies than Sheffield. In three years, the number of crack cocaine users in the city had increased five-fold and drug agencies suggested it could hit the levels first predicted in 1988. Wythenshawe saw its own self-contained drug war, with a number of people shot. Officers carrying carbines and sidearms took to

317

the streets of Moss Side, Rusholme and Longsight in April 2003 following intelligence that the Gooch and Doddington gangs were about to resume their twelve-year rivalry.

None of this detracts from the great achievements of Manchester, the first industrial city, as vital and entrepreneurial a place, pound-for-pound, as any in Europe. Writers and critics continue to celebrate its legacy and extol its outlook, the best contemporary account being *Manchester, England* by former Hacienda DJ Dave Haslam. And it is also easy to exaggerate the dangers. Crimes involving firearms still account for less than one per cent of all crimes in Greater Manchester Police area. To put the gang scene into trans-Atlantic perspective, when researchers from Operation Chrome compared Manchester (population 600,000) with Boston (population 500,000), they found the British city had fewer than ten gangs, compared to sixty in Boston, and Boston had twice as many youth homicides, even with a death rate enviably small by US standards.

The story of Manchester is still, however, what it was in Friedrich Engels's time: a tale of two cities. Nowhere in the British Isles have wealth and poverty stood in such stark proximity; nowhere has civic confidence been greater nor crime levels higher. Nothing illustrated this dichotomy better than the Commonwealth Games of 1992, an event which showcased the city at its best: friendly, involved and efficient. The purpose-built stadium at Eastlands was magnificent, a leading architect was brought in to re-design the mess of Piccadilly Gardens, the free bus system worked like clockwork and everything passed off with barely a hitch. Even the weather was *reasonably* kind. Yet security at the Eastlands site during its construction was controlled by PMS Ltd, the company once linked to Paul Massey, who at the time was serving a long jail sentence. 'The police see us as organised crime – run by gangsters,' complained manager Steve Kent. 'It is simply not true. They stop our vans and say, "How's your boss doing in jail?"'[92]

And there performing at the opening ceremony, before the Queen and millions of television viewers, were rappers Moss-Sidaz, whose members bear bullet scars and sing of life on the streets. One of the band was kicked out of his junior school at ten for burning it down, then thrown out of high school for smoking weed, and says most of his friends have been in jail. He found his voice through rap; the tragedy for so many others is that they can find articulacy only in the least creative language of all: violence.

Patsy McKie, the chairman of Mothers Against Violence, likes to tell the story of an acquaintance who asked a young gang member, 'Why do you have a gun?'

'Because no-one listens to me,' replied the youth. 'But when I have a gun in my hand, people listen.'

Postscript

In January 2005, eighteen months after the publication of the first edition of this book, the *Manchester Evening News* carried one of its periodic reports on anti-gang interdictions. 'NINE HELD IN DAWN BLITZ,' announced the headline.

> One hundred police today staged dawn raids on 16 homes across Manchester in a hunt for armed criminals. Nine suspected gangsters were arrested and homes in north and south Manchester and Trafford were searched. Of those captured, three were being questioned about attempted murders. Others were quizzed over possession of guns and drugs offences. One firearm and ammunition were seized during the raids. Supt David Keller said: 'These individuals are believed to have been involved in a number of serious firearms incidents, including the theft of cars at gunpoint. I want to send a strong message to those people involved in gun violence that their actions will not be tolerated in our communities.'

The raids merely confirmed that the saga of Manchester's gangland is never-ending. Violence and shootings fluctuate, but the drug trade, in particular the increasingly ubiquitous cocaine, continues to fan the flames.

Police successes have made sizeable dents in the fabric of the gang world. Despite reports of the emergence of a Young Doddington Crew, the Doddies seem all but finished. The Longsight Crew suffered a heavy blow with the demise of its leader, Julian Bell. In March 2004, the wheelchair-bound gangster was found guilty of possession of drugs with intent to supply and sentenced to six years. He had earlier been sentenced to fourteen years for possession of firearms with intent to endanger life and will serve the latest term consecutively, a total of twenty years. His chief minder, Richard Solomon, from Hulme, was already serving a life term for murder. 'They were known gang members who regularly carried firearms,' said Detective Chief Inspector Mick Lay. 'I'm delighted that two highly dangerous men have been taken off the streets.'

The Pitt Bull Crew had already been smashed. The Cheetham Hill mob, no longer a unified gang but a number of smaller outfits, saw various soldiers jailed for long terms for kidnapping, torturing and taxing other drug dealers. In January 2004, four alleged members of the Gooch were slapped with anti-social behaviour orders restricting their movements, what they could wear and who they could associate with, while at a loftier end of the scale an international gang supplying the Gooch and others with large quantities of Class A drugs was dismantled with the aid of a supergrass. The Salford underworld, meanwhile, saw a number of high-profile, drug-related murders.

The most significant police action has been Operation Xcalibre, an on-going campaign under the auspices of an assistant chief constable. Focusing more of Greater Manchester Police's resources on armed gangs than ever, it includes a specialist intelligence cell to gather and study all firearms-related information to identify and locate the chief perpetrators. Its main focus will be what the police call 'high profile, tough operational policing activities and law enforcement', with a long-term strategy to develop preventative measures within communities.

'What we have to understand is what drives these young people to embark on this lifestyle in the first place,' said ACC Dave Whatton. 'Being part of a group gives them a feeling of belonging. They think that society has given up on them. They see others enjoying items of wealth and they want to be a part of it. The communities have the best understanding of how to tackle this issue and by continuing to work and build relationships with them, we aim to help educate young people on the consequences of getting involved in the first place. We will also continue to support the role the police play in the Manchester Multi-Agency Gang Strategy, the only gang intervention project of its kind in the UK that aims to prevent people from becoming involved in gangs in the first place and prevent current gang members from offending.'

Their hardest task will be rooting out the gang culture now it has become ingrained. Members of the anti-gang community group CARISMA have begun to take their message to primary schools because they found that by the time the children reach secondary school, it is too late. One member gave a presentation to students aged thirteen and fourteen. 'I asked them to come up with reasons for joining a gang, and they had no trouble filling the flip chart,' she said. 'Then I asked how they would get the money to buy an expensive piece of jewellery if they did not turn to crime, and they struggled. That is scary. And these weren't bad kids – they were just average. That is how deeply the gang lifestyle is ingrained.'

Notes on Sources

Unless otherwise indicated in the text or endnotes, all interviews for this book were conducted by the author except for John Stalker, which is reproduced with the kind permission of Tony Barnes of Edge TV, makers of the Granada Television series *Mean Streets*. I am especially grateful to the BBC for permission to quote from unbroadcast interviews with Paul Massey recorded for the *Modern Times* series.

Newspapers and Periodicals
City Life
Daily Mail
Economist, The
Face, The
Guardian, The
Independent, The
Manchester Evening News
Mirror, The
Mixmag
Police Review
Sale and Altrincham Messenger
Salford Advertiser
Salford City Reporter
South Manchester Reporter
Stockport Express and Advertiser
Sun, The
Sunday Times
What's Doing (Manchester CAMRA magazine)
Yorkshire Post

TV
The Cook Report
Close Up North
Dispatches
Look North-West
Mean Streets
Modern Times
Open Eye
World In Action

Reports

Brennan, Det Supt David. *Drugs and Inner City Violence.* Unpublished.

Bullock, Karen and Nick Tilley. *Shootings, Gangs and Violent Incidents in Manchester.* Home Office.

Calvey, David. *Getting on the Door and Staying There,* in *Danger In The Field.* Routledge.

Evans, Karen, Penny Fraser and Sandra Walklate. *Whom can you trust? The politics of 'grassing' on an inner city housing estate.* The Sociological Review, 1996.

Goggins, Paul. *Poverty – Hope's Deadly Enemy.* Child Poverty Action Group.

Institute of Social Research. *Towards a Safer Salford.* University of Salford 1994.

Greater Manchester Police. *A Factual Guide to Drugs.*

Her Majesty's Inspectorate. *North West Regional Crime Squad 1994: A Report.* Home Office.

Home Affairs Committee. *Third Report on Organised Crime 1995.* The Stationery Office.

Mares, Dennis. *Gangchester: Youth Gangs in Manchester.* Unpublished paper, Utrecht University, 1998.

Morris, Sheridan. *Clubs, Drugs and Doormen.* Home Office Police Research Group 1998.

Power, Anne and Rebecca Tunstall in association with the Joseph Rowntree Foundation. *Dangerous Disorder: riots and violent disturbances in thirteen areas of Britain, 1991–1992.* York Publishing Services.

Shropshire, Steve and Michael McFarquhar. *Strategies to Address the Gang and Gun Culture*.

Stelfox, Detective Chief Inspector Peter. *Gang Violence – Strategic and Tactical Options*. Home Office.

Wood, Detective Superintendent Chris. *The Use of Intelligence-based Policing and Surveillance of Target Criminals*. National Criminal Intelligence Service.

Books

Several books provided key background and are essential reading to understand the time and place. *Altered State* by Matthew Collin (with contributions by John Godfrey) is an atmospheric and enviably well-written account of Ecstasy and acid house. Dave Haslam's *Manchester, England* is easily the best book about the modern city and another pleasure to read. *Crack of Doom*, Jon Silverman's chronicle of the menace of crack cocaine, is particularly good on Manchester.

Ashdown, Paddy. *Beyond Westminster: Finding Hope in Britain*. Simon and Schuster.

Barnes, Tony, Richard Elias and Peter Walsh. *Cocky: the Rise and Fall of Curtis Warren*. Milo Books.

Barnes, Tony. *Mean Streets*. Milo Books.

Bronson, Charles and Stephen Richards. *Legends Volume 1*. Mirage Publishing.

Collin, Matthew. *Altered State*. Serpent's Tail.

Davies, Nick. *Dark Heart*. Chatto & Windus.

Dorn, Nicholas and Nigel South (editors). *A Land Fit For Heroin?* Macmillan Education.

Ferris, Paul with McKay, Reg. *The Ferris Conspiracy*. Mainstream Publishing.

Fleming, Denis. *The Manchester Fighters*. Neil Richardson.

Francis, Mickey. *Guvnors*. Milo Books.

Freemantle, Brian. *The Octopus*. Orion.

Hailwood, Andy. *Gun Law*. Milo Books.

Haslam, Dave. *Manchester, England*. Fourth Estate.

Kidd, Alan. *Manchester*. Edinburgh University Press.

MacPhee, John. *The Silent Cry*. Empire Publications.

Mason, Eric. *The Inside Story*. Pan.

Morton, James. *Gangland 2*. Little, Brown.

Murphy, David. *The Stalker Affair and the Press*. Routledge.

Prince, Michael. *God's Cop*. Frederick Muller.

Rea, Anthony. *Manchester's Little Italy*. Neil Richardson.

Redhead, Steve (editor). *Rave Off: Politics and Deviance in Contemporary Rave Culture*. Avebury.

Savage, Jon (editor). *The Hacienda Must Be Built!* International Music Publications.

Schill, Paul. *The History of The Ardwick Lads' and Men's Club*. 1935.

Silverman, Jon. *Crack of Doom*. Headline.

Stalker, John. *Stalker*. Viking.

Taylor, Peter. Stalker: The Search for the Truth. Faber and Faber.

Thompson, Tony. *Gangland Britain*. Hodder and Stoughton.

Twemlow, Cliff. *Tuxedo Warrior*. Summersdale Publishing.

Wilson, Tony. *24 Hour Party People*. Channel 4 Books.

Notes

1 Dave Haslam, *Manchester, England*, Fourth Estate.
2 Social historian Dr Andrew Davies, of Liverpool University, is the acknowledged authority on the scuttlers, and has for several years been working on a research project to document their activities. One day he might even write that book he has been promising.
3 *The Independent*, 31/10/94.
4 *Manchester Evening News*.
5 Chief Constable Colin Sampson, *The Sampson Report*.
6 Eric Mason, *The Inside Story*.
7 Peter Taylor, *Stalker: The Search for the Truth*.
8 Evidence at Liverpool Crown Court.
9 What turned out to be an extraordinary hearing began in mid-May, 1995, but only after the Northern Ireland Secretary had made a successful application to prevent a public airing of certain evidence by Stalker relating to his work on the shoot-to-kill inquiry, on the grounds of national security. The dossiers of the drugs intelligence unit were opened and read out by Kevin Taylor's barrister, Roger Farley QC, and for the first time alleged members of the 'syndicate' were named at a public hearing. At the forefront was said to be James Monaghan, otherwise known as 'Jim Swords', alleged to be a professional criminal who the QSG had 'grown around'. Monaghan had been a popular middleweight boxer in the sixties. Others named as gang members or associates included boxing promoter Jack Trickett, Jimmy 'the Weed' Donnelly, Vincent Schiavo, Joe Leach, Les Simms, Michael Roy Brown and Mark Klapish. One member, described in court as 'M', was said to be closely linked to IRA members who regularly visited his home. Four men were implicated in running guns for the terrorists. A regional crime squad report alleged that the QSG had a 'top jolly' – slang for corrupt senior policeman – and named him as John Stalker.

Intelligence reports made during observations on Kevin Taylor between 1973–83 reported that he was a big gambler and his business phone number was found at the QSG's Manchester HQ, a car pitch. The same dossier alleged that Mr Taylor had financed a drugs deal and laundered cash for Jim Swords, neither of which was ever proven. Mr Taylor claimed in court that his life had been ruined by a police conspiracy and that his name was blackened to discredit his friend John Stalker with the intention of removing him from the 'shoot-to-kill' inquiry. Clearly the information in the files, despite its limited circulation, was extremely damaging to Taylor's reputation. 'It was intended to do serious harm to a man on whom there was no evidence of wrong-doing whatsoever,' said Mr Farley.

Stalker was the first witness and angrily rejected the allegations about him. 'These are absolute lies,' he said. 'They are a complete fabrication.' Perhaps worst of all from Stalker's point of view was the suggestion that he might be sympathetic to the IRA, which was contained in a report to the police authority prepared by Topping and signed by James Anderton. Stalker was almost apoplectic. 'This is a smear campaign of the absolute worst,' he said, gripping the sides of the witness box. 'I'm almost speechless. They suddenly dredge up this awful phrase which is grossly libellous.'

Articulate and often pungent in his rebuttal, Stalker went on, 'Whether or not it had happened to me, the essence of good police work is to realise the power and authority you have in your hands and to examine it as responsibly as possible because of the repercussions if handled badly. If handled maliciously it is even worse. If what has happened was a result of this dross, it is a disgrace to the people involved. I don't blame the police force. I blame the people who misused such information to the detriment of so many other people.' Stalker dismissed the various informants as 'Walter Mitty' and rejected the 'myth' of the QSG. He was backed up by testimony from John Thorburn, former head of Manchester CID, who criticised the quality of the DIU's intelligence reports.

As the hearing wore on, the claims became more sensational. It was alleged that Jim Swords had been behind a £50,000 'contract' on the lives of two supergrasses called Pilot and Cook and the detective Harry Exton. Another document said that London crook Ronnie Knight – once the husband of actress Barbara Windsor – had been seen on a yacht in Gibraltar with alleged QSG associates. Some of the 5,000-plus names in the DIU files were also read out. They ranged from soccer manager Malcolm Allison and leading libel lawyer George Carman to Sinn Fein president Gerry Adams. No reason was given in court for their inclusion on the list and there was no suggestion they were under any suspicion, though an Iranian-born businessman who had run a radio station and several nightclubs and had no criminal record was described as 'a very prominent drug dealer in the north-west.

Seven weeks into the hearing, Greater Manchester Police were told by their insurance company that almost £6 million had been spent on costs and their legal insurance cover was running out. They settled with Mr Taylor for an undisclosed amount, which they had no intention of publicising. In 1998, however, a report to the Commons Home Affairs select committee revealed that Taylor received more than £2.3 million in damages and costs. He died in October 2001, seven weeks after major heart surgery.

Despite the huge financial loss to the taxpayer, Sir James Anderton was unrepentant after the hearing. 'What I did was right and professional,' he said. 'I would handle it in exactly the same way today. I have done nothing wrong and my conscience is clear. There was no conspiracy and no malicious prosecution of Mr Taylor. It is unfortunate that the truth will never come out because of a commercial decision to settle. Of course the public will be left with lingering doubts but I can assure them that the investigation was perfectly professional. I had no choice but to keep Her Majesty's Inspector of Constabulary informed about allegations made against Mr Stalker. The matter had to be referred to the police authority and I gave a verbal briefing to the chairman and the clerk in 1986. If I had taken precipitate action instead, it would not have been right.' Retired CID boss Peter Topping also defended himself against the 'very hurtful' comments of Stalker in the witness box. 'As far as the investigation went, we analysed the evidence very carefully and the police team acted perfectly properly,' he said.

10 Testimony at Liverpool Crown Court.
11 Dave Haslam, *Manchester, England.*
12 *Manchester Evening News.*
13 *Manchester Evening News.*
14 John Silverman, *Crack of Doom.*
15 *The Independent,* 11/7/91.
16 Quoted in James Morton, *Gangland 2.*
17 Open Eye, *In The Firing Line,* Granada Televison, 13/12/90.
18 *Manchester Evening News.*
19 The interviews with Paul Massey were conducted from an unscreened documentary in the BBC Two series *Modern Times.* Extracts are reproduced with kind permission of the BBC, unless otherwise indicated.
20 *Daily Mail,* 24/7/69.
21 Dave Haslam, *Manchester, England.* Fourth Estate.
22 Sleevenotes, *Techno! The New Dance Sound of Detroit,* ZTSE Productions, 1988.
23 Redhead, Steve, *Rave Off!*
24 Sean O'Hagan, *The Times,* 22/2/92.

25 Matthew Collin, *Altered State*.
26 Quoted in Matthew Collin, *Altered State*.
27 Quoted in Matthew Collin, *Altered State*.
28 Quoted in Matthew Collin, *Altered State*.
29 Open Eye, *In The Firing Line*, Granada Televison, 13/12/90.
30 Open Eye, *In The Firing Line*, Granada Televison, 13/12/90.
31 Quoted in *Mancunion*, Manchester University student newspaper.
32 Quoted in Matthew Collin, *Altered State*.
33 Quoted in *The Hacienda Must Be Built!*, International Music Productions.
34 Flannery later sued the police for his injuries, claiming they had been heavy-handed in storming the flat and had then exacerbated his injuries after the fall caused the problem by dragging him 100 yards along the ground to a van. He sought £1.3 million in damages. Police defended their actions, saying his injuries were self-inflicted. The case took nine years to reach court, but he was awarded £30,000 and the judge said the officers in the case who had insisted they had carried, rather than dragged, him were both untruthful and negligent and their actions amounted to an assault.
35 *Manchester Evening News*.
36 *Manchester Evening News*.
37 *The Guardian*, undated.
38 Detective Superintendent David Brennan, *Drugs and Inner City Violence*.
39 Sonia Stewart quotes from an interview given to BBC *North West Tonight*.
40 *Manchester Evening News*.
41 *The Independent*, 11/7/91.
42 *Manchester Evening News*.
43 *Manchester Evening News*.
44 *Manchester Evening News*.
45 Tony Wilson, *24 Hour Party People*.
46 Dave Haslam, *Manchester, England*.
47 *Manchester Evening News*.
48 A Colt 45 from the same batch was later used to shoot dead a security guard on the steps of Farnworth town hall in a bungled robbery, another was used to pistol-whip a man in north Manchester, and a third was used to shoot a man in a Bradford nightclub.
49 *Manchester Evening News*.
50 One crude protection racket was uncovered in Lower Kersal, where several young men threatened shopkeepers and small businesses with arson if they didn't pay up. A car spares business was badly damaged by fire and an elderly man who lived above it had to scramble through a broken window onto a ledge and then climb

onto the roof of a van to escape. Detectives set up a sting at the car
parts shop and filmed the gang demanding cash from the owner.
'No shop, no work,' one was heard to say. They told the newsagents
who refused them that they wanted a different answer by the end of
the week or all the windows would be put through. On one occasion
the newsagent was told, 'This is Salford '95. If you don't pay us,
we'll put your windows through and burn your car and the insurance
will go up.' Two months later, the building was torched again and
effectively destroyed. Five young men – three of them brothers –
were jailed for a total of twenty-two years.

51 *Manchester Evening News.*
52 *Manchester Evening News.*
53 Dave Haslam, *Manchester, England.*
54 Evans, Karen, Penny Fraser and Sandra Walklate, *Whom can you
trust? The politics of 'grassing' on an inner city council estate.*
55 *Manchester Evening News.*
56 Institute of Social Research, *Towards a Safer Salford.*
57 *Manchester Evening News.*
58 Sonia Stewart quotes from an interview given to BBC *North-West
Tonight.*
59 Haslam, Dave, *Manchester, England.*
60 A number of small Salford mobs became known by the postal
districts they came from.
61 Minutes of the Manchester City Centre Pub and Club Watch
Network.
62 Calvey, David, *Danger in the Field,* Routledge.
63 *The Guardian,* 18/2/96.
64 *On The Line,* BBC Radio 5 Live.
65 *Manchester Evening News.*
66 *Towards A Safer Salford.*
67 Billy Webb's gang held regular 'board meetings' in Debbie's Diner, a
small café beneath a railway arch in Bolton, and enforced their rule
with some brutality: they beat people with baseball bats, smashed
their hands with hammers and even raped their girlfriends. The
most terrible crime with which Webb was associated was the murder
of a five-year-old boy, Dillon Hull, who was shot in the head on a
Bolton street. Dillon had been walking hand-in-hand with his
stepfather, a small-time drug dealer who had refused to work for
Webb, when a hired killer opened up on them. The stepfather
survived but Dillon died as he tried to run away. Webb was never
convicted of the crime, though others were, but was finally arrested
after detectives bugged the café where he held his meetings and
taped lengthy and incriminating conversations. While on bail
awaiting charges of conspiracy to supply drugs, Webb was shot

dead at the age of forty-one in a Wigan flat by an unknown gunman.

68 I am indebted for much of the material in this chapter to the *Stockport Express*, which produced an excellent profile of Little after his death.

69 *Manchester Evening News.*

70 *Stockport Express Advertiser.*

71 One of those acquitted was Graham Mansell, a stocky, shaven-headed figure with a goatee beard who went on to run his own drugs business from safehouses in Stockport. Mansell was arrested after leaving a flat in Manchester's trendy Didsbury district. He ran off, dumping a one kilo bag of amphetamines, but was cornered after taking refuge on a garage roof. A search of his flat revealed a substantial drugs-making operation and a stash of guns and ammunition in a cupboard. Mansell, twenty-four, of Stalybridge, admitted supply and intent to supply drugs and was found guilty of possessing firearms and ammo. He claimed to have been a foot soldier and denied any knowledge of the weapons but this was rejected by the judge at Manchester Crown Court, who said, 'It is quite clear to me that you were a major mover in the drugs trade, earning up to £1,000 a week.' He was jailed for twelve years.

72 *Manchester Evening News.*

73 At the time of writing, several men charged with Barnshaw's murder were facing a lengthy trial.

74 A description given at Manchester Crown Court in 2003.

75 *Manchester Evening News.*

76 *Manchester Evening News.*

77 *Manchester Evening News.*

78 The breakthrough against gunsmith Anthony Mitchell came when a Scotsman was arrested on the London to Glasgow train, ostensibly for being drunk and disorderly. He was carrying a pistol, silencer and ammo. The Scotsman worked for a security company connected to the Glasgow gangster Paul Ferris. In May 1997, more than sixty officers mounted a surveillance operation at John Ackerman's home in Islington, north London. Paul Ferris and another man arrived. A box was taken from the house and put in a car driven by Constance Howarth, of Pendleton, Salford. Police stopped the car and found three MAC-10s and 360 rounds. Howarth claimed she had been asked to collect money by an Eccles car dealer she knew and had no idea it was guns.

Mitchell, however, remained at large; he had been connected to Ackerman by a middleman and without him the police did not have a case. 'During his interviews he was extremely arrogant,' says detective Cliff Purvis. 'Mitchell knew that as long as the middleman was not in custody, he could claim that Ackerman was a liar. He likes to toy with authority. His ego wouldn't let him accept that he may get caught.' In October 1997, the middleman was arrested in Kent, and Mitchell was picked up before he could flee the country. A search of his workshop uncovered more than forty deactivated MAC-10s and a stash of working parts to restore them. The Forensic Science Service was able to link him to more than fifty reactivated guns recovered around the country and in Ireland. Mitchell admitted several weapons offences and was jailed for eight years in April 1999. Ferris was jailed for ten – reduced to seven on appeal – and Constance Howarth for five. The exact number of illegal weapons Mitchell sold is unknown.

79 A twenty-year-old man was later cleared of the killing but was jailed for five years after he admitted trying to sell cocaine and heroin to an undercover cop. The judge was forced to acquit him of the murder of Zeus King and the attempted murder of two other men after witness Sharon White, aged eighteen, sniggered, chewed gum and refused to answer questions in the witness box. 'I'm not interested,' she told the prosecutor. 'I didn't want to come here. You might as well just take me to Risley. I refuse to answer any questions for the rest of my life if I have to. It's done my head in now. I am going to keep my mouth shut. I am going to ignore you.'

80 *Manchester Evening News.*
81 *Manchester Evening News.*
82 *Manchester Evening News.*
83 Dean 'OG' Ogle, who acted as the Doddington's armourer, was later charged with supplying the .22 Smith and Wesson automatic and .357 Magnum used to kill McKie and injure his friend. Ogle and his twenty-four-year-old uncle, Leon Simms, were described in court as leaders of the Doddington and were both convicted of possessing firearms with intent to endanger life and of attempting to pervert the course of justice. 'You moved loaded guns around Moss Side and Hulme for use should the occasion arise,' said Judge Simon Fawcus. 'You should be put out of the way of the public for a long time.' Ogle was jailed for sixteen years and Simms for ten.
84 Quoted in *Manchester Graduate*, Manchester University, 2003.
85 Haslam, Dave, *Manchester, England.*
86 Court of Appeal judgment, Massey v Regina.
87 Bullock, Karen and Nick Tilley, *Shootings, Gangs and Violent Incidents in Manchester,* Home Office.
88 Bullock, Karen and Nick Tilley, *Shootings, Gangs and Violent Incidents in Manchester.*
89 Bullock, Karen and Nick Tilley, *Shootings, Gangs and Violent Incidents in Manchester.*
90 Recommendation from ACPO, the Police Federation and the Super-

intendents' Association to the Home Affairs select committee, reported in *Police Review*, 9/12/94.

91 Quoted in *Manchester Evening News*.

92 Quoted in *Manchester Evening News*.

Picture credits

Press Association (photo pages 1, 14, 15); Ignition (1, 7), *Manchester Evening News* (2, 3, 4, 5, 6, 8, 9, 12, 13); Aidan O'Rourke (12); Greater Manchester Police (15, 16); Carol Stokes (8); the *Guardian* (16); j.henry.com (11).